MW01688812

Microsoft® Visual FoxPro 3

For Windows®

Step by Step

Other titles in the *Step by Step* series:

For Microsoft Windows 95

(available in Fall 1995)

Integrating Microsoft Office Applications Step by Step, for Windows 95

Microsoft Access for Windows 95 Step by Step

Microsoft Access/Visual Basic Step by Step

Microsoft Excel for Windows 95 Step by Step

Microsoft Excel/Visual Basic Step by Step

Microsoft PowerPoint for Windows 95 Step by Step

Microsoft Project for Windows 95 Step by Step

Microsoft Visual Basic 4 Step by Step

Microsoft Windows 95 Step by Step

Microsoft Word for Windows 95 Step by Step

Microsoft Works for Windows 95 Step by Step

More Microsoft Windows 95 Step by Step

Upgrading to Microsoft Windows 95 Step by Step

For Microsoft Windows 3.1

(available now)

Microsoft Access 2 for Windows Step by Step

Microsoft Excel 5 for Windows Step by Step

Microsoft Excel Visual Basic for Applications Step by Step, for Windows

Microsoft Mail for Windows Step by Step, versions 3.0b, version 5 and later

Microsoft Office for Windows Step by Step, version 4

Microsoft PowerPoint 4 for Windows Step by Step

Microsoft Project 4 for Windows Step by Step

Microsoft Word 6 for Windows Step by Step

Microsoft Works 3 for Windows Step by Step

Microsoft®

VISUAL FOXPRO 3

For Windows®

Step by Step

tlr

Microsoft® Press

PUBLISHED BY
Microsoft Press
A Division of Microsoft Corporation
One Microsoft Way
Redmond, Washington 98052-6399

Library of Congress Cataloging-in-Publication Data
Microsoft Visual FoxPro 3 for Windows step by step / by Technical Learning Resources, Inc.
p. cm.
Includes index.
ISBN 1-55615-846-7
1. Visual FoxPro for Windows. 2. Database managment.
I. Technical Learning Resources, Inc.
QA76.9.D3M574 1995
005.75'65--dc20 95-17567
CIP

Printed and bound in the United States of America.

1 2 3 4 5 6 7 8 9 QMQM 9 8 7 6 5 4

Distributed to the book trade in Canada by Macmillan of Canada, a division of Canada Publishing Corporation.

A CIP catalogue record for this book is available from the British Library.

Microsoft Press books are available through booksellers and distributors worldwide. For further information about international editions, contact your local Microsoft Corporation office. Or contact Microsoft Press International directly at fax (206) 936-7329.

For Technical Learning Resources, Inc.
Project Manager: Kathryn L. Hogan
Writers: Mark Ganchrow, John F. Grace
Contributing Writers: Robert Parshall, Joseph N. Trapp
Application Development: Dallas C. Miller
Project Editor: Bonnie W. Hayman
Production/Layout: A. Sharon Pelletier
Technical Advisors: William Gilmore, Patrick E. Marino
Indexer: Patricia Johns

For Microsoft Press
Acquisitions Editor: Casey D. Doyle
Project Editor: Wallis Bolz
Technical Editor: Dail Magee, Jr.

Technical Learning Resources, Inc., and Microsoft Press

Microsoft Visual FoxPro 3 for Windows Step by Step has been created by the professional trainers and writers at Technical Learning Resources, Inc., to the exacting standards you've come to expect from Microsoft Press. Together, we are pleased to present this self-paced training guide, which you can use individually or as part of a class.

Technical Learning Resources, Inc. (TLR) is dedicated to providing end users and training organizations nationwide with high performance training manuals designed for both classroom instruction and self-paced learning. TLR's exclusive micro-modular design and reusable practice disk ensure quick and easy learning of new skills for users at all levels. Each micro-modular lesson is self contained and allows the end user to choose exactly what lesson modules they wish to learn, when they wish to learn them. This results in a much higher level of control, flexibility and quality instruction without undue time or cost. TLR's manuals provide instruction on consumer software applications commonly used in home office and small office environments, as well as instruction on the more popular business software applications.

The development of *Microsoft Visual FoxPro 3 for Windows Step by Step*, in conjunction with Microsoft Press, allows TLR to reach a new audience of users. We appreciate the opportunity to provide you with the quality instruction presented in this book.

Technical Learning Resources, Inc., is located in Rochester, New York.

Microsoft Press is the independent—and independent-minded—book publishing division of Microsoft Corporation. The leading publisher of information on Microsoft software, Microsoft Press is dedicated to providing the highest quality end-user training, reference, and technical books that make using Microsoft software easier, more enjoyable, and more productive.

After you've used this *Step by Step* book, please fill out the feedback form in the back of the book and let us know what you think! Incorporating feedback from readers is a key component in continuously improving the books in the *Step by Step* series, and your help ensures that our materials remain as useful to you as possible.

Contents at a Glance

Table of Contents

Building a New Database,
see Lesson 4, page 31

Creating Queries,
see Lesson 10, page 179

Creating Forms,
see Lesson 5, page 57

Using Classes,
see Lesson 7, page 101

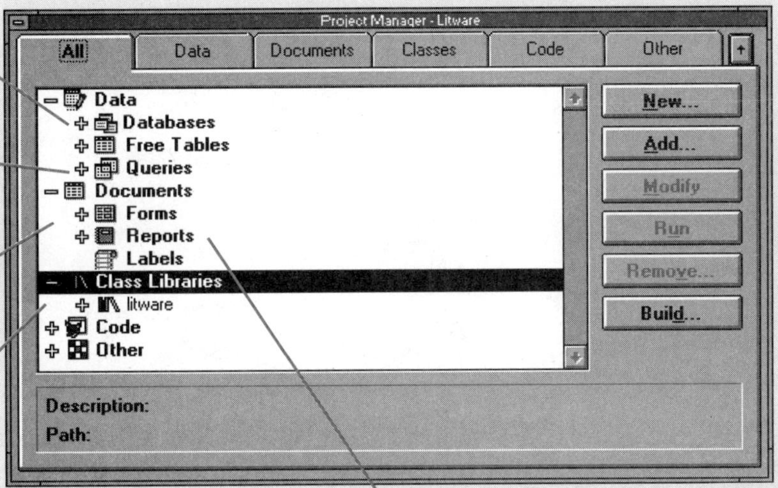

Designing Reports,
see Lesson 11, page 197

Creating Table Fields,
see Lesson 4, page 38

Creating a Table,
see Lesson 4, page 36

Creating Table Relationships,
see Lesson 4, page 50

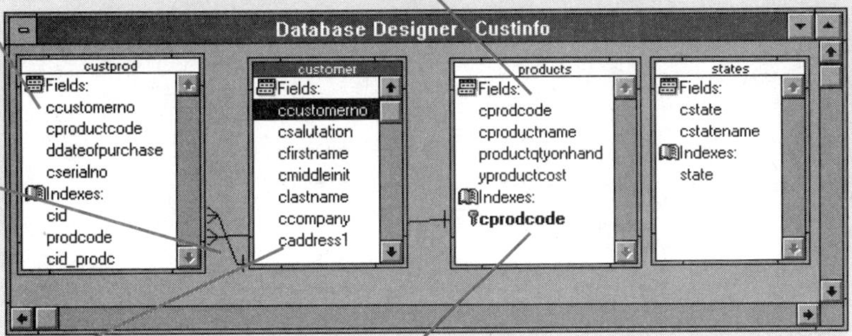

Adding Tables,
see Lesson 4, page 42

Defining Indexes,
see Lesson 4, page 45

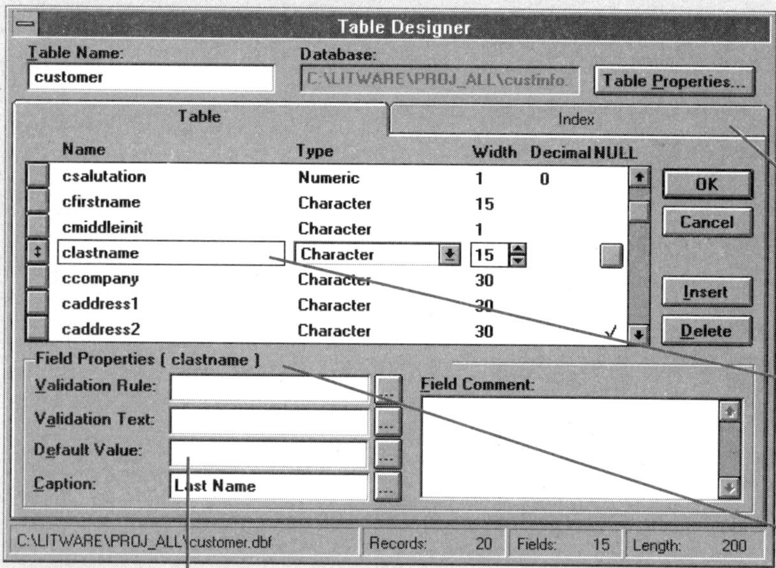

Setting Indexes, see Lesson 4, page 45

Assigning Field Names, see Lesson 4, page 38

Setting Field Properties, see Lesson 4, page 39

Setting Captions, see Lesson 4, page 39

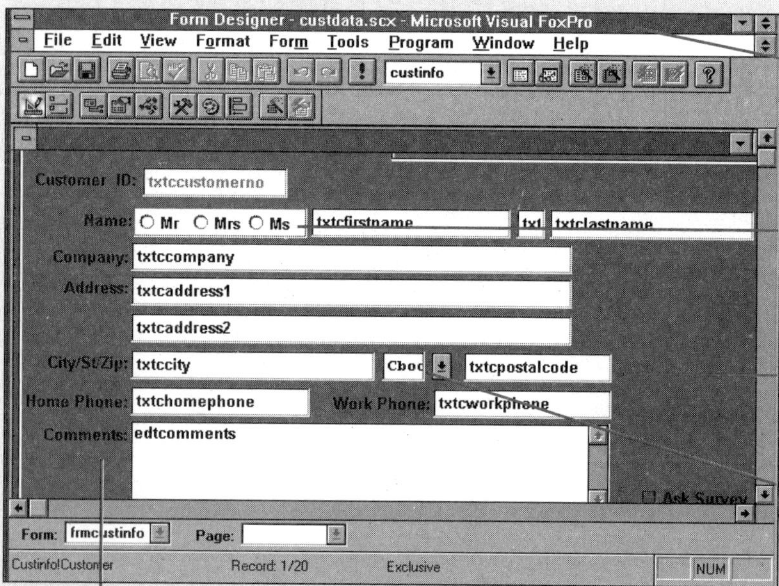

Creating a New Form, see Lesson 5, page 59

Placing Option Boxes, see Lesson 5, page 74

Adding Text Boxes, see Lesson 5, page 63

Creating List Boxes, see Lesson 5, page 74

Creating Labels, see Lesson 6, page 91

Using Class Designer,
see Lesson 7, page 103

Creating a Command Button Class,
see Lesson 7, page 104

Setting Class Properties,
see Lesson 7, page 105

Creating a New Class,
see Lesson 7, page 107

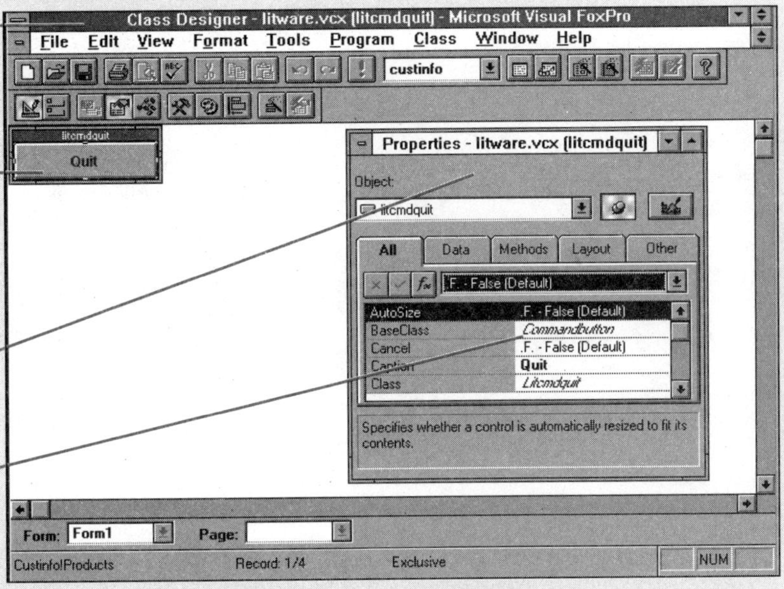

Creating Menu Prompts,
see Lesson 8, page 127

Creating Menu Options,
see Lesson 8, page 128

Previewing Menus,
see Lesson 8, page 132

Specify Submenu Options,
see Lesson 8, page 128

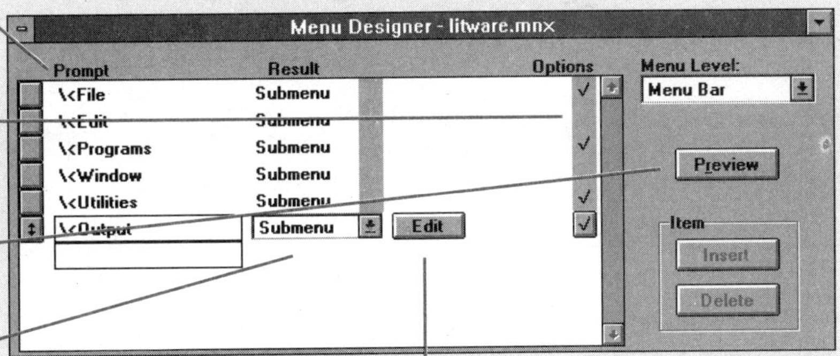

Editing Menu Results,
see Lesson 8, page 132

Adding Tables,
see Lesson 10, page 182

Ordering Queries,
see Lesson 10, page 184

Grouping Queries,
see Lesson 10, page 185

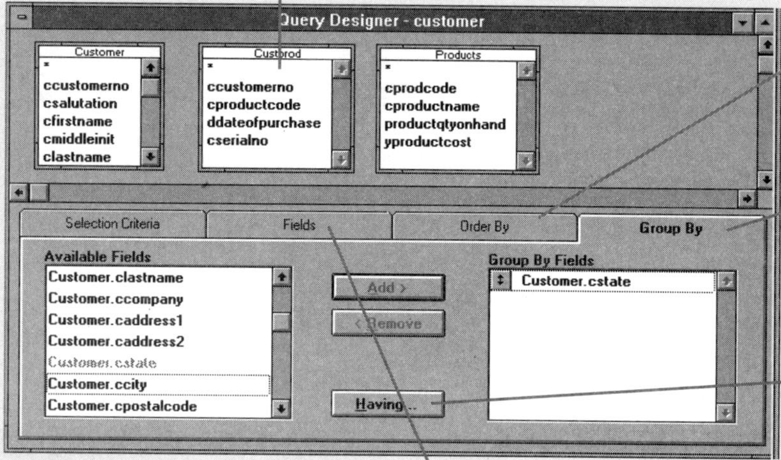

Selecting Groups,
see Lesson 10, page 191

Selecting Query Fields,
see Lesson 10, page 183

Creating Report Column Headings,
see Lesson 11, page 201

Using Report Designer,
see Lesson 11, page 203

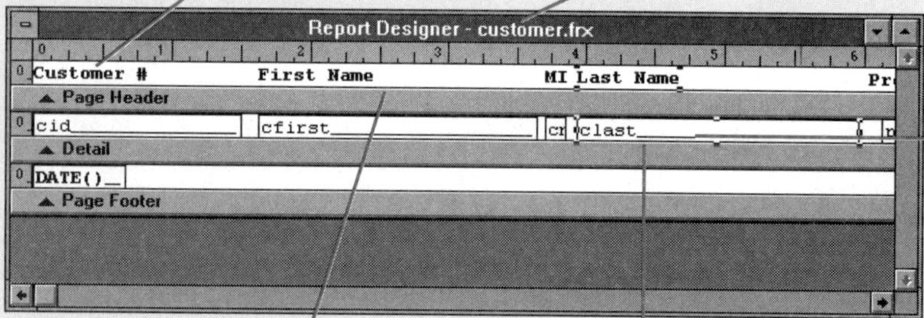

Creating Report Fields,
see Lesson 11, page 205

Formatting Text,
see Lesson 11, page 208

Resizing Field Columns,
see Lesson 11, page 202

About This Book

In "About This Book" you will learn:

- The best starting point for you.
- How to use this book as a classroom aid.
- The conventions used in this book.

Microsoft Visual FoxPro 3 for Windows is a powerful new application development package that you can use to create dynamic databases and high-performance client/server interfaces. Visual FoxPro provides you with the tools to create visual objects that can be used over and over again when developing any application, through the use of an easy-to-use object-oriented environment. By taking advantage of Visual FoxPro's tools you will be able to develop applications rapidly. Designers, Wizards, and Builders in Visual FoxPro have eliminated some of the more tedious aspects of application development, allowing you to spend more time producing a quality product.

IMPORTANT This book is for use with Visual FoxPro 3 for the Windows 3.1 operating system. Visual FoxPro 3 will run on Windows 95, Windows NT, and Windows for Workgroups 3.11, but the screen shots and text in this book reflect a Windows 3.1 bias.

Microsoft Visual FoxPro 3 for Windows Step by Step is a tutorial that shows you how to use Visual FoxPro to harness the power of objects and build flexibility into your applications. You will learn how to develop a Visual FoxPro application rapidly using the Visual FoxPro feature set (Designers, Wizards, Builders, and Tools). You will use the

Table Designer to build Visual FoxPro tables and the Form Designer to create Visual FoxPro forms. Using Visual FoxPro's base classes, you will create your own classes, and then create objects from the classes. You will use Wizards to create reports.

You can use this book to learn Visual FoxPro at your own pace, or you can adapt it for use in a classroom setting. Each lesson contains a set of practice files, allowing you to pinpoint the skills you need to learn quickly. To get the biggest benefit from this book and an understanding of everything that Visual FoxPro can do for you, we suggest that you work through all of the lessons in order.

Finding the Best Starting Point

This book is designed for new users who need detailed instructions, as well as experienced users who may want to read only about the new features of Visual FoxPro. To help you customize your learning plan, the following table provides recommended starting points based on your application development experience.

If you	Follow these steps
Have never used FoxPro or a visual-development environment, and are unfamiliar with object-oriented programming	Read *Getting Ready*, *Lesson 1*, and *Lesson 2*. Then work through the remaining lessons in chapter order since the dialogue follows the development of a typical application.
Have never used FoxPro but are familiar with object-oriented programming	Read *Getting Ready* and *Lesson 2*. Work through the remaining lessons in any order.
Are new to object-oriented programming but have used versions of FoxPro	Read *Getting Ready*, *Lesson 1*, and *Lesson 2*. Work through the remaining lessons in any prior order.
Are familiar with object-oriented programming and FoxPro	Read *Getting Ready* and *Lesson 2*. Work through the remaining lessons in any order.

Using This Book As a Classroom Aid

As an instructor, you can use *Microsoft Visual FoxPro 3 for Windows Step by Step* for teaching Visual FoxPro to developers with a wide variety of backgrounds: those experienced in FoxPro, those familiar with object-oriented programming (OOP), those who are new to object-oriented programming, and those who are familiar or unfamiliar with visual development tools. You can customize the lessons to meet the needs of your students.

Each lesson in *Microsoft Visual FoxPro 3 for Windows Step by Step* has a set of practice files. You may want to select lessons to teach a particular concept, while incorporating your own experiences and demonstrations into the lessons. At the beginning of each lesson the estimated lesson time is posted, allowing you to plan your class day. If you are going to teach the entire book, you should set aside at least three full days to allow for discussion, questions, and practice.

Conventions Used in This Book

Microsoft Visual FoxPro 3 for Windows Step by Step is designed to lead you through the development of a database application. To explain important concepts and procedures along the way, this book uses several instructional conventions.

Notational Conventions

- Characters you are to type appear in **bold**.
- Titles of books appear in *italic*.

Keyboard Conventions

- Names of keys are in small capital letters—for example, TAB and SHIFT.
- A plus sign (+) between two key names means that you must press those keys at the same time. For example, "Press SHIFT+ SPACEBAR" means that you hold down the SHIFT key while you press the Spacebar.
- A comma (,) between two keys means that you must press those keys sequentially. For example, "Press ALT,F,O" means that you first press and release the ALT key, and then the F key, and then the O key.

Other Features of This Book

- The optional "One Step Further" exercises at the end of each lesson build on the skills and topics covered in the lesson, often exploring a new option or shortcut technique.
- This book is divided into three sections: an introduction to Visual FoxPro and object-oriented programming, the basics of Visual FoxPro, and how to optimize Visual FoxPro. At the end of each section is an optional "Review & Practice" scenario. Using real-life situations, these less structured activities allow you to learn more about the features that were introduced in that section. You will be introduced to typical business challenges and provided with general guidelines for solving these challenges on your own.

- You can perform many commands by clicking a button in a window, dialog box, or toolbar. If a step instructs you to click a button, a picture of the button appears in the left margin, as the New Table button does here.
- Text in the margin summarizes main points, gives tips, or provides additional useful information.
- The appendix, "Smart Naming Strategies," shows you some popular methods for naming variables and objects in object-oriented applications, and includes examples of how to implement these naming strategies.
- The glossary at the end of the book provides a useful reference to the many new terms and concepts you'll encounter in this book.

Cross-references to Microsoft Visual FoxPro Documentation

Microsoft Visual FoxPro 3 for Windows Step by Step helps you get quickly acquainted with Visual FoxPro documentation. At the end of each lesson, there are references to the documentation that comes with Visual FoxPro. While working through a lesson, you might want to learn more about the feature described in the lesson. Using the chapter or online lesson referenced at the end of the lesson, you will find cross-references to the following Visual FoxPro documentation and features.

- *Microsoft Visual FoxPro Developer's Guide* contains background information, procedures, and examples for developing Visual FoxPro applications. The *Developer's Guide* covers important topics, including setting up your database, creating forms and controls, using classes, and compiling and debugging an application.
- *Microsoft Visual FoxPro User's Guide* provides information about how to use Visual FoxPro as an interactive data management tool, including how to create tables and build a database, and how to perform queries and run reports.
- *Microsoft Visual FoxPro Language Reference* is a reference to the Visual FoxPro programming language and covers the three platforms: Windows, Macintosh, and MS-DOS.
- *Microsoft Visual FoxPro Help* gives you online access to a wide variety of topics about programming with Visual FoxPro. Visual FoxPro Help also includes an online language reference with explanations of Visual FoxPro commands, properties, and controls; a guide to using Visual FoxPro's interface, including information on designers, Wizards, dialog boxes, menus, and tool bars; and a technical reference section containing information on error messages and Visual FoxPro file structures, optimizing Visual FoxPro applications, and upgrading from previous versions of FoxPro.
- *Microsoft Visual FoxPro Wizards* coach you through the process of creating items such as forms, tables, queries, and reports.

Getting Ready

In "Getting Ready" you will learn:

- How to install the practice files on your computer's hard disk.
- Important new terms in Visual FoxPro.
- How to get the most out of Visual FoxPro Help.

This section of the book prepares you for your first steps into the Microsoft Visual FoxPro 3 for Windows environment. There are several things you need to do before you begin the lessons. First you will need to install the practice files onto your computer's hard disk; this section describes the installation process and each of the practice files. You will also learn some new terms used in Visual FoxPro, and you will explore Visual FoxPro's online Help system.

IMPORTANT Before you break the seal on the practice disk in the back of this book, be sure that you have the correct version of the software. This book is designed for use with Microsoft Visual FoxPro 3, an application that runs on the Windows 3.1 operating system. To determine what software you are running, you can either check the software documentation, the installation disk labels, or the exterior product packaging, or you can click the About Microsoft Visual FoxPro command on the Help menu.

Installing the Step by Step Practice Files

Inside the back cover of this book, you'll find a disk labeled "Microsoft Visual FoxPro 3 for Windows Step by Step Practice Files." You will use this disk with Visual FoxPro 3 to construct the LitWare application in this book. A special program on the practice files disk copies these files onto your hard drive into a directory named LITWARE. Within the LITWARE directory, the installation program also creates a subdirectory for each lesson and copies the files required by each lesson into the appropriate subdirectory.

Copy the practice files onto your hard disk

1. Insert the practice disk into your computer's 3.5 inch disk drive.
2. From the Program Manager, choose Run from the File menu.

   The Run dialog box appears.
3. In the Command Line text box, type **a:\install** (type **b:\install** if your computer's 3.5 inch drive is the b drive).
4. Click the OK button.

   The Step by Step installation program starts.
5. Follow the instructions on the screen to complete the installation process.

Using the Practice Files

The lessons in *Microsoft Visual FoxPro 3 for Windows Step by Step* teach you how to build a Visual FoxPro application from the ground up. In each lesson, you will create and change the various files that make up the application. You will begin each lesson (with the exception of Lesson 2 "Analyzing the Problem" and Lesson 4 "Building a New Database") by opening files from an existing Visual FoxPro application. Lesson 2 walks you through the analysis of the LitWare application, and Lesson 4 shows you how to begin a Visual FoxPro application from scratch.

Lesson Background

You are a database application developer who has been hired by LitWare, Inc. LitWare is a small software company poised to grow as a result of some ground-breaking upgrades to their existing products. LitWare has opened an 800 line to receive upgrade requests directly from their customers. You are assigned to design and develop an order processing system that LitWare's sales representatives can use to handle incoming calls for upgrade requests.

The table below lists the names of the practice files that you will need to start each lesson and identifies any files you create or save after you complete a lesson. Following the lessons for each part of the book is a list of review files that provide additional practice for the lessons discussed in that part.

New Visual FoxPro Terms

If you are familiar with previous versions of FoxPro, you will notice that some new terms have been introduced in Visual FoxPro. The list below defines some of the new terms and provides the equivalent terms in previous versions of FoxPro.

Previous Versions	Visual FoxPro	Description
NEW	Database	A database file has a .DBC extension and can contain one or more tables, views, connections to remote data sources, and stored procedures.
Database	Table	A table stores data in records (rows) and fields (columns). Each Visual FoxPro table can be stored in its own file with a .DBF extension or contained in a database.
View	View	A customized virtual table definition that can be local, remote, or parameterized. Views reference one or more tables or other views. They can be updatable, and they can reference remote tables.
Screen	Form	A dialog box, window, or other device used for displaying information and controls to the user.
Lists	List Boxes	Scrollable list of information items or options.
Popup	Combo Box	Control that provides a scrollable list of options and a text box in which the user can type new information.
Push Button	Command Button	A control that is associated with a particular command. When you click the command button at run time, the command executes.
Radio button	Option button	A control used to select a single setting or preference from multiple choices.
Text Edit Region	(Gets)	Edit BoxA control that provides a place to enter or view text in a form. Edit boxes hold multiple lines of text.

Locating Information in Help

Online Help in Visual FoxPro provides several ways in which you can get more information about a feature. When you want general information, you can choose the Contents command from the Help menu. This Help window works like a table of contents to give you access to the entire online help system. When you want to look up information about a specific command or property, you can use the Search For Help On command.

This Help window works like an index; you enter a word or phrase, and then select from a list of related topics what you want to see. In addition, when you are in a dialog box, you can press the F1 key to view information about the currently open dialog box.

Search for a topic in Help

Visual FoxPro does not have to be running in order for you to access Help information. You can access Help from the Help menu in Visual FoxPro, or you can start Visual FoxPro Help directly from the Program Manager.

1 In the Program Manager, open the Microsoft Visual FoxPro program group.

The program group contains program icons for Visual FoxPro and a variety of programs related to Visual FoxPro, including Visual FoxPro Help, Image Edit, Hotspot Editor, and Setup.

2 Double-click the Microsoft Visual FoxPro Help program icon.

Visual FoxPro Help starts and displays the Contents window. The Contents window includes a toolbar at the top of the window for navigating through Help topics, or for quickly returning to the Contents window and searching for specific Help topics.

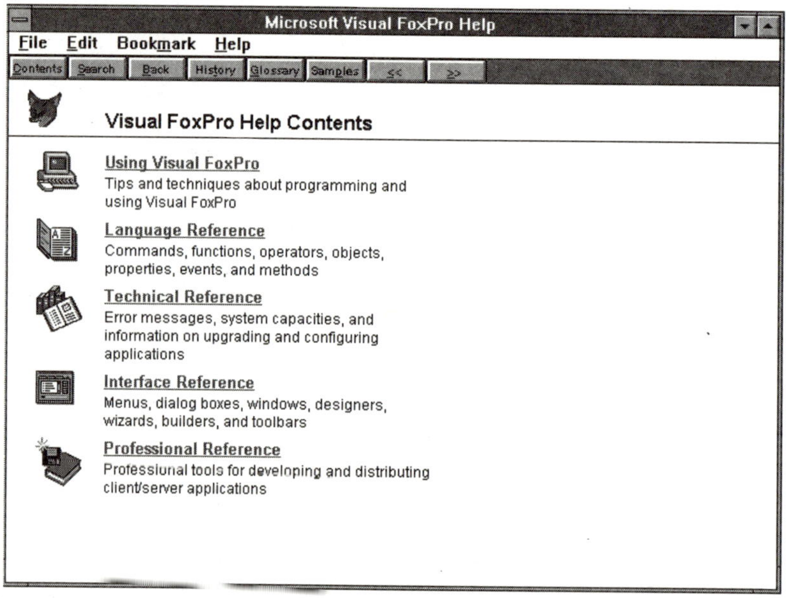

3 Click the Search button at the top of the Contents window.

The Search dialog box appears. You can type the name of a category of information about which you want to know more.

4 Type **Controls** but do not press Enter.

As you type, Visual FoxPro searches for categories of information associated with the word Controls, and displays those categories in the center list box.

5 In the center list box, click the category *controls and objects* if it is not already selected.

6 Click the Show Topics button.

Help displays a list of topics related to the *controls and objects* category in the bottom list box.

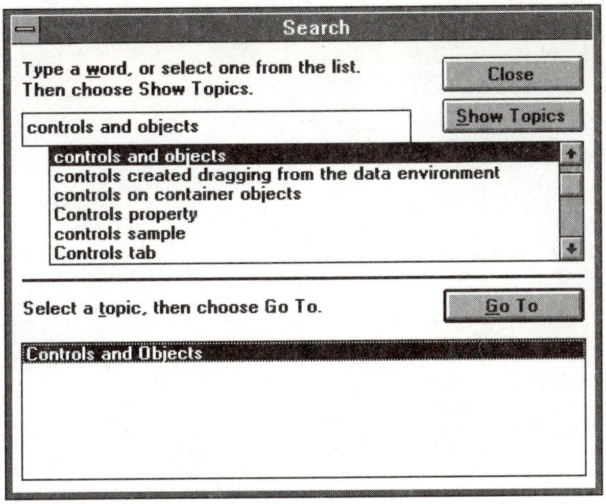

7 In the list of related topics at the bottom of the screen, click Controls and Objects.

8 Click the Go To button.

Information about a sample form containing examples of controls and objects appears. If you think you will look up a particular Help topic often, you can use the Define command in the Bookmark menu to mark the topic for future reference.

9 Click the Contents button at the top of the Help window.

The Controls topic closes and the Contents window appears.

Jump to related topics

You will often find a link to related topics in Visual FoxPro Help. The most common link is called a "hyperlink" and is indicated by green underlined text. Using hyperlinks, you can follow topic threads to obtain all the Visual FoxPro Help included on a particular subject.

1 In the Help Contents window, point to the green underlined phrase Language Reference.

The arrow pointer changes to a pointing hand, indicating that you are pointing to a hyperlink.

2 Click the left mouse button.

Help displays a new window that summarizes topics included on Language Reference.

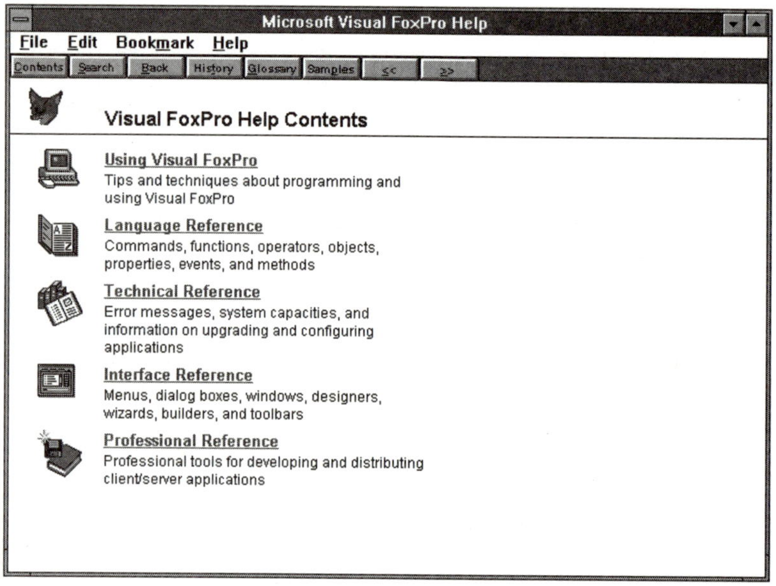

3 Click on the green underlined word Introduction at the top of the window.

Help displays a new window that contains an introduction to information contained in the Language Reference.

4 Click the Back button at the top of the window.

Help returns to the previous Help window.

5 Click the Back button again.

Help returns to the Contents window.

6 From the File menu, choose Exit.

Visual FoxPro Help closes and the Windows Program Manager appears.

Using Wizards

A Wizard is a sequence of dialog boxes that presents specific questions about what you want to create. Once you answer the questions, the wizard completes the task. You can use Visual FoxPro Wizards to accomplish common programming tasks quickly, such as creating new forms, and designing reports and queries. For example, if you use the Table Wizard, you can indicate which fields you wish to create and set field and table properties. The Wizard will create a new table that matches your specifications. Once you have completed a task using a wizard, you can modify the results of the task to customize it for your application, allowing it to look and function as if it had been created specifically for the application.

New Features in Visual FoxPro 3

The following table lists the major new features in Microsoft Visual FoxPro 3 for Windows that are covered in this book. The table shows the lesson in which you can learn about each new feature. For more information about new features see the *Installation Guide and Master Index*.

To learn how to	See
Create application components with Designers	Lessons 1, 4, 5, 6, 7, 8, 10, and 11
Take shortcuts with Toolbars	Lessons 5, 6, 7, and 8
Create application interfaces without programming	Lessons 5, 6, 7, and 8
Manage your work with the Project Manager	Lessons 4, 5, 6, 7, 8, 9, 10, 11, and 12
Harness the power of object-oriented programming	Lessons 1, 5, 6, 7, and 8
Handle events with ease	Lesson 6
Optimize your system	Lesson 12
Program for shared access	Lesson 9
Create your own classes	Lesson 7
Use Wizards and Builders	Lesson 4, 5, and 11

Part

1

Presenting Visual FoxPro

Lesson

1

What's New and Different in Visual FoxPro

Estimated time
30 min.

In this lesson you will learn:

- About the new features of Visual FoxPro.
- About objects.
- Why using objects and object-oriented technology when developing applications benefits you.

If you have used FoxPro before, you are familiar with its powerful features; the speed with which it searches large databases using the Rushmore database engine; its design tools, such as the Report Writer, Relational Query By Example, and Menu and Screen builders; and its debugging tools such as the Trace, Debug, Command and View windows. Microsoft Visual FoxPro 3 for Windows, a more dynamic version of FoxPro, provides more and advanced tools to help you develop complex applications quickly and efficiently.

Visual FoxPro Development Tools

Visual FoxPro, a powerful database management system and application-development environment, provides tools to manage data directly that you can access with the mouse. With the power and speed of Visual FoxPro, many data management tasks that were accomplished on a mainframe can now be accomplished easily on the desktop. Here is a quick overview of the Visual FoxPro tools:

- You can use Visual FoxPro's Class Designer to create new classes quickly. Your programming time is cut dramatically as you use these classes over and over again in the same application or other applications. You can make changes to the properties of a class, and Visual FoxPro automatically changes the properties in related subclasses.
- Client/server tools and language enhancements permit access to data from a remote location as well as to data stored in a format other than the Xbase-.DBF format. You can use these Client/server tools to create a prototype application on your local machine, and then move the final application to a client/server environment without having to make last-minute code changes.
- Visual design tools, such as toolbars and designers, allow you to create and modify items such as forms, queries, and reports quickly and graphically.
- The data dictionary allows you to enforce business rules—rules that govern data and validity—at the table level, using field-level and record-level validations. You can also use longer—up to 128 characters—names for fields, set permanent relationships between tables, and use the Referential Integrity builder to generate code to enforce data integrity.
- Wizards and builders guide you through the process of creating application components such as tables, forms, queries, and reports by asking you questions and creating or modifying the item based on your answers.
- Event-driven, nonmodal applications can be written with no additional code. This allows the user to open multiple windows, even multiple instances of the same window, and switch between them, saving the status of each.
- Multi-user systems require little additional code. Using Visual FoxPro, you can set record and table buffering and locking to insulate one user's changes from another's; in addition, transaction processing allows a reversal of unsuccessful update attempts.

An Overview of Object-Oriented Programming

Visual FoxPro uses object-oriented programming to create applications. Object-oriented programming is not a difficult concept to understand; it is merely a new way of thinking about programming. As with any new concept, there is some new syntax to learn, but for most programmers, learning the syntax is easy. What you'll find more challenging is learning the logic of isolating operations into objects.

Defining the Terms

Knowing some of the basic terms of object-oriented programming will help get you started programming with objects. Here are some brief definitions.

Abstraction refers to each routine being a "black box"; it models an item in the real world, and hides its complexity from the user. The user of an item needs to know only *what* an object does, not *how* it does it. When you drive a car, you need to know what steps you need to take to make the car go in the direction you desire, but you don't need to know what the engine does when you step on the gas, or how your turning the steering wheel translates into the car's wheels turning in the desired direction.

Classes and subclasses are the blueprints, or templates, for objects. Objects are created from the class at the time the application is run; an object is the result of turning the blueprint design into actuality.

Class hierarchy refers to the parent class/subclass/object relationship.

Encapsulation refers to an object's being self-contained, meaning that its function is set, and the user needs to know only how to use the object. The functionality and characteristics of the object are contained within the object's definition.

Inheritance refers to the way objects take on the properties and methods of the class from which they are created (defined). Subclasses inherit properties from base classes; objects inherit properties from subclasses and their parent classes. If you make changes to the parent class, subclasses and objects belonging to that parent automatically reflect the change.

Instance of a class is another term for an object.

Methods are procedures (programs) attached to objects, and are executed in response to a command or an event.

Objects are made up of classes combining both data and properties. A form is an object, and the controls on the form are also objects.

Polymorphism means that objects can call methods with the same name, but the behavior is based on the functions of the object and not on the method. In a real-life example, you might tell three people to go to the store. One might walk, another might ride a bicycle, and the third might drive, but they would all be following your instructions to "go."

Properties are the characteristics, or attributes, of an object or class.

The Benefits of Object-Oriented Programming

Object-oriented programming is an environmentally conscious way to develop systems; it encourages the developer to reduce, reuse, and recycle code and objects. Because of this, it can lead to faster, more efficient development, and more accurate prototypes.

Here are some benefits of object-oriented programming:

- Reusable objects: Once a class has been developed and debugged, it can be added to new applications with no additional testing. You can also combine objects to create a "superclass," which can be used to create newer, more dynamic objects.
- Faster development: Because objects are reusable, you can save hours by adding objects to the program rather than having to write long and tedious code strings.
- Less code: Because you generate fewer lines of code, there is less opportunity for errors.

- Easier and reduced maintenance: Because changes are required in fewer locations, maintenance of the application is kept to a minimum.
- Easy to modify objects: You can make a change to an object with minimal impact on the rest of the system.

What is an object?

An object is simply a self-contained class or collection of classes that perform a specific function.

For example, a command button is an object. You may have programmed a Quit button as a means of going back to the previous screen, or you may have programmed it to take the user completely out of the application. Whatever happens as a result of the user clicking on a button is determined by you when you create the button (object).

The command button, like other objects, always contains two types of information: characteristics and behavior. Characteristics are also called *properties* or *attributes*, and behaviors are also called *methods*.

Objects may have properties and methods in common with other objects; those objects should be created from the same *class*. A class defines the properties and methods for objects that belong to the class; this is called *inheritance*. Since all objects within a class inherit their characteristics from the class, any changes to the class update all objects in that class. This makes maintenance much easier than it would be if you had to change each object individually.

How Objects Work

Events

Objects have a set of *events* associated with them—anything that happens involving that object. A mouse click, double-click, or the cursor moving onto an object are examples of events. When an event occurs, it *fires*—causes execution of—methods with the same name as the event.

Methods

Methods are procedures or programs attached to objects and invoked by the object's associated events. As mentioned above, different classes can have methods of the same name. For example, the Quit button could cause the user to exit a form or close the entire application.

Understanding Classes

All objects are created from classes; classes define the characteristics of objects. Because of *inheritance*, any changes made to the *base* class or any *subclasses* to which the object belongs are reflected in all objects in that class.

Suppose you create a class called Customer. The delete logic for this class would be to delete the current record. The code for that method would be invoked by the click event for a Delete button and would exist in the objects created from the class. The Delete button is an object unrelated to the People class, but when it is used in conjunction with the Customer class, it executes the proper behavior and deletes the current record.

Each time that button is used in a form based on the class Customer, it behaves exactly the same way—invoking the Delete method for the class. If you decide to change the behavior so that you must confirm the deletion, you make the change only in the Customer class, not to each instance of the Delete button or the class from which the Delete button is created.

You might not want to delete active customers just because the user clicks on the Delete button; first you might want to verify that there are no outstanding invoices for this active customer. In all other ways, however, you want the active customer to be the same as the other entities in the Customer class. You can create a subclass called Active Customer, whose base class is Customer. Because of inheritance, the new Active Customer class automatically takes on the properties and methods of its parent class, Customer. You can override any of the properties or methods of the parent class in order to create a new Delete method for the Active Customer class, in which the logic says: "If there are no open invoices for this customer, ask the user to confirm the deletion, and then delete if appropriate; otherwise, don't."

Faster Development

Because of *abstraction* and *encapsulation*, the fact that each routine is self-defined and models a real-world event regardless of its environment, objects can easily be reused and inserted into new places in any application. Because an object invokes the proper method for the associated class (*polymorphism*), the developer can reuse objects from other applications as well as from other developers, knowing only the name of the routine called by the object. Since there is much less code written, development and debugging time are greatly reduced. Since the object itself does not need to be debugged each time it is used, more time is saved, and reliability increases.

Easier Maintenance

Under procedural code, changing the behavior of a module may mean making changes to a called procedure, a calling program, and anything else that might be affected by the change. A system-wide change probably needs to be coded in multiple programs. Any programmer, especially one who isn't the original developer, is likely to spend a great deal of time and effort simply tracing through programs and figuring out relationships between calling and called routines.

In Visual FoxPro, however, the implementation of object-oriented programming ensures that a design change would not require a major rewrite. Since each object stands alone and does not need to interact with its environment, the changing of an object's methods or properties is unlikely to have a major effect on other system components. You can make the required modification with much less worry about "breaking" any other part of the system. Making a system-wide change is easier as well—simply make the necessary change to the relevant class or classes.

Object-Oriented Programming and Visual FoxPro

Visual FoxPro provides the ability to create objects and classes using the interface or the language. The Visual Class Designer has the same interface as the Forms Designer, so creating a class visually is the same as creating a form. In addition, once you have created a form or object, you can save the object or a combination of objects as a class, even if you hadn't originally designated it as a class. You can set the properties of a class or object using the language, or you can set the properties visually, using the Properties Designer. Because you can create classes and objects with as little or as much coding as you want, Visual FoxPro provides a simple and powerful way to become familiar with and use object-oriented techniques.

A Tour of Visual FoxPro

You will now take a look at Visual FoxPro. You will open the Project Manager, Database Designer, and the Form Designer. These new tools will make your application development easier and faster.

Taking a look at Visual FoxPro

When you launch Visual FoxPro, the Project Manager creates a new, empty project so you can add existing items to your project or create new items to include in the project.

Start Visual FoxPro

1. From the Program Manager, select the Visual FoxPro program group.
2. Select and click the Visual FoxPro 3.0 icon.

   FoxPro starts and the Project Manager appears.

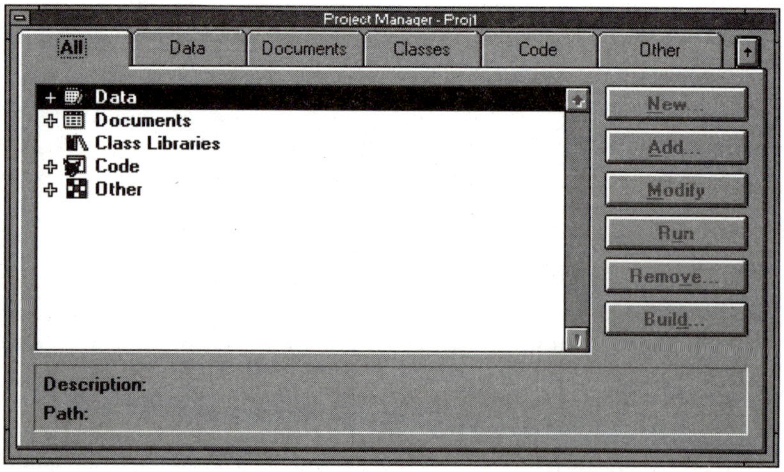

The Project Manager

You can use the Project Manager to organize and manage your files. A project is a collection of files, data, documents, and Visual FoxPro objects that are saved as a file with a .PJX extension. When the Project Manager window is active, Visual FoxPro displays the Project menu on the menu bar.

The items in the Project Manager are organized in an outline that you can expand or collapse. A plus sign appears next to a symbol if there are one or more items of that type in the project. Click the plus sign next to a symbol to see items in the list. Click the minus sign to collapse an expanded list.

The Project Manager is used as the basis for building the LitWare application described in this book, and will be used in almost all of the lessons in the book.

The Database Designer

You use the Database Designer to add, modify, and remove tables, set relationships between tables, edit stored procedures, and work with local and remote views of the database. The Database Designer displays all the tables, views, and relationships contained in a database. When the Database Designer window is active, Visual FoxPro displays the Database menu and the Database Designer toolbar.

Each table is represented by a resizeable window that lists the table's fields and indexes, if any exist. The Database Designer shows persistent relationships by displaying lines between tables that connect the indexes.

Open the Database Designer

1. In the Project Manager, click the plus sign next to Data.
2. Select Databases.
3. Click New.

   The Create dialog box appears.
4. Type **data1.dbc** in the database name field.
5. Click Create.

   The Database Designer and Toolbar appear.

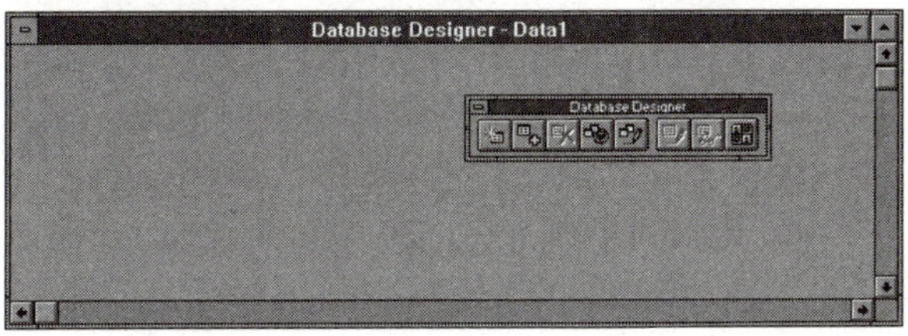

The Database Designer toolbar is displayed when the Database Designer is active.

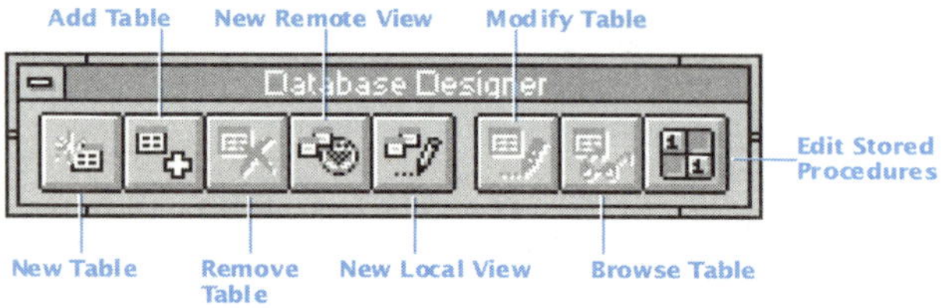

The Database Designer will be used in Lesson 4.

6 Close the Database Designer.

The Form Designer

You can use the Form Designer to create and modify forms and form sets visually. A form set consists of one or more forms that can be manipulated as a unit. Forms and form sets are objects with their own properties, events, and methods.

When the Form Designer window is active, Visual FoxPro displays the Form menu, the Form Controls toolbar, the Form Designer toolbar, and the Properties window.

Open the Form Designer

1 In the Project Manager, click the plus sign next to Documents.

2 Select Forms.

3 Click New.

The New Form dialog box appears.

4 Click New Form.

The Form Designer for FormDoc1 and the Properties Window for FormDoc1 appear.

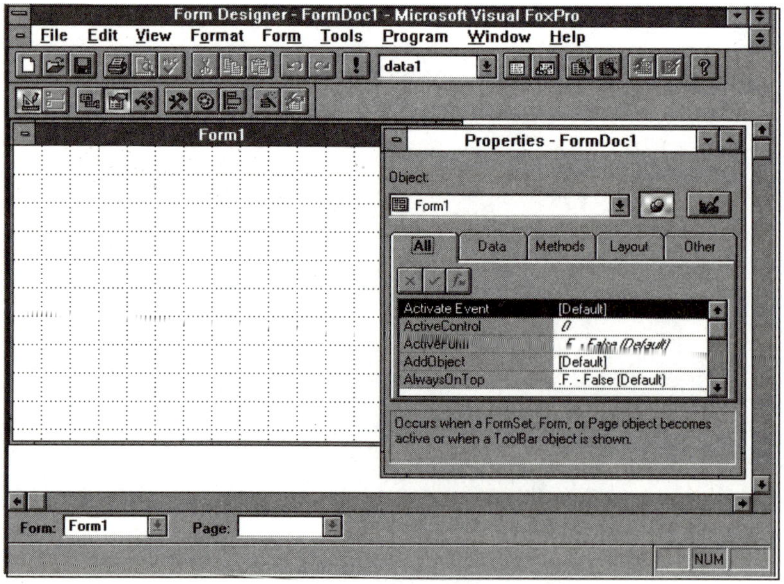

FormDoc1 is the name assigned by Visual FoxPro to the new form until you give it a name. The Form Designer will be used in Lessons 5 and 6.

5 Close the Form Designer.

The Menu Bar

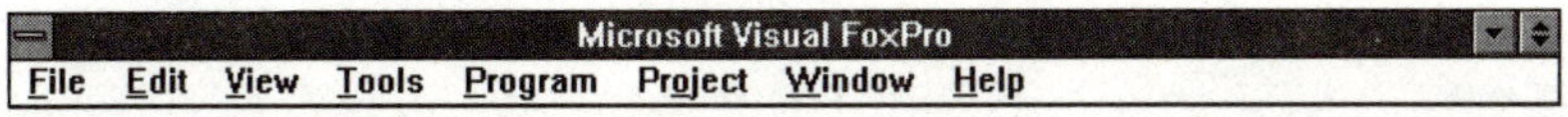

Commands and functions used to operate Visual FoxPro are grouped under eight different menus in the Menu Bar, which is located at the top of the screen. Each menu's commands are grouped according to their functions. Below is a summary of the commands found in each menu.

Menu	Contains Command For
File	Opening, saving, closing, reverting, importing, exporting, printing and page setup, opening recently used files and exiting a file or Visual FoxPro.
Edit	Undoing operations; selecting and editing text; search and replace features; links and object information.
View	Viewing the toolbars.
Tools	Wizards, spelling, macros, class browser, trace and debug windows and options.
Program	Do, cancel, resume, suspend, and compile.
Project	New, add, modify, run, remove and rename files; Include, set main and edit description; project information, errors and build; cleanup project.
Window	Displaying windows.
Help	Contents, search and technical help.

Now that you have briefly toured the Visual FoxPro development environment, you can close Visual FoxPro.

If you want to continue to the next lesson

1 Click File on the Menu bar.

2 Select Close.

If you want to quit Visual FoxPro for now

1 Click File on the Menu bar.

2 Select Exit.

Lesson Summary

In this lesson, you were given a quick overview of some of the new features in Visual FoxPro. You also learned the terms related to object-oriented programming, and how they apply to real-world examples.

You learned the major benefits of object-oriented programming. Because you generate less code using Visual FoxPro, there is likely to be fewer errors. You can easily modify the objects with minimal impact on the rest of a system because they are self-contained. And the same object can be used in different systems to perform functionally similar but executionally different code. In the example of the Delete button, you saw how the same object can be used to perform the same function on two different types of items.

Preview of the Next Lesson

In the next lesson, you'll assume the role of a systems analyst for the LitWare Corporation. As a systems analyst for LitWare, you will identify the problem LitWare is having with its current system, and design a new application using Visual FoxPro.

Lesson

2

Analyzing the Problem

In this lesson you will learn:

- About the challenge that faces LitWare.
- Why Visual FoxPro is the answer.
- How to use Visual FoxPro to get to a solution.

Estimated time
30 min.

LitWare, Inc., charged you, a systems analyst, with the task of developing a customer service data management system. The company's decision was based on an internal analysis that determined a need for an on-line system specifically designed to meet their requirements. This lesson describes why LitWare contacted you and defines your recommended solution.

LitWare, Inc., Company History

LitWare, Inc., a software development company, has been selling its core products for over two years. It is a small company and has been able to utilize manual systems for all of its data maintenance and customer service needs. To maintain their rather small database, LitWare was utilizing space on a shared mainframe for inventory control. Suddenly, two of their products began to sell beyond all expectations, overburdening the manual system.

As sales continued to soar, LitWare released upgrades for their products, adding features that made the products more attractive to an even larger audience. LitWare now had to deal with the sales of the upgraded products. The company needed a system that could provide faster and more effective processing of product sales and support. The manual system, although it had worked in the past, was now inefficient, time consuming, and costly. The initial reaction was to add more phone lines and Customer Service Representatives (CSR). A new quality team evaluated the needs of the customer service department.

As the number of customer calls continued to rise, so did the level of customer dissatisfaction. Customers waited on the telephone for too long a time, some clients were accidentally abandoned while on hold, and others just hung up, never to call back again. The result was lost sales, unhappy customers, disgruntled CSRs, and LitWare's quality team scrambling for a solution.

Realizing that customer satisfaction was critical to LitWare's success, LitWare's quality team decided to do a workflow analysis of the customer service department. The quality team defined and charted the existing manual workflow process, and defined the requirements for converting to an on-line data management system. Once the team defined the tasks of the customer service department, they would be able to develop the requirements necessary to improve the level of service.

Customer Service, Information, and Access Requirements for the LitWare Application

The manual system used by LitWare customer service was first developed to track the customers and number of products owned by the customers. This system met the needs of a small company with limited resources and customers.

CSRs were responsible for logging customer information received through phone calls or mailed warranty cards. The CSR completed a form containing basic customer information:

- Customer name
- Customer address
- City, State, Zip code
- Phone
- Fax
- Product owned
- Product code

The form was filed in the customer service office. When a customer called, the CSR put the caller on hold, went to the filing cabinet, pulled the file, and completed the customer call. The call included completing information regarding customer file updates, (i.e. change of residence, new phone number etc.), the ordering of new products, the ordering of an upgrade product, and checking inventory status. If there was more than one customer with the same name, the CSR took more time to go back and forth to the filing cabinet to get the right file. Mistakes were made. Time was lost.

Sales ballooned and new product upgrades were completed and released for sale, but the manual customer service process remained. The forms changed to include more products and upgrades, but the process was not updated and became a nightmare for the CSRs. Once the CSR had the correct file, he or she had to verify customer information and products owned by the customer. The CSR recorded changes, took new orders, and hopefully had time to conduct a customer satisfaction survey. Inventory information was at least one day old and the CSR had to thumb through the inventory pages to verify stock, another time-consuming process.

As an order was taken, the CSR wrote the information on an order form and sent the form to shipping at the end of the day for entry into the shared mainframe system.

The manual system was no longer working.

As the quality team looked at the existing system they discovered:

- Customer calls were too long.
- Many customers just hung up.
- Information in the files was incorrect: when customers had similar names, often the incorrect file was pulled during a customer call, and customers purchased products at upgrade prices without having purchased the original product.
- Shipments were late due to lack of inventory, resulting in additional customer calls.
- Sales declined as customer dissatisfaction increased.
- The customer service staff had a large turnover rate due to stress.
- There was no method to query information and generate reports except the month-end physical inventory reports.

The quality team realized that something must be done, immediately.

The team implemented a needs analysis process to gather input from customers, CSRs, and LitWare executives. This needs analysis resulted in a new set of requirements for the customer service program.

Information and access requirements

Customer Service Representatives must be able to:

- View and update customer data information
- View and update customer product ownership information
- View current inventory status
- Process orders with automatic inventory updates
- Have customers complete customer satisfaction surveys immediately

Other LitWare departments, such as Sales and Marketing must be able to:

- Query data
- Print reports
- Customize queries and reports

Application requirements

Customer Service Representatives must be able to:

- Verify customers
- Enter new customers into the system
- Update current customer data files
- Process orders
- Verify and update inventory
- Gather survey information
- Generate reports from available data
- Provide other CSRs access to the data files at the same time
- Grow and expand capabilities

Inventory personnel must have the ability to:

- Provide daily inventory reports

LitWare Executives must have the ability to:

- Generate daily inventory reports
- Query and view data on demand
- Query and generate reports on demand
- Expand the application as LitWare grows

Given these requirements, the quality team decided to seek outside assistance for a solution. They contracted you to develop a solution based on the defined requirements.

Application specifications

Reviewing the workflow process requirements provided by LitWare, you concluded that the new application solution must include:

- Immediate access to customer information
- Verification of customer identity
- Ability to immediately update customer data file
- Ability to conduct customer survey quickly
- Access to customer product table to verify customer ownership of the product
- Order processing
- Access to remote inventory data files for status review
- Time-of-purchase inventory updating
- Security access for data protection

- On-demand query and reporting
- User-friendly graphical interface
- On-screen language easily understood by the user
- Easy-to-use data entry screens
- Simultaneous multiple-user access to screens and tables
- Flexibility and ability to upgrade
- Short learning curve for CSRs
- Transparent data processing

You determined that the best solution for LitWare would include a database management application running on a LAN, with a client-server hardware configuration linked to the shared mainframe. The customer data files would reside on the server while inventory would reside on the remote mainframe, all accessible by the CSRs. Inventory staff would have access to only the inventory data files, while LitWare executives would have security access for data integrity, querying, and reporting.

NOTE Our focus is on the software solution; we will not go into detail about the hardware solution. However, it is critical to remember that the hardware utilized for any application is as critical as the application itself. An application running on an inadequate hardware platform will fail. It is also important for database management applications to access data from a variety of sources.

Creating the Solution

The solution for the successful development and implementation of the LitWare application includes four data tables. These four tables include information about the customer and the products owned by the customer, as well as product and inventory information.

The customer table contains:

- Customer identification number
- First name
- Middle initial
- Last name
- Some address
- Work address
- City

- State
- Postal zip code
- Home telephone
- Work telephone

The customer owned product table links the customers to the products they own and includes the following information:

- Customer identification number
- Product serial number
- Date of purchase

The product table contains:

- Product name
- Product number
- Product code
- Cost of product
- Product quantity in inventory

The items of most interest to LitWare included level of customer satisfaction; accuracy of customer data and elimination of duplicate customer records; accuracy of customer purchasing history, including the identification of products the customer owns as well as the date of purchase; accuracy of inventory data, including the quantity on hand and inventory adjustments at time of purchase; and the ability to query and generate reports for above items.

Now that you have determined the data requirements, you developed a flow chart charting the path traveled by the data.

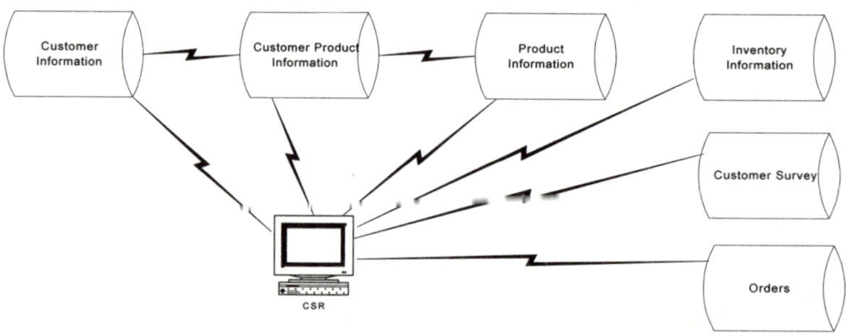

Application requirements

In seeking a solution for LitWare, you develop the following list of application requirements:

- Established in the industry with a high level of technical support
- Has the capabilities to access and integrate data from a variety of sources
- Emphasizes design over coding
- Provides a visual interface for development
- Provides on screen forms with data fields
- Adheres to all standard Windows events and protocol
- Has customized menus and toolbars
- Allows reusable objects that be can utilized in a variety of situations
- Provides button usage
- Uses classes, libraries, and inheritance to maximize the flexibility of coding
- Maintains data stability
- Operates efficiently on a client-server LAN
- Has an easy user interface

The final design

Now that the specifications and requirements have been defined from the LitWare perspective, what about the developer perspective? What are the developer's requirements for a tool used to develop, maintain, and continually upgrade the LitWare application?

You recommended Microsoft Visual FoxPro 3 for Windows from Microsoft Corporation as the development application for the LitWare solution. This product meets and exceeds the data and application requirements set forth by LitWare. Visual FoxPro provides the following advantages to the developer:

- Quick prototype
- Multi-user support
- Rapid application development
- Robust form builder
- Easy maintenance
- Transaction processing
- Ability to develop locally and move to remote
- Works equally well with local and remote data

- Ease of query and report generation
- Superior graphical interface

An Overview Before the Quick Tour

The LitWare application will consist of five on-screen forms that allow the CSR to effectively complete a call. The first is the custfind form, which allows the CSR to identify the customer:

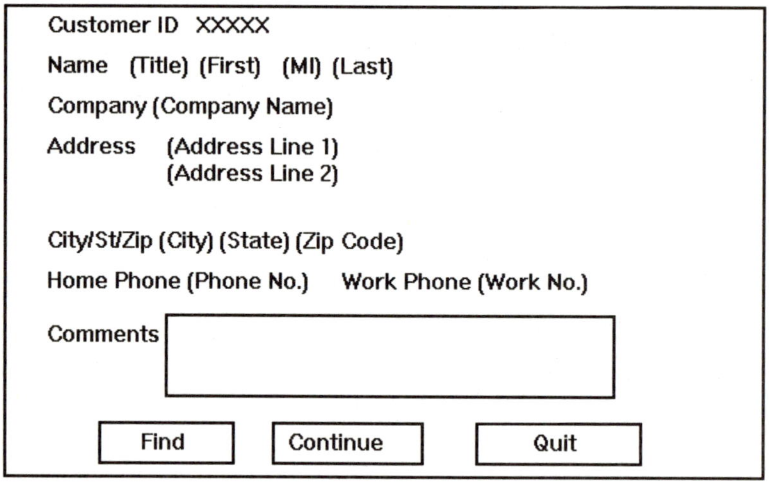

If there is another customer with the same name, the custmore form will appear, allowing selection and verification of the customer.

First Name	Middle I.	Last Name	Address 1	City	State	Zip

Once verified, the custdata form appears, and the CSR verifies or adds new customer information:

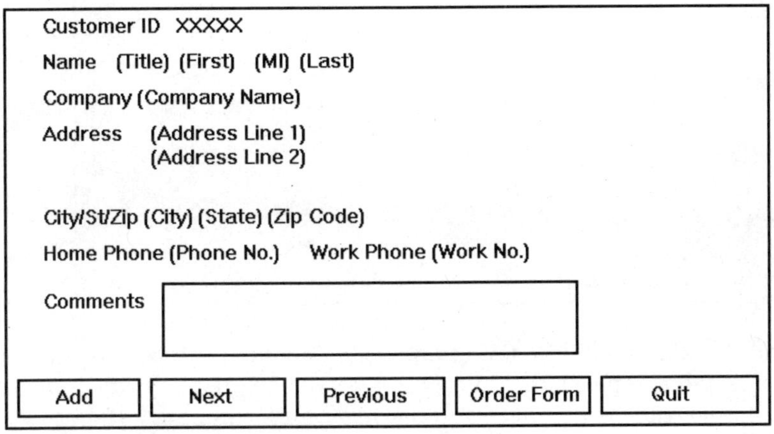

The call is processed and as the order is placed, the custinvc form appears to present current inventory information:

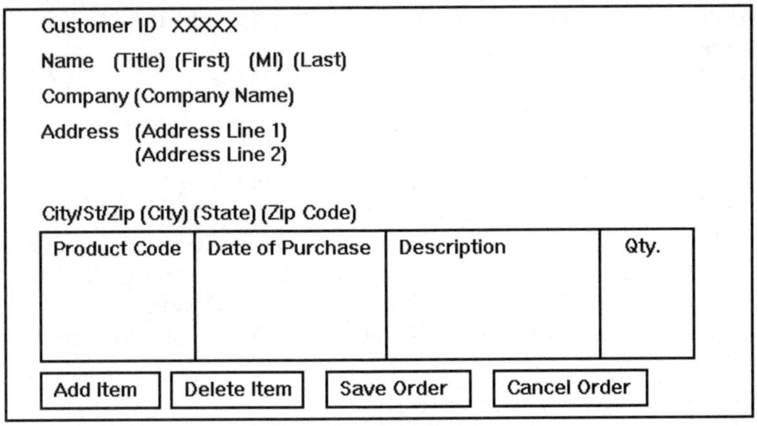

Once the order is placed, shipping is scheduled, and the inventory is updated (all done by Visual FoxPro as the CSR enters data). Now the CSR will ask the customer a few survey questions:

Were you satisfied with the service you received during this call? (Y/N)

Would you like to be placed on our mailing list? (Y/N)

Would you like to be entered into a free drawing? (Y/N)

Comments and Suggestions

When the call is closed, the CSR prepares for the next call by returning to the custfind form. The CSR completes the data processing as he or she moves from screen to screen. The customer table is updated, and the inventory is updated and accessible for querying and report generation.

The Visual FoxPro solution is efficient, and easy-to-use and maintain. The time per call is decreased to better than acceptable levels. The information available to the CSR and the customer is current, and action is taken and closure achieved at each call. Inventory is up-to-date and the LitWare executive staff has the information they need to monitor, plan, and grow.

Lesson Summary

This lesson provided the LitWare challenge of upgrading from a manual to an electronic customer service program, and a database design for the solution to that problem. As the systems analyst, you evaluated specifications and requirements for a new system, and established and designed a solution based on those specifications and requirements. You viewed some of the forms and tables in the final design. You have completed the specifications and requirements, but how will you make it all come together?

Preview of the Next Lesson

In Lesson 3 you will be given a quick tour of the LitWare application. You will temporarily become a LitWare CSR and process a call. The tour will prepare you for the application you will develop in this book and begin to introduce you to the power of Visual FoxPro.

Lesson

3

Using a Visual FoxPro Prototype

Estimated time
20 min.

In this lesson you will learn how to:

- Use a prototype to view an application.
- Use objects in a Visual FoxPro application.

As the system analyst who developed the design for the LitWare application discussed in Lesson 2, you decided that a prototype of the Visual FoxPro application would provide an opportunity to test the design early in the development cycle. The prototype, a fully functioning application using limited amounts of data, allows users to test the application in a real-life situation. The prototype becomes a tool for you; you can make enhancements to the application during development based upon the information you gather from observing users.

You will use a prototype to work through a customer call, verify customer identity, take an order, complete a customer survey, and close the call.

As you work through a customer call, you will use an application developed with the many new powerful features of Visual FoxPro. After using the final product, you will use this step-by-step book to learn how to develop your own Visual FoxPro application.

Start the lesson

1. Open Visual FoxPro.
2. From the File menu, click open.
3. In the Directories List box, select c:\Litware\proj_03.
4. Select litware.pjx, and click the OK button.
5. From the Documents Tab, run the Custdata form.

The first screen displayed is the Customer Find screen. This screen displays a form that allows the user to locate, add, and modify data. You will notice a number of on-screen objects that help the user access and display data.

Using the Prototype

LitWare CSRs are responsible for receiving inbound calls from customers. These calls include the following tasks: verifying customer identity and product ownership, taking orders, and gathering customer information for a customer survey. You will test a prototype application developed in Visual FoxPro to determine if these tasks are easy to accomplish and whether the application provides the data desired.

Some of the items you should take notice of include: the form, the text boxes (name, address, and so forth), the command buttons (find, next, previous, and so forth), and the combo box (states). All of these objects have been given certain characteristics (properties) to perform pre-defined tasks.

Determine the identity of the customer

Upon answering the phone, you discover that the customer's last name is Barraco.

1. With the Customer Find Screen open, click the last name field.
2. Type **Barraco.**

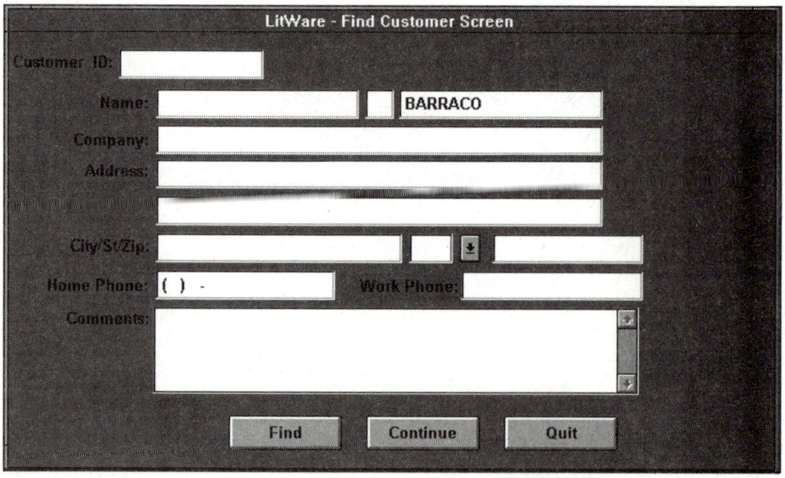

3 Click the Find command button.

A customer list appears.

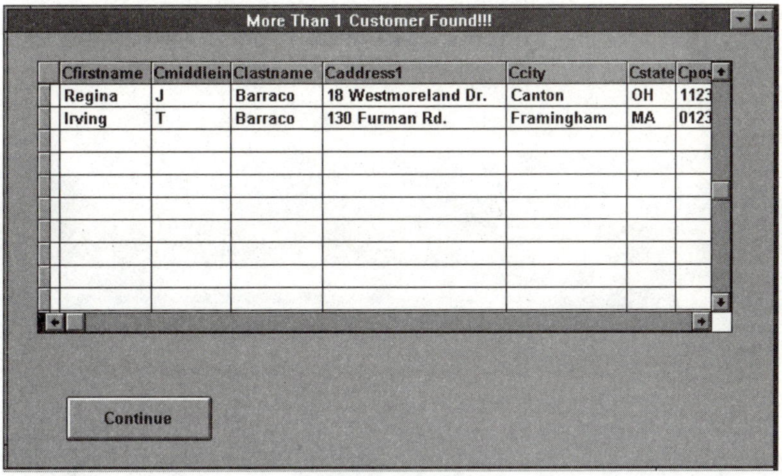

There are two customers with the last name Barraco. In this Visual FoxPro prototype, the application automatically searches the customer table to determine if there are any duplicates of a last name. If a duplicate is found, the information for both customers is displayed on the screen.

4 Verify the first name of the caller.

This customer gave her first name as Regina. The other Barraco has a first name of Irving.

5 Click on Regina Barraco on the Customer List.

The customer information screen for Regina Barraco appears on the screen.

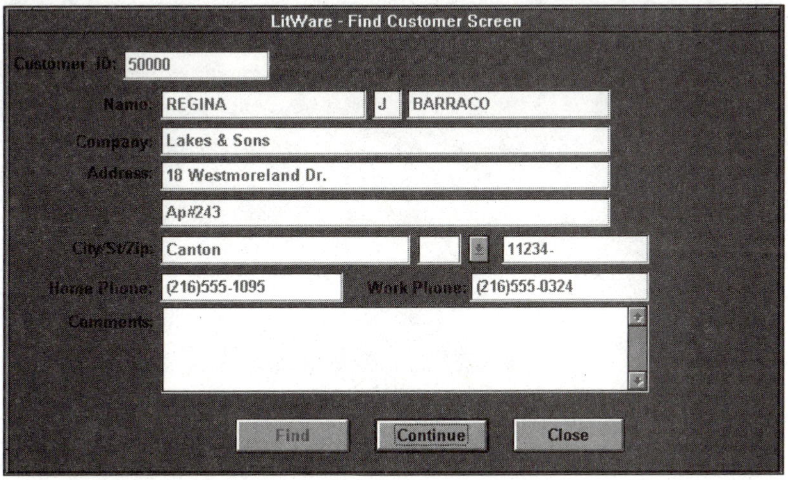

Review and verify the information for Regina Barraco. Once you are certain that Regina is who she says she is, you are now ready to take her order.

Take an order

1 Click the Continue command button.

The Customer Information Screen appears.

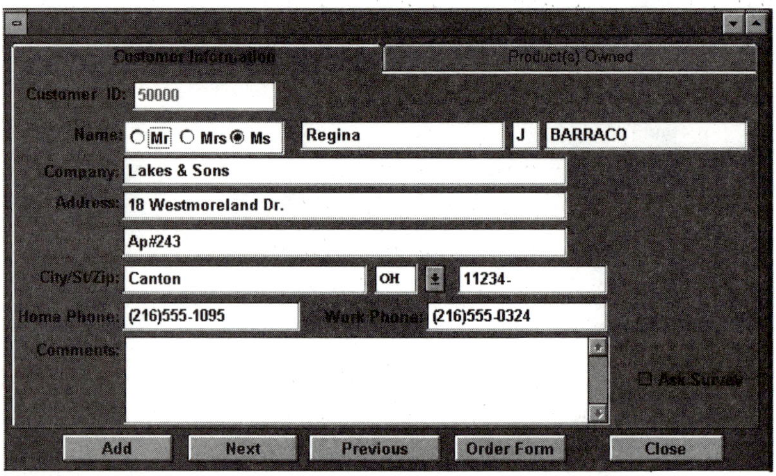

2 Click the Order Form command button.

The order form appears.

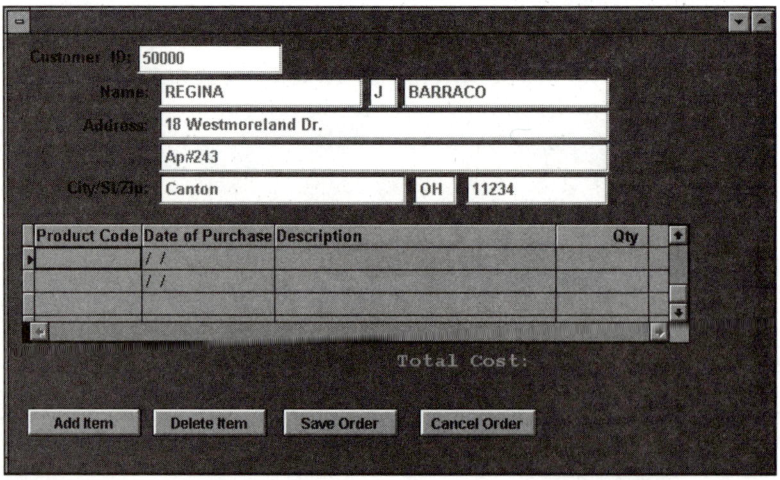

3 Click the Add Item command button.

The product inventory list appears from a remote data source. Visual FoxPro provides the tools to access data from a variety of sources with the click of a command button.

With the inventory list on the screen, verify price and availability. Ask Regina which product she wishes to order. She says she is interested in ordering product #1002, Government Database Update.

4 Select product #1002.

The Government Database Update is added to the customer data information showing that the product has been purchased by Regina. Confirm with Regina the price of $79.99 and Visual FoxPro automatically updates the remote inventory file.

5 With the order complete, click the Save Order command button.

The customer information screen reappears.

Take a customer survey

Inform Regina that you would like to ask her a few questions.

1 If the Ask Survey checkbox is selected, select the Quit button to access the survey screen.

The survey screen appears.

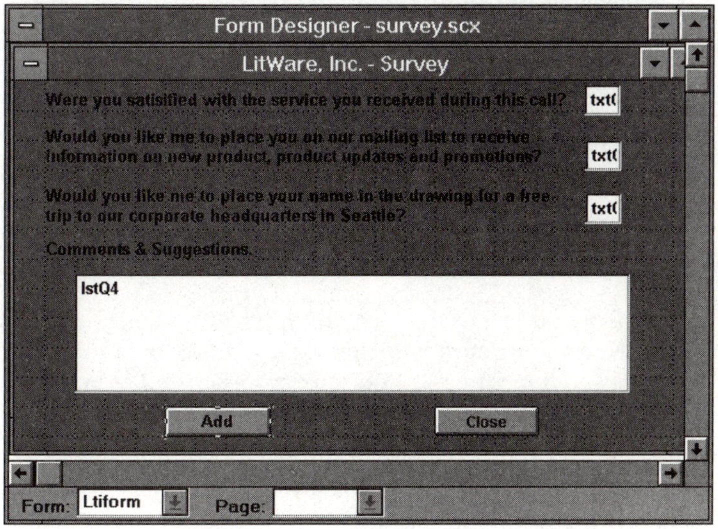

2 Ask the customer each of the following questions:

- Were you satisfied with the service you received during this call?
- Would you like me to place you on our mailing list to receive information on new products, product updates, and promotions?

- Would you like me to place your name in the drawing for a free trip to our corporate headquarters in Seattle?
- Any comments?

Check the **yes** or **no** box based on the responses to questions 1, 2, and 3. If Regina had given any comments you would type them into the comment field. When you have finished the survey, thank Regina for her time and order, wish her a good day (evening), and hang up the phone.

3. Select the Close command button.

   The Customer Find Screen appears.

   You are now ready for the next call.

One Step Further: Reviewing the Application Prototype

You have the opportunity to go back and review the prototype any number of times. This is an excellent time to go back and spend a few minutes on each screen and examine each of the objects that were not used in the call with Regina.

If you want to continue to the next lesson

1. Click File on the Menu bar.
2. Select Close.

If you want to quit Visual FoxPro for now

1. Click File on the Menu bar.
2. Select Exit.

Lesson Summary

The prototype was a test of the LitWare application design. You viewed forms and used data from a variety of sources, including a remote inventory file from a mainframe (simulated) using a local view. You took an order and completed a customer survey. You witnessed the use of objects, forms, command buttons, and check boxes to access and display data. Now it is time for you to learn how to develop the application.

Preview of the Next Lesson

Lesson 4, Building a New Database, is the first step in the process of developing the application. You will learn how to use Project Manager, create a new table, add tables, and append data to the tables. You will also learn to link tables and establish referential integrity.

Part

2

Developing the Visual FoxPro Solution

Lesson

4

Building a New Database

Estimated time

60 min.

In this lesson you will learn how to:

- Create a new project and database.
- Build a new table, and define fields and indexes.
- Append data to existing tables.
- Link tables.
- Define relationships between tables.
- Ensure referential integrity.

At the core of a Microsoft Visual FoxPro 3 for Windows application are tables that contain data. The tables can be free tables that you have created in FoxPro or another database system, or tables that you have built and related to each other using Visual FoxPro. The tables that you create in this lesson will be placed in a database that you will access when you use the Visual FoxPro Project Manager to develop the LitWare application.

You will now start developing the LitWare application based on the analysis of the LitWare problem you read in Lesson 2, and the prototype of the LitWare application you toured in Lesson 3. Realizing that the power of any application lies in the organization of its data, and the accessibility and flexibility of that data, the LitWare quality team developed a complete list of the data items that the application will need to include.

The quality team determined that a customer table containing information about LitWare customers and a product table containing information about LitWare products are needed to drive the LitWare application. From these parent tables, other tables, including one that lists the LitWare products each customer owns, will also be developed for the LitWare application. The application is designed to provide easy access to customer information for LitWare CSRs. The CSR can verify the customer's identity and product ownership, submit purchase orders, and update a remote inventory database.

The data items contained in the Customer table are:

- Unique customer number
- Title
- Customer name
- Company
- Home address
- Work address
- City
- State
- Postal code
- Home telephone
- Work telephone
- Date customer was added to the database
- Customer comments

The data items contained in the Product table are:

- Product code
- Product quantity on hand
- Product cost
- Product name

The data items contained in the Customer Product table are:

- Unique customer number
- Product code
- Date of product purchase by customer
- Product serial number

Now that you've read the analysis, viewed the prototype, and examined the list of data items, it's time to get started building the application. In this lesson, you will concentrate on building tables and defining the relationships between tables.

Start the lesson

1. Open Visual FoxPro.
2. Close all open projects.

Getting Started with Projects and Databases

You will begin developing your application by creating a project, database, and tables. In this lesson, you will use the Visual FoxPro Project Manager, Table Designer, and Database Designer to create the LitWare project, build tables, and attach data to the tables. First you will create the LitWare project file as the container for the tools and database. From Project Manager, you will use the Table and Database Designers to build tables, append data to a table, add tables, and define indexes. In this lesson, you'll use expression builders, drop-down menus and pop-up menus—all designed to save time in the development process and provide an easy and efficient means to building your application.

Creating a New Project

The Project Manager is organized much like a file cabinet and consists of several tabs, such as All, Data, Documents, and Classes. These tabs give you rapid and easy access to objects that you will use in the project. As the application is developed, you will use point-and-click or drag-and-drop mouse techniques to access and manipulate the application components.

Create a new project

1. From the Visual FoxPro File menu, select New.

   A New dialog box appears.

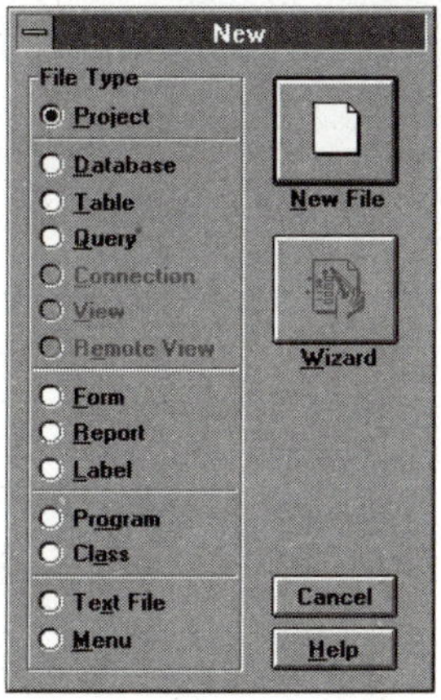

2. Under File Type, select Project.

New File

3 Click the New File button.

The Create dialog box appears.

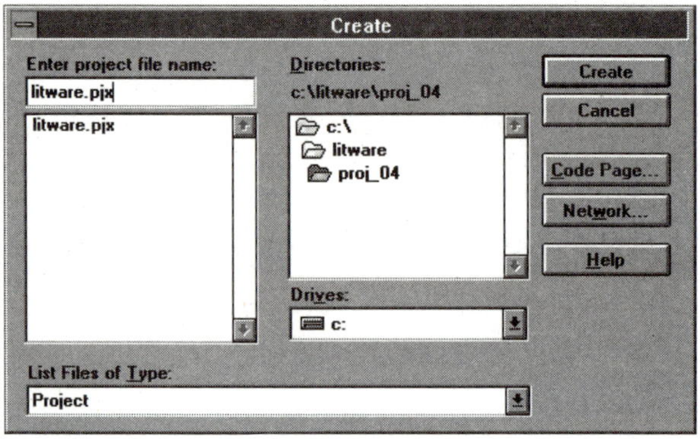

4 Type **LitWare** as the project name.

5 Set the drive and directory path to read: c:\litware\proj_04.

You may need to modify the path if you installed the lesson files in a different drive.

6 Click the Create button.

The Project Manager dialog box appears. Notice that the name LitWare appears in the title bar. Visual FoxPro displays the name of the project in its title bar.

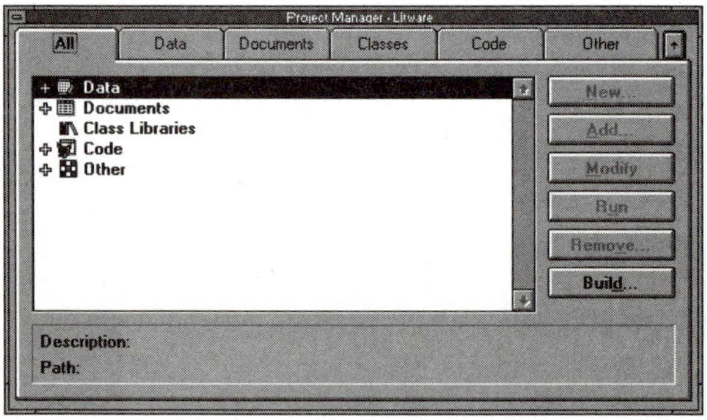

Creating a New Database

Within a project, you create a database by placing information in tables. You will use the Database Designer to create the database. The LitWare project will consist of a database containing tables for customer data, product information, and customer-owned product information, with the customer-owned product information table linked to the products inventory table located on a remote server.

Create a new database

1. From the Project Manager, click the Data Tab.

   Items contained in the Data Tab appear.

2. From the list of Data items, select Databases.

New

3. Click the New button.

   The Create dialog box appears.

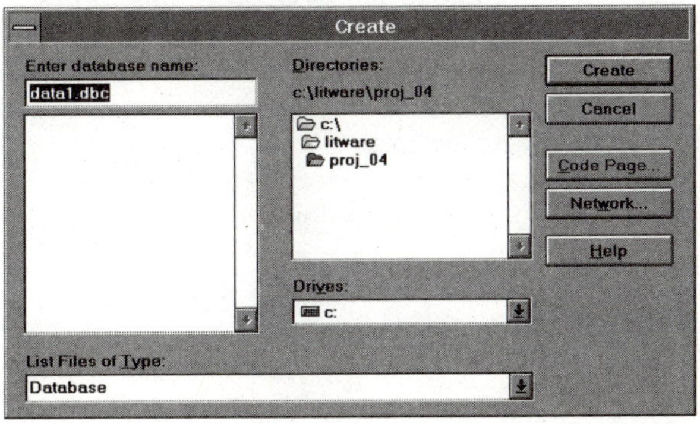

4. Enter **custinfo** for the database container name.

5. Set the drive and directory path to read: c:\litware\proj_04.

   You may need to modify the path if you installed the lesson files in a different drive.

6. Click the Create button.

7. From the View menu, select toolbars, click Database Designer

   The Database Designer appears.

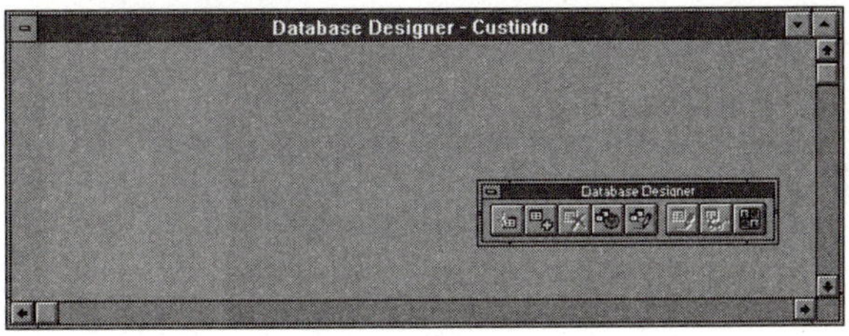

When you begin a new project, the Database Designer is empty. You must create the tables to store information in the custinfo database container. First you will create the customer table, and then you will add the custprod (customer-owned products) table.

Creating a New Table

Tables can be added to a database using two different tools: Table Designer or Table Wizards. You can make use of the greater flexibility of the Table Designer to create and modify tables, fields, and indexes. You can also implement validation rules, default values, and null values with ease.

TIP Use the Table Wizard to develop simple tables such as a mailing list. The Table Wizard asks a series of questions that guide you through the table creation process. The Table Wizard contains predetermined table types and field names. After the Table Wizard has created the table, you can modify the results for your application.

In this exercise you will use the Table Designer to create the Customer table, add fields, and create indexes.

Create a new table

1 From the Database Designer toolbar, click the New Table button.

The New Table dialog box appears.

New Table

2 Click the New Table Button.

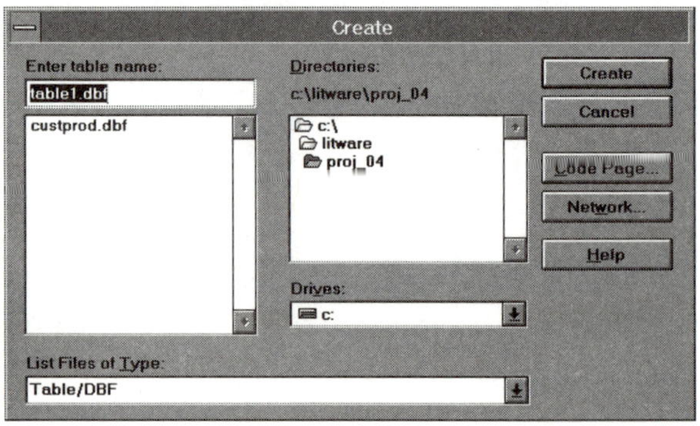

The Create dialog box lists the custprod. This table has already been created and is part of the practice files; it will be used throughout this book.

3 Type **customer** as the table name.

4 Set the drive and directory path to read: c:\litware\proj_04.

You may need to modify the path if you installed the lesson files in a different drive.

5 Click the Create button.

The Table Designer appears.

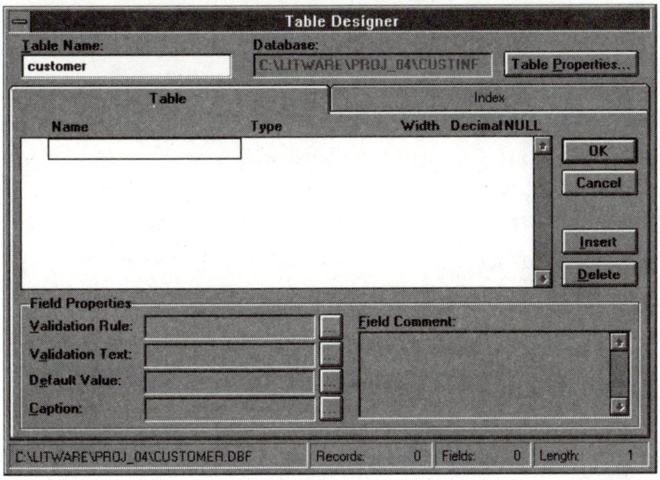

Adding and Defining Fields in a Table

Customer data is contained in the customer table. You determined the data items that must be included in the customer table when you listed the information that LitWare required for each customer. To reflect those data requirements, you must define the type and size of each field, and then assign a field name to each item. These field names will be the names used by the database. You will also assign a caption to each field. The field names are the names used by the database; the captions are the names that will appear as the column headers in reports.

The following field names are used for the customer table:

Field Name	Field Contents
csalutation	title
ccustomerno	customer unique identification number
cfirstname	customer first name
cmiddleinit	customer middle initial
clastname	customer last name

Field Name	Field Contents
ccompany	customer company
caddress1	customer address 1
caddress2	customer address 2
ccity	customer city
cstate	customer state
cpostalcode	customer zip code
chomephone	customer home phone
cworkphone	customer work phone
ddateadded	date customer added to the database
mcomment	comment field

You will also need to define the type and width of each field. Data type needs to reflect the type of data that will be displayed in the data field. For example, below you will find a list of data types and the relevant LitWare data item.

Data type	Format	Data item
Character	Alphanumeric	Customer name and address
Currency	Monetary Units	Product costs
Date	Month, day, and year	Date product was purchased
Memo	Alphanumeric text of an indeterminate length	Notes about a phone call

You must set the field width wide enough to accommodate the number of characters needed to display the information.

Add and define fields

1. In the Table Designer, click the outlined box under field name.

   The cursor may already be in place.
2. Type **ccustomerno** as the field name.
3. Press TAB to move to the highlighted Type text box.

Select field types

1. Press the spacebar or click the drop-down arrow button to the right of the Type text box.
2. Select Character.
3. TAB to Width.
4. Set width to 5.

Edit field captions

Field captions appear when you are browsing or editing tables, and are displayed in grid column headers. To make column headers in the LitWare fields more readable, you'll edit the field captions to give the fields more meaningful names.

1 Click the selection box to the left of ccustomerno in the list of field names in the Name text box to select the field.

2 Click the Caption text box under Field Properties.

3 Type **Customer #**

4 Click the selection box under the ccustomerno name field.

Continue editing field captions in the customer table by clicking the next field name and adding data from the following table into the Table Designer.

Field Name	Type	Width	Caption
csalutation	numeric	3	Title
cfirstname	character	15	First Name
cmiddleinit	character	1	Middle Initial
clastname	character	15	Last Name
ccompany	character	30	Company
caddress1	character	30	Address1
caddress2	character	30	Address2
ccity	character	20	City
cstate	character	2	State
cpostalcode	character	10	Postal Code
chomephone	character	14	Home Phone
cworkphone	character	14	Work Phone
ddateadded	date	8	Date Customer was added
mcomment	memo	4	Comment

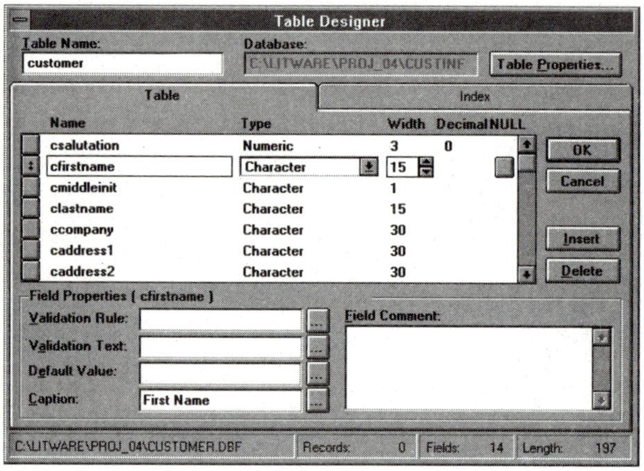

5 Click the OK button.

The Add Input Data Dialog box appears.

6 Click No. You will be appending (adding) data from an existing table.

The Database Designer window now contains the customer table.

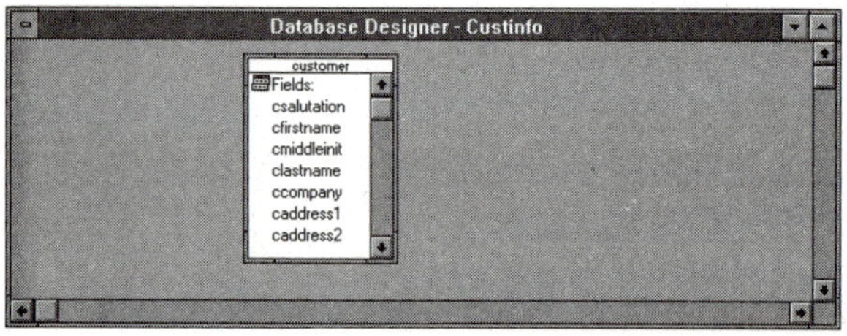

Browse the table

The browse table displays the data contained in the table and provides a place for you to add, modify, and append data.

You can double-click the Customer table title bar, instead of selecting Browse.

1. Select the Customer table by clicking it.
2. From the main menu, select Database.
3. Select Browse.
4. Using the right mouse button, click the table.
5. Select Browse from the pop-up menu.
6. Close the Browse window.

At this point the Customer table is empty and contains no data. You will need to enter data into each of the fields to populate the table.

Appending data to the Customer table

To save yourself some data entry time, you will append (copy) data from the Customer table shown in Lesson 3.

1 Browse the Customer table.

2 From the Table menu, select Append Records.

3 The Append From dialog box appears.

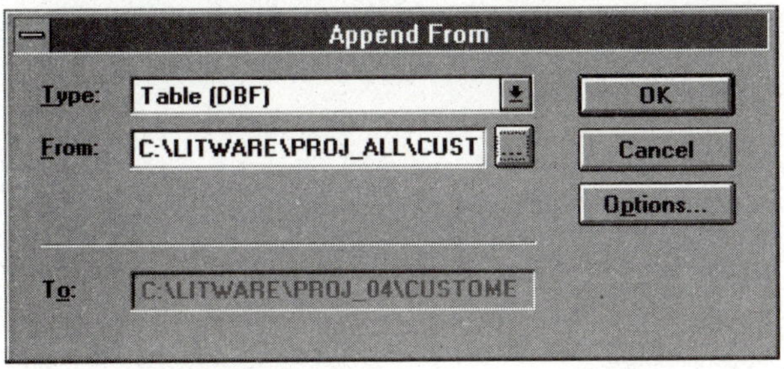

Do not change Type as you will be adding a .dbf file created in Visual FoxPro. Visual FoxPro also provides the tools for appending data from a variety of sources, including remote servers.

4 Click the ellipses button "..." next to From in the selection box.

5 Set the drive and directory path to c:\litware\proj_all.

6 Select customer.dbf.

7 Click the OK button.

The Append From dialog box is displayed with the drive and directory path selection.

8 Click the OK button.

The browse window appears with new data.

You can add, modify and append data using the Edit view. You apply the Edit view by selecting Edit from the View menu.

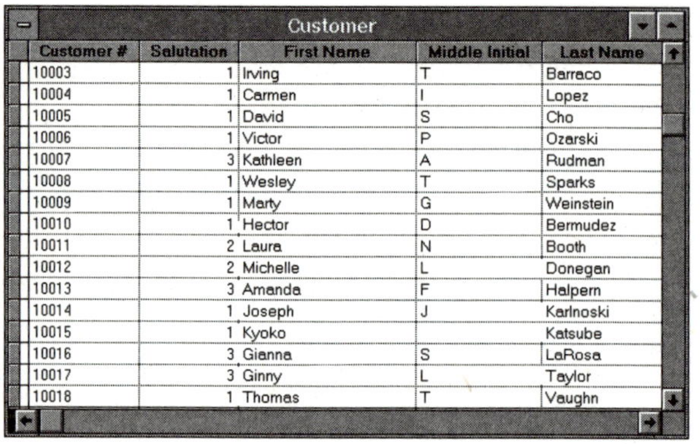

Customer

Customer #	Salutation	First Name	Middle Initial	Last Name
10003	1	Irving	T	Barraco
10004	1	Carmen	I	Lopez
10005	1	David	S	Cho
10006	1	Victor	P	Ozarski
10007	3	Kathleen	A	Rudman
10008	1	Wesley	T	Sparks
10009	1	Marty	G	Weinstein
10010	1	Hector	D	Bermudez
10011	2	Laura	N	Booth
10012	2	Michelle	L	Donegan
10013	3	Amanda	F	Halpern
10014	1	Joseph	J	Karlnoski
10015	1	Kyoko		Katsube
10016	3	Gianna	S	LaRosa
10017	3	Ginny	L	Taylor
10018	1	Thomas	T	Vaughn

9 Close the Browse window.

TIP There may be a time when you will want to view both the Edit and Browse windows at the same time. You can look at the same or different records simultaneously in the split browse window.

Adding Tables

When you add tables, you have the ability to incorporate data from a wide variety of outside sources. This allows you to take tables that have already been created and incorporate them into your application.

Add a table

In the exercise below you will add a table that lists the LitWare products each customer owns. The table that will be added is a free table and is not yet associated with a database. Field names and column headings in a free table are restricted to ten characters. After adding the table, you will need to rename the fields to match the other tables used in the LitWare application.

Add Table

1 Click the Add Table button on the Database Designer toolbar.

The Open dialog box appears.

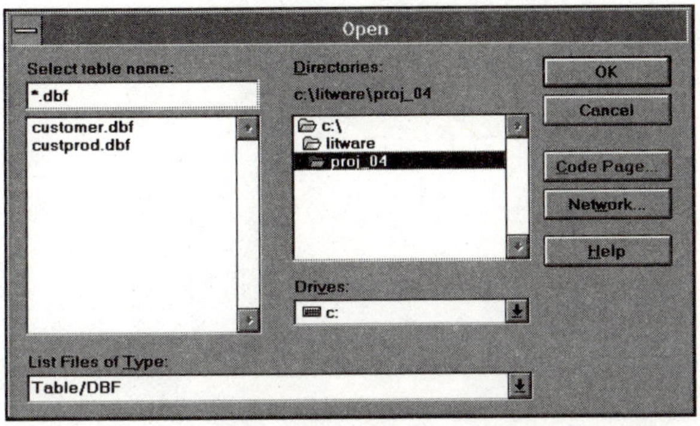

2 Set the drive and directory path to read: c:\litware\proj_04.

A list of .dbf files appears.

3 From the Select table name text box, select custprod.

4 Click the OK button.

The table appears in the Database Designer.

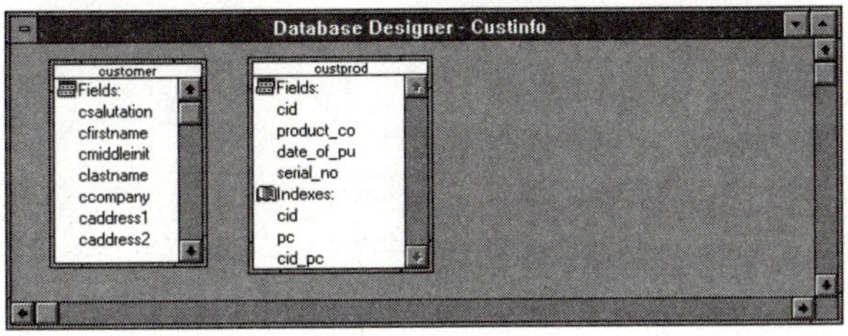

Change the field names

In this exercise you will change the field names in the custprod table to make them consistent with the field names in the other tables.

1 Select the custprod table by clicking on it.

2 Use the right mouse button to click the custprod table.

3 Click modify from the pop-up menu.

The Table Designer appears.

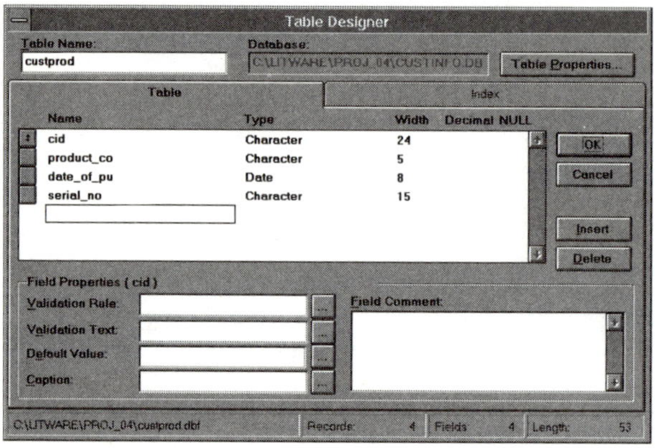

4 Select the cid (customer id number index in custprod table) field name.

5 Type **ccustomerno**

6 TAB to type, and select character.

7 TAB to width, and set the width to 5.

8 Click the Caption text block.

9 Type **customer #** in the caption text block.

10 Click the product_co field name.

11 Repeat steps 4-10 to rename each of the following fields:

Field Name	New Field Name	Type	Width	Caption
product_co	cproductcode	character	5	Product Code
date_of_pur	ddateofpurchase	date	8	Date of Purchase
serial_no	cserialno	character	15	Serial #

12 Click OK to close the Table Designer.

13 Click Yes to make structure changes permanent.

Making Your New Database Work

Now that you have created and added the tables required for LitWare's application, you can establish the relationships between the tables that will allow the tables to function together within the application. For example, in the exercises below you will link the customer table to the custprod table in order to identify which products are owned by the customer. Table and Database Designers make defining indexes and links quick and easy.

Defining Indexes

Indexes determine the order in which applications access table records and the types of relationships that exist between database tables. There are four types of indexes:

Primary A primary index ensures that only unique values are entered into a field and determines the order in which the records are processed. Each table can have only one primary index. This ensures referential integrity in a persistent relationship.

Candidate A candidate index enforces unique values and can be a candidate for use as a primary index. You can have multiple candidates per table.

Unique A unique index allows duplicate values and stores a list of each unique value in the table's index.

Regular A regular index does not enforce uniqueness on data but can be used for ordering and searching data for queries and reports.

Using any of these index types in a table automatically creates a separate compound index file (.cdx), which contains all the indexes used within the database. A .cdx file contains record pointers for each index in the table and is used for ordering records and establishing relational links. The .cdx file opens each time you use the table.

Define the indexes in the Customer table

Using the right mouse button to click the Customer table, select Modify from the pop-up menu.

Modify Table

One of the primary system requirements of the LitWare upgrade system is to be able to search and find the products owned by a particular customer. For this requirement to be met, the Customer table must be linked to the custprod table, which is in turn linked to the Products tables. Each LitWare customer must have a unique identification number. This number will be the primary index for the customer database.

1. Click the Customer table.
2. Click the Modify Table button on the Database Designer tool bar.

   The Table Designer for the Customer table appears with "Customer" displayed in the table name text box.
3. Click the Index Tab.
4. Type **name** as the index name in the Name text box.
5. Use the TAB key to move to the Type text box. This action will highlight the Type text box.
6. Select regular.

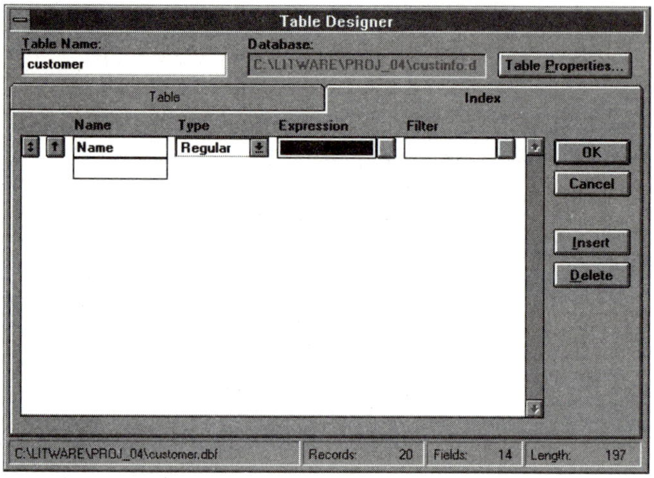

7 Use the TAB key to move to the Expression text box.

Use the Expression Builder

You can use the Expression Builder to define indexes. In this exercise you will create an index to prevent duplication of customer identification numbers that will be linked to the products owned by that customer. Setting this index at regular intervals allows you to sort and order on the customer last name for queries and reports.

Expression Builder

1 Click the Expression Builder button to the right of the Expression text box.

2 With the cursor in the Expression text box, double-click clastname in the fields list.

   You will notice that clastname now appears in the Expression text box.

3 Click the string scroll arrow, and select the "+" sign.

   The "+" sign appears in the Expression text box.

4 Double-click on cfirstname in the fields list.

   You will notice that cfirstname appears in the Expression text box.

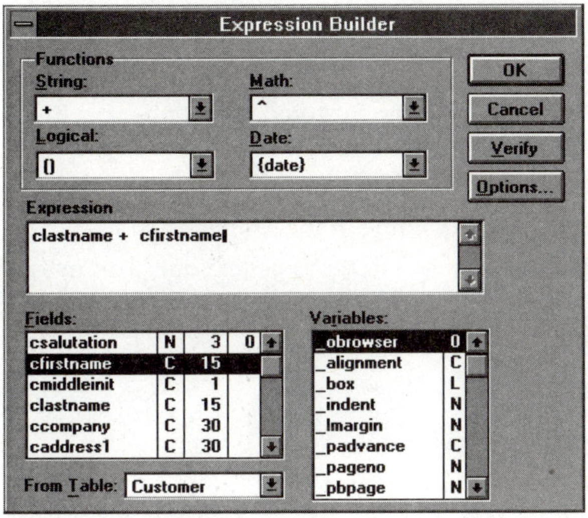

5 Select Verify to test the validity of the expression.

If the expression is valid, a message appears in the lower left-hand corner of the screen.

If you receive an error message stating that the syntax is in error, you will need to review and redefine the indexes.

6 Click the OK button.

The Table Designer appears.

7 Click the field name below Name.

8 Type **cid**

9 Press the TAB key until Type is selected and select Primary.

10 Press the TAB key until Expression is highlighted, and type **ccustomerno** in the Expression text box.

This establishes the unique customer number as the primary index.

11 Click the OK button.

12 Click Yes to make structure changes permanent.

Define the indexes in the Custprod table

1 Click the Custprod table.

2 Click the Modify Table button on the Database Designer tool bar.

or

Using the right mouse button to click the Custprod table, select Modify from the pop-up menu.

The Table Designer for the Custprod table appears with "Custprodr" displayed in the table name text box.

3 Click the Index Tab.

4 Type **cid** as the index name in the Name text box.

5 Use the TAB key to move to the Type text box. This action will highlight the Type text box.

6 Select regular.

7 Click OK.

Create a validation rule

The LitWare application requires that the customer identification number must be between 10000 and 50000. To meet this requirement, you must develop a validation rule to ensure data integrity. In other words, a CSR should not be able to enter a customer whose identification number is not in the correct range.

1 Click Customer table on the Database Designer.

2 Click the Modify Table button.

3 Click ccustomerno in the list of field names.

Validation Rule

4 Click the Validation Rule button.

The Expression Builder appears.

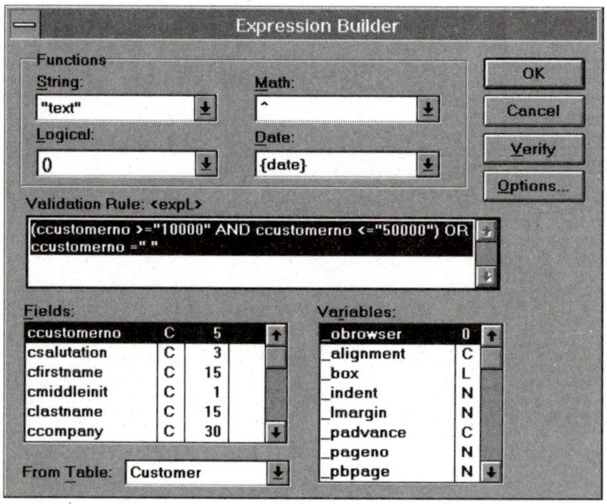

5 Double-click on ccustomerno in the Fields text box; ccustomerno appears on the prompt text box.

6 Click the Logical menu button, and select the greater than or equal symbol (>=).

7 Click the Prompt text box next to the >= sign and type "**10000**" (include the quotes).

8 Click the Logical menu button, scroll down, and select AND.

Press the space bar.

9 Double-click the ccustomerno field on the list of fields.

Press the space bar.

10 Click the Logical menu button, scroll down, and select the less than or equal to sign (<=).

Press the space bar.

You can type the expression in the Prompt text box. This works well with short expressions like the one used here.

11 Click the expression text box next to the <= sign and type "**50000**" (include the quotes).

12 Add open parentheses [(] in front of the first ccustomerno and add closed parentheses [)] after the 50000".

13 After the new expression type **or ccustomerno=**" ".

14 Select Verify.

15 Click the OK button.

Visual FoxPro checks the expression to verify its syntax. If a Syntax error box appears, check the validation rule.

The expression in the prompt box should read (ccustomerno >= "10000" AND ccustomerno <= "50000") or ccustomerno=" ".

Create a validation rule error message

When a CSR attempts to enter a customer number outside of the specified range, an error message appears. You will now create your own custom error message.

1 In the Table Designer, click the Validation Text button.

The Expression Builder appears.

2 Click the String menu button.

3 Click Text.

4 Between the quotation marks, type **You must enter a customer number between 10000 and 50000**.

5 Click the OK button.

The Table Designer appears.

Set a default field value

You want to record the date that new customers are added to the database. To make this task automatic, you can set the date field default to enter the current date when a new customer is added to the table.

1. From the Table Designer, locate and click the ddateadded field.
2. Click the Expression Builder button next to Default Value.

   The Expression Builder appears.
3. From the Date drop-down menu, select Date().

   When you enter a new customer, the current date automatically appears in the date field.
4. Click the OK button to close the Expression Builder.
5. Click the OK button to close the Table Designer.
6. Click Yes to make structure changes permanent.

Test the validation rule and default date field value

1. Browse the Customer table. (Use the right mouse button to click on the Customer table, and select Browse from the pop-up menu.)
2. From the Table menu, select Append new record.

   The current date appears in the date added field.
3. Add a new customer with the number 50010.

   A message box appears with the message you created.
4. Click the OK button.
5. Delete the number 50010.
6. From the File menu select Close to close the Browse Table.

Linking Tables

You can access records in multiple tables by creating relationships between indexes in different tables. Three relationships exist within Visual FoxPro: one-to-many, many-to-many, and one-to-one.

One-to-many Use a one-to-many relationship to link a single record in one table to multiple records in another. In the LitWare project, a one-to-many relationship exists between the customer and custprod tables. The customer table is the parent that owns many products listed in the custprod table, the child.

Many-to-many Use a many-to-many relationship to access many records in one table and many records in another. A many-to-many relationship exists between the orders and products tables, so that many products can exist on many orders and many orders can include many products.

One-to-one Use a one-to-one relationship to access one record in each of two tables. One-to-one relationships are rare because the records can usually be contained in the same table.

Link the customer and custprod tables

One of the relationships in LitWare's application allows the CSR to display a list of products owned by the caller based on the caller identification. To establish this relationship, you'll need to link the key indexes in each table.

1. Click and hold on the cid index in the customer table.
2. Drag the mouse to position the pointer (the cursor becomes a small rectangle) directly over the cid index on the custprod table.
3. Release the mouse button. This action drops the cid index from the customer table into the custprod table.

   The pointer becomes a thin rectangle.

   The Edit Relationship dialog box appears.

   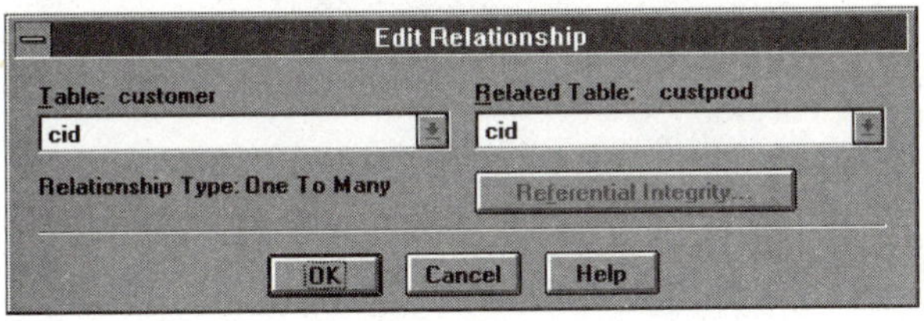

   You can now view the indexes from each of the tables. The first link shows a one-to-many relationship between the ccustno (customer identification number) on the customer table to the ccustno (customer identification number) on the custprod table. The customer table is now linked to the customer product table, creating a one-to-many relationship between customers and products.
4. Click the OK button.

Ensuring Referential Integrity

Referential Integrity refers to rules that you set up to control how records are inserted, updated, or deleted in related tables. The LitWare application requires that records from parent (customer, product) tables cannot be deleted if a related record exists in a child (custprod) table, and that records of the child tables cannot be modified unless there is a corresponding key value in the parent table.

Ensure referential integrity

1 Double-click the link line between the Customer and Custprod tables.

The Edit Relationship dialog box appears. Note the Referential Integrity button.

Referential Integrity

2 Click the Referential Integrity button.

The Referential Integrity Builder appears.

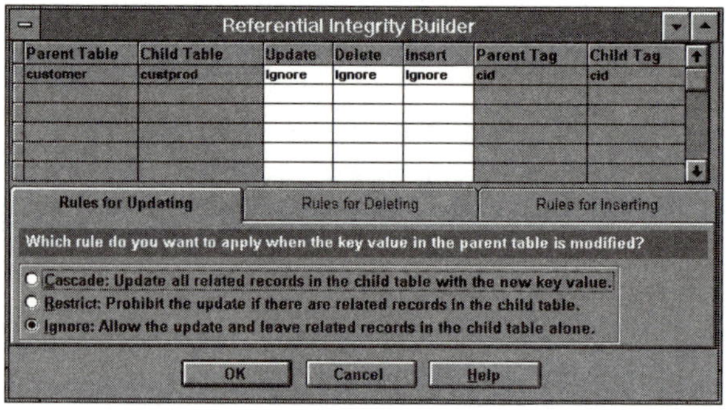

3 Click the Rules for Updating tab. It may already be selected.

4 Review the rules, but leave them intact.

5 Click the Rules for Deleting tab.

6 Click the Restrict option button.

By clicking this button you restrict the deletion of records from the customer parent tables if there are related records in the custprod child tables.

Restrict deletion

You also determined that records in the child tables should not be modified or added to unless there is a key value, in this case the customer number, in a parent table. In this exercise you will restrict the deletion of the child tables if there is a related customer identification number in a customer table.

1 Click the Rules for Inserting tab.

2 Click the Restrict option button.

3 Click the OK button.

A warning box appears.

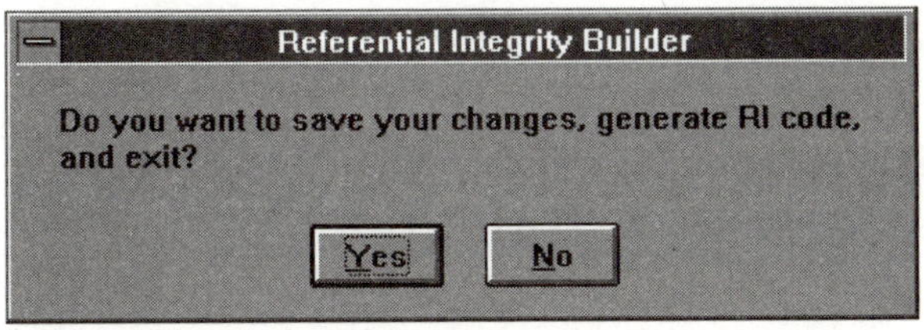

4 Click Yes.

A second warning box appears.

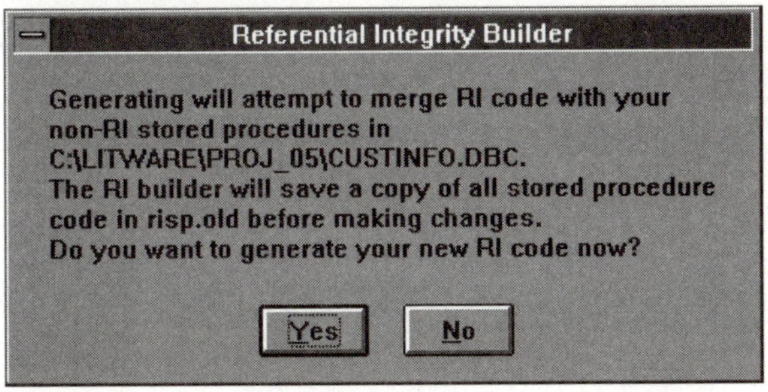

5 Select Yes for Visual FoxPro to rewrite the code.

6 Click the OK button.

7 Close the Database Designer

One Step Further: Creating Triggers

A trigger is an expression that is activated when the user modifies table records by using the insert, update, or delete commands. Activated triggers perform specific operations.

In this exercise, you will create a trigger that makes it impossible for the CSR to delete records.

1 Locate and select the Customer table.

2 Click Modify.

Add Table Properties

3 Click the Add Table Properties button.

The Table Properties window appears.

4 Click the Delete Trigger button.

The Expression Builder appears.

5 Type **.F.** in the prompt text box (include the periods).

This makes it impossible for the CSRs to delete customer records.

6 Click OK.

7 Click in the Comment field.

8 Type **Customer records cannot be deleted without the assistance of the system administrator.**

9 Click the OK button in the Table Properties window.

10 Click the OK button in the Table Designer.

A Question box appears, asking if you want to make the changes permanent.

11 Click the Yes button.

If you want to continue to the next lesson

1 Click File on the Menu bar.

2 Select Close.

If you want to quit Visual FoxPro for now

1 Click File on the Menu bar.

2 Select Exit.

Lesson Summary

To	Do this	Button
Create a project	Open Visual FoxPro. Click File. Click the New button. Click Project. Type the new project name.	
Create a database	In the Project Manager, Click the Data Tab. Click Database. Type the new database name. Locate the directory in which to store the database, and select Create.	
Create a table	In the Database Designer, click the New Table button. Type the name for the table. Locate the directory that contains the database, and then click the Create button.	
Add a table	In the Database Designer, click the Add table button. Locate the directory that contains the table. Click the table name.	
Link a table	Click the index in one table and drag that index to the table with which you wish to link. Drop the index directly on top of the index you wish to link.	

For online information about	From the Visual FoxPro Help Menu, choose Contents, select "Using Visual FoxPro," and then
Databases	Select the topic, "Databases and Tables"
Tables	Select the topic, "Databases and Tables"

For more information on	See in the *Microsoft Visual FoxPro Developer's Guide*
Databases	Chapter 6, "Using Databases"
Tables	Chapter 7, "Working with Tables"

Preview of the Next Lesson

In the next lesson, you will learn how to build forms that will allow LitWare CSRs to interact with the application. Forms are on-screen controls that provide the visual tools for the user to access, enter, and retrieve data.

Lesson

5

Creating Forms

Estimated time
60 min.

In this lesson you will learn how to:

- Create a new form.
- Add objects to a form.
- Create a pageframe showing multiple pages.
- Add text and edit boxes.
- Add labels to text boxes.
- Add command buttons.
- Add a grid.
- Create a grid using grid builder.

Once you have created the LitWare project file, database, and tables for your application, your next step is to develop the forms the LitWare Customer Service Representative (CSR) will use to access information in the database application. When these forms are displayed on the computer screen, the CSR will be able to enter, access, and manipulate customer records.

Just as you had to define the data requirements for each table before designing the table, you must also create forms based on the needs of the CSR. In the LitWare application, forms provide an easy-to-use visual interface for the CSR to use when answering a customer call. Using the forms created from the Customer screen, the CSR can now verify customer information and assist the customer in ordering product immediately, thus saving valuable time.

You can use Form Designer to help you design an easy-to-use graphical interface for your database application. Form Designer provides the means for you to create and manipulate forms and control objects.

Start the lesson

1. Open Visual FoxPro.
2. From the File menu, select Open.
3. In the Drives and Directories lists, select c:\litware\proj_05.
4. Select litware.pjx.
5. Click the OK button.

   The Project Manager displays the LitWare project.

The Custdata and Custmore Forms

The CSRs use the custdata and custmore forms to verify the identity of the customer, check which products the customer owns, and take orders for new products. The main form in the LitWare application is the custdata form, also known as the customer information form.

The custdata form that you will design will consist of two pages. Page one will display customer data: name, home address, home and work telephone numbers, and customer identification number. You must clearly label each field so that the CSR understands what information must be entered. Page two provides a means for the CSR to access the table that contains information about the products owned by the customer. The form will contain command buttons to add, delete, select the order form, quit, and manipulate customer records. In this lesson you will create the custdata form shown below. The custdata form has two pages.

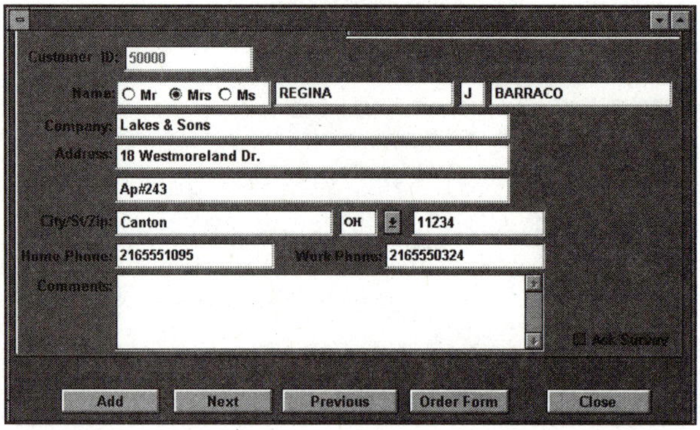

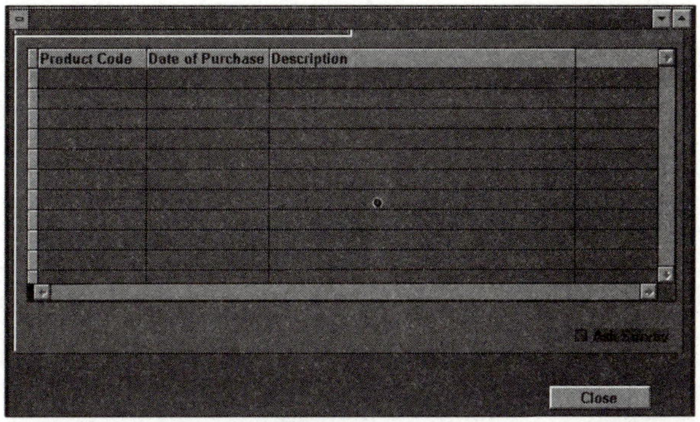

The custmore form displays a customer list that the CSR can use to verify a customer's identity when the records of two or more customers have similar information.

The custmore form you will create in this lesson looks like the illustration below.

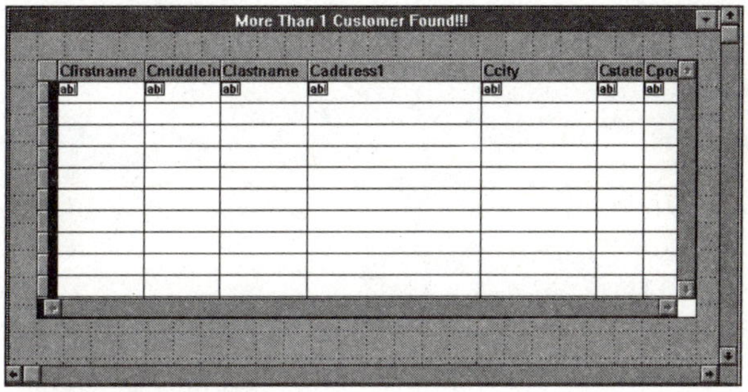

Creating a New Form

You will use the Form Designer to create the custdata form. The Form Designer is a design tool that allows you to use objects to create forms. Using objects makes form design and creation easier and faster. In Form Designer you can drag and drop data fields from an existing table to create text boxes, create labels using the label button, and align objects on the form using tools from the Layout toolbar. You can also add grids, command buttons, option boxes, combo boxes, and check boxes with ease.

The Properties Window in Form Designer provides the tools for assigning properties to each of the objects used in a form. You can easily assign file names and captions, apply color, or resize objects on the form. You can also apply methods to objects on the form. In this lesson you will be introduced to properties, but you will use them more extensively in Lesson 6.

Create a new form

1 In Project Manager, click the Documents tab.

2 Click Forms to select the category.

3 Click the New button.

The New Form dialog box appears. The dialog box indicates that you have the option to use the Form Wizard or to build your own new form.

TIP Use the Form Wizard to develop simple forms for data entry. The Form Wizard asks a series of questions that guide you through the form creation process. The Form Wizard allows for creation of a single table form or a one-to-many, parent-child table form.

4 Click the New Form button.

The Form Designer appears.

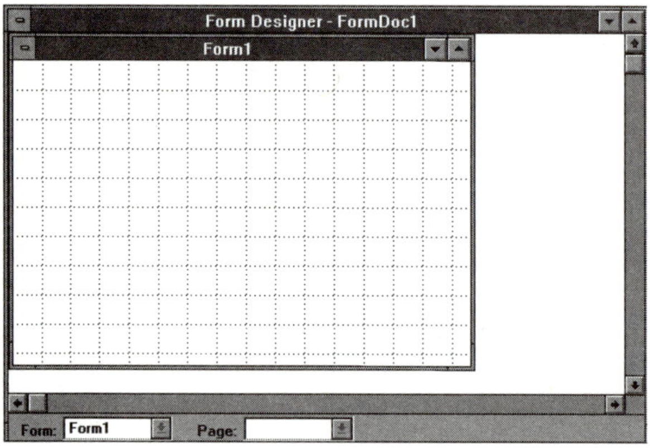

Form Designer displays Form1 in the FormDoc1 window, indicating that this is the first form that you have opened in this project. The FormDoc1 name will change to the name you choose when you save the form. Form1 is the blank workspace, or form window that you will use to create the custdata form. You will rename and caption this form in Lesson 6.

In the following exercise, you will use the Form Controls toolbar. If the Form Controls toolbar is not open, you must open it.

Open the Form Controls toolbar

➤ From the View menu, select the Form Controls toolbar.

Maximize

TIP You can maximize the Form Designer to give yourself the greatest amount of work space. Click the Maximize button in the Form Designer window to make the window bigger.

Adding Objects to Your Form

Now that you have displayed a blank form window, Form1, you will add objects to the form window to create the custdata form.

Microsoft Visual FoxPro 3 for Windows offers two types of objects that you can add to a new form: container objects and control objects. You can access both types of objects from the Form Controls toolbar or the Project Manager.

Container Objects A container object is a parent object that holds other subordinate objects. For example, a form is a container object that is the parent of a command button displayed on the form. Other container objects can include page frames, grids, and command button groups.

Control Objects A control object allows the user to select options, enter data, and choose actions. On a form, control objects can include check boxes, command buttons, text boxes, and grids.

In this lesson, you will add both types of objects to the custdata form.

Using Multiple Pages in a Single Form

In Visual FoxPro, a single form can use multiple pages to display several sets of data and controls. A tab at the top of the form represents each page. You can click on the tab to display the contents of the page.

The two-page custdata form that you are about to create will display two groups of customer information: customer data, and data about the products that the customer owns.

Create a two-page form

Page Frame

1. On the Form Controls toolbar, click the Page Frame button.
2. Position the pointer in the upper-left corner of Form1.

   The pointer changes to a cross hair.
3. Click the cross hair on the upper-left corner of the form and drag it to the lower-right corner of the page, creating a page frame that covers most of the Form1 window. Leave a 1-inch space across the bottom of the form for the command buttons you will add a little later in this lesson. A two-page form appears.

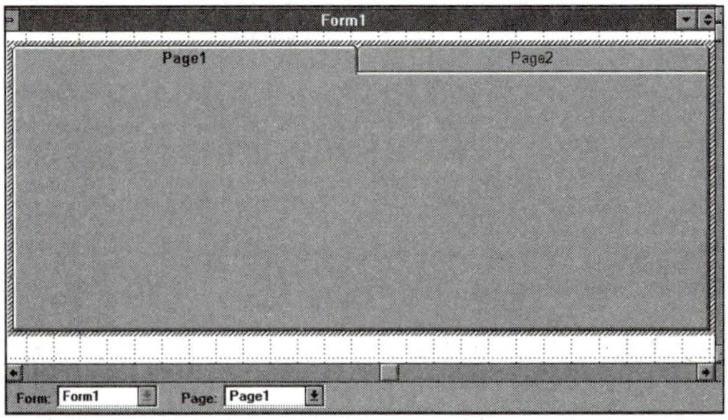

Adding Text and Edit Boxes

You will use text boxes to display the customer information contained in the LitWare customer table. You will add text boxes, or control objects, that will display the following data items to page1 of the custdata form:

- Unique customer number
- Customer last name
- Customer first name
- Customer middle initial
- Company
- Address 1
- Address 2
- City
- State
- Postal zip code
- Phone number 1 (home)
- Phone number 2 (work)
- Date customer added to the database
- Comment Field

Add the objects to Page1

1 Use the right mouse button to click on Page1 of the form.

A pop-up menu box appears.

2 Click Properties.

The Properties dialog box appears, showing Page1 in the object text box.

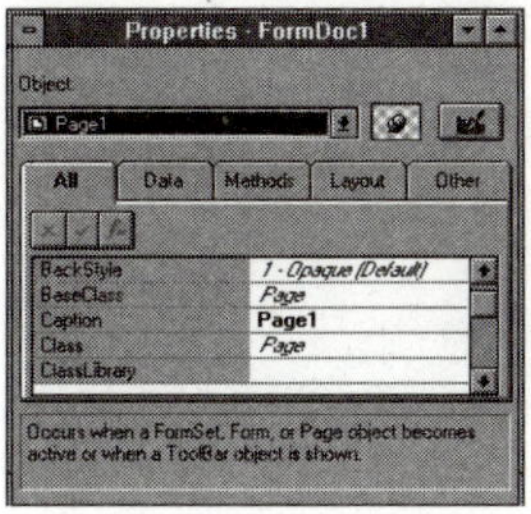

3 Click the Scroll Arrow button.

4 Select Page1 from the object text box.

TIP Each time you add an object to a form, pageframe, page, or grid, check Properties to ensure that you are placing the object in the right container.

In order to use the fields from the customer table that you have already created on the custdata form, you must open the LitWare project data environment. The data environment will allow you to access tables and view contained in the project. When you place these fields onto the form, the customer table is recorded as the control source property for the text boxes. When adding text boxes to Page1 of the form, open properties and make sure that Page1 is selected in the object text box. A shaded line outlines the page frame on the form.

Add text boxes

1 From the Form Designer menu, select View.

2 Select Data Environment.

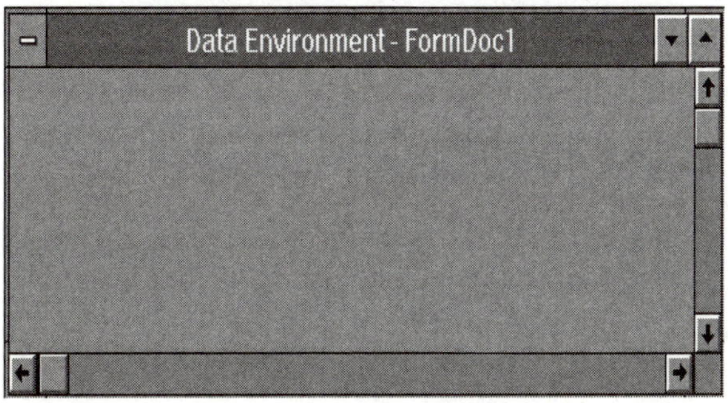

3 From the Visual FoxPro menu, select Data Environment, and then select Add.

TIP You can also open the Add Table or View window with the right mouse button. Using the right mouse button, click anywhere on the Data Environment, and then select Add. To get the Data Environment or Properties window to appear, use the right mouse button to click off the pageframe but on the form. The pop-up menu appears for you to make your selection.

The Add Table or View window appears.

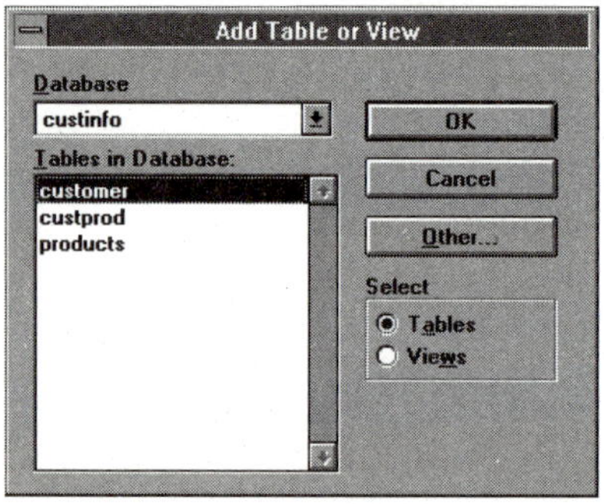

4 Confirm that custinfo is the selected database in the Database text box.

5 Double click on customer from the Tables listed in the Database text box.

The customer table appears in the Data Environment.

6 Select ccustomerno from the list of fields in the customer table, drag it to the form, and drop it anywhere on the form.

The text1 text box appears on the form.

7 Click and drag the text1 text box to the position shown below.

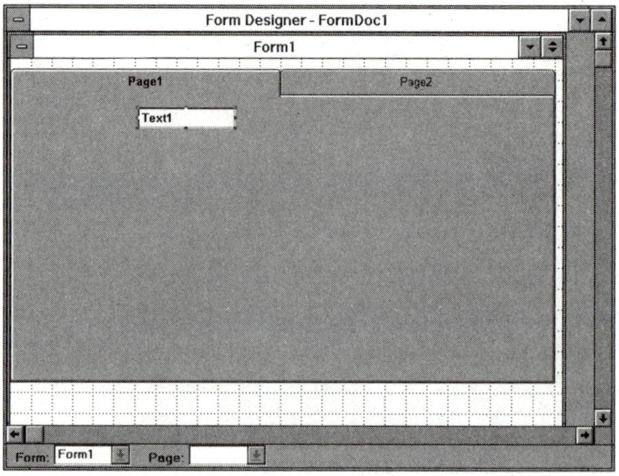

Use this drag-and-drop method to add the following fields from the customer table to the form. Later in the lesson, you will add file names and captions to the text boxes.

text2 = csalutation

text3 = cfirstname

text4 = cmiddleinit

text5 = clastname

text6 = ccompany

text7 = caddress1

text8 = caddress2

text9 = ccity

text10 = cstate

text11 = cpostalcode

text12 = chomephone

text13 = cworkphone

TIP You can move a text box by clicking on it and dragging it to a new location on the form. You can resize a text box by clicking on it, and then clicking and dragging any of the resize handles.

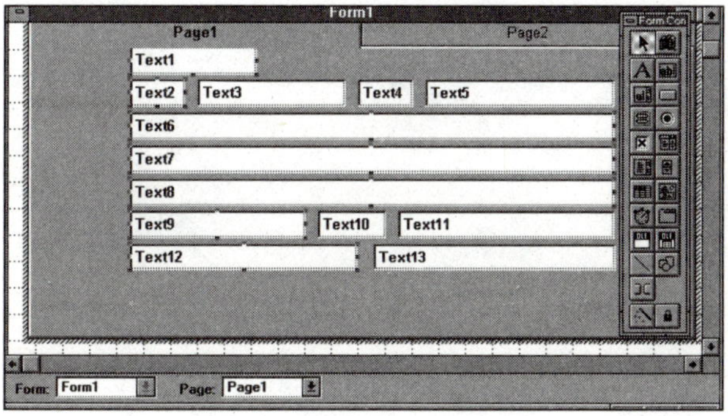

Try using the mouse to select boxes. Click and drag a selection box to select the text boxes. The selection box does not stay on the screen, but the selected boxes are displayed with resize handles.

Align the text boxes

The Layout toolbar contains the tools that will help you align the objects and create a visually appealing and functional form. Before you begin the following exercise, make sure that the you are still working on Page1. Use the right mouse button to click on the pageframe, and then check to make sure that Page1 appears in the object text box. The pageframe will have a lightly screened line around it if it is selected.

1. From the View menu, select the layout toolbar.
2. Holding down the shift key, click to select text boxes 1, 2, 6, 7, 8, 9, and 12.
3. On the Layout toolbar, click the Align Left Sides button.

   The selected boxes move so that their left sides align.
4. Select text boxes 2, 3, 4, and 5.
5. On the Layout toolbar, click the Align Top Edges button.

   The selected boxes move so that their top edges align.

Add an Edit Box

An Edit Box allows the CSR to enter comments using an unlimited number of characters.

Edit Box

1. On the Form Controls toolbar, click the Edit Box button.
2. Click and drag to draw the Edit Box on the lower portion of page one.

   The Edit1 box appears.

   Resize and reposition the text boxes and edit box to match the following figure.

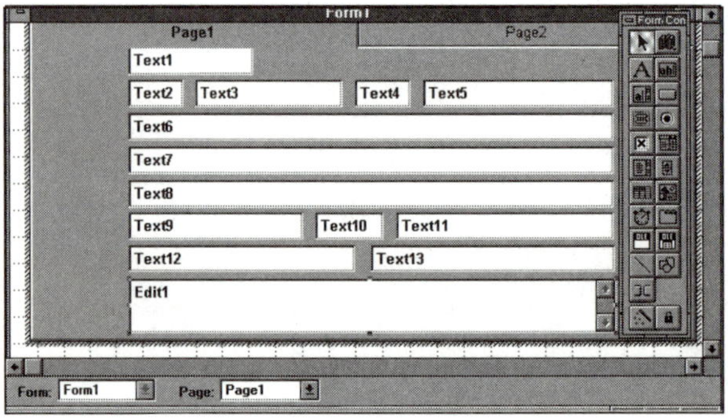

Add names to text and edit boxes

1. Using the right mouse button, click on Page1 of the form, and select Properties.

   The Properties window appears.
2. Click the drop-down arrow to the right of the Object box to display a list that includes all objects contained on the form: pageframes, pages, text boxes, edit boxes, command buttons, and so forth.

3 Click the Text1 box.

4 Choose the Other tab.

5 Click Name property.

6 Type **txtcustomerno** in the Text1 box.

7 Press Enter.

The text box now reads txtcustomerno.

8 Click the drop-down arrow to the right of the Object box and select Text2 from the list. Follow the steps above to add names to the text and edit boxes listed.

Text Box	**Name**
text2	txtcsalutation = customer title
text3	txtcfirstname = customer first name
text4	txtcmiddleinit = customer middle initial
text5	txtclastname = customer last name
text6	txtccompany = customer company name
text7	txtcaddress1 = customer address
text8	txtcaddress2 = customer second address
text9	txtccity = customer city
text10	txtcstate = customer state
text11	txtcpostalcode = customer postal code
text12	txtchomephone = customer home phone
text13	txtcworkphone = customer work phone
edit1	edtmcomments = customer comments

When finished your form should look like the following figure.

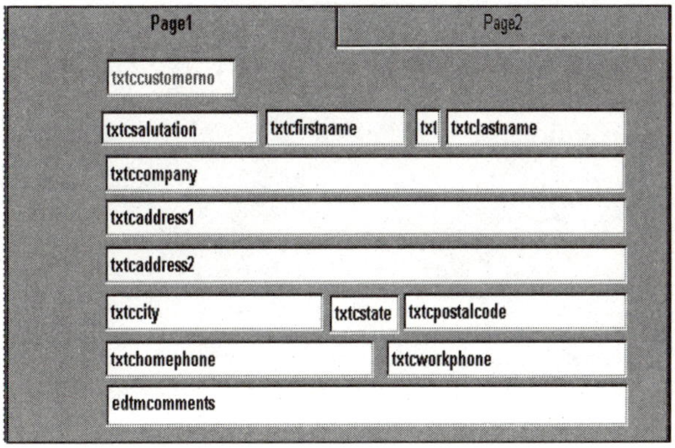

Adding Labels without Captions

In order to make the job of the CSR easier, you can add labels to the text boxes and name them to indicate the information contained in the text box. In this exercise you will add labels to the text boxes, but you'll refrain from naming them. Captions are properties that you will add in Lesson 6.

Add labels to the custdata form

Label

1. Click the Label button on the Form Controls toolbar.
2. Position the pointer approximately 2 grid squares to the left of the txtccustomerno text box.

   The pointer changes to a cross hair.
3. Click and drag the cross hair to draw a label approximately 2x1 grid squares in dimension.

   A Label1 box appears to the left of the txtcustomerno text box. In Lesson 6, you will add a caption to Label1. The caption, Customer's Identification Number, will indicate that the txtcustomerno text box will contain a customer's I.D. number.
4. Repeat steps 1-3 to place a label in front of the following text boxes.

Label	**Text box**
Label2	txtcsalutation, txtcfirstname, txtmiddleinit, and txtclastname boxes
Label3	txtccompany
Label4	txtcaddress1

Leave the label on the second address blank

Label5	txtcaddress2
Label6	txtccity, txtcstate, txtcpostalcode
Label7	txtchomephone and txtcworkphone boxes
Label8	edtmcomments

Reposition the text boxes and labels to give the form a visually appealing look. Make sure that the text boxes are placed in such a way that data entry is easy for the CSR. Use the figure below as a guide.

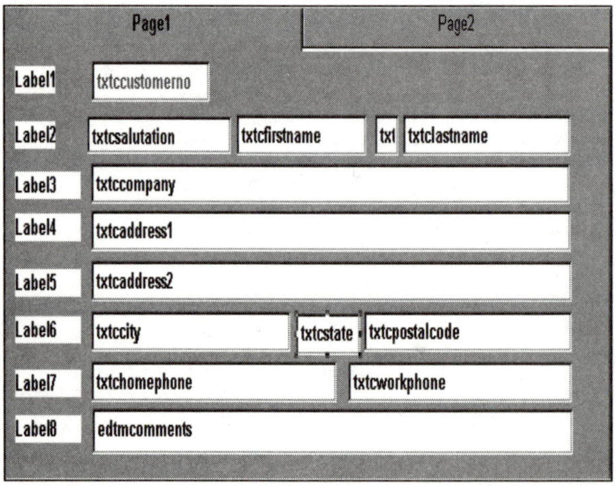

Adding Command Buttons

In the custdata form, command buttons allow the CSR to add new customer records, display previous customer records, activate the Orders form, and quit the custdata form.

Add command button to the custdata form

Command Button

1 Click the Command button on the Form Controls toolbar.

2 Position the pointer in the lower-left corner of the custdata form below the page frame. The pointer changes to a cross hair.

3 Click and drag the cross hair to draw a rectangular command button approximately 1x4 grids in size.

A command button appears.

4 Use the method described above to add four more command buttons.

5 Reposition the command buttons so that they are equally spaced across the bottom of the form.

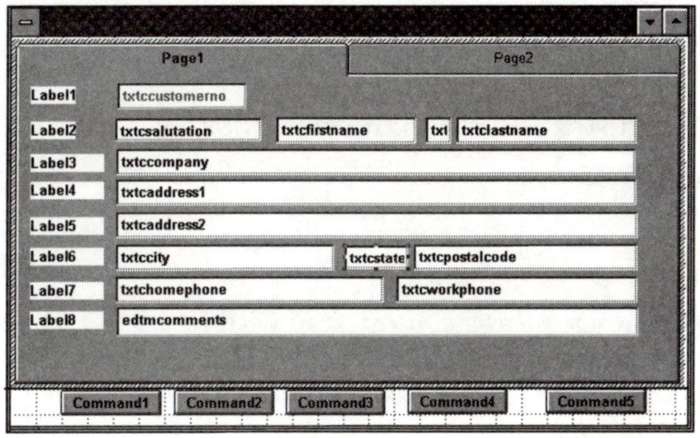

TIP You can use the Command Group Builder to create several buttons at once. The Command Group Builder makes it easy to set properties for a Command Group control. You set properties by selecting options displayed in a familiar dialog box format.

In Lesson 6 you will add names, properties and events to these buttons.

Adding a Grid

Adding a grid to a form allows you to display and manipulate data using multiple rows and columns. Each grid column contains its own set of properties, events, and methods. The custdata form contains a grid on page two that displays the product code, product name, and quantity of product owned by each LitWare customer.

Add a grid to page2 of the custdata form

1. Using the right mouse button, click on the custdata form.
2. Select Properties from the pop-up menu that appears.

   The Properties window appears.
3. Click the drop-down arrow to the right of the Object box.
4. Scroll down through the list to find and select Page2.
5. Click the Grid button on the Form Controls toolbar.

   Grid
6. Place the cursor in the upper-left corner of Page2, click the mouse button, and then drag with the mouse until you have created a rectangle that covers Page2. This rectangle forms a grid.

Add columns to the grid

1. From the Properties window, select the Layout tab.

   If the Properties window is not open, click on the grid using the right mouse button, and then select Properties from the shortcut menu. Then click the Layout tab.

   Verify that grid1 is selected in the object box.
2. Select Column Count.
3. Type **3**
4. Press the Enter key.

   The grid becomes a three column grid with headers 1, 2, and 3. You will name and add other properties to the grid in Lesson 6.
5. Close the Properties window.

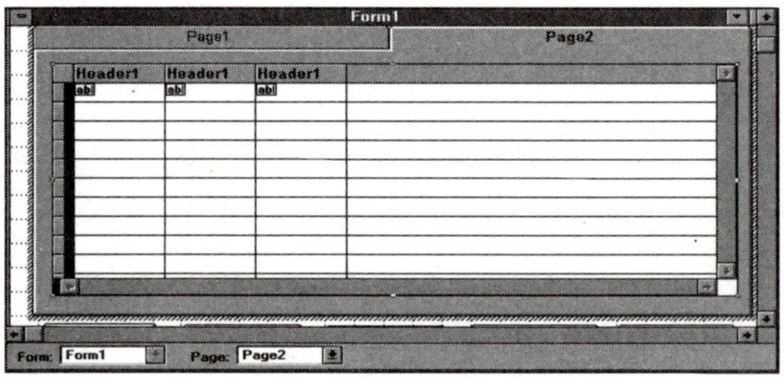

Save the new form

1. Click File on the main menu.
2. Select Save.

   The Save dialog box appears.
3. Type **custdata.scx** as the form name.
4. Set the Drive and Directories path to c:\LitWare\proj_05.
5. Click the Save button.
6. Close the custdata form.

Save

Using Grid Builder

You will use Grid Builder to create the custmore form, which is the form that the CSR uses to enter customer information. Grid Builder can copy fields and column headers from existing tables, eliminating the need to re-key data and recreate the form. When the CSR needs to find or search for duplicate customer information, he or she will call up the custmore form to display the existing LitWare customer database.

Create the custmore form

1. From Project Manager, click the Document tab.
2. Click Forms.
3. Click the New button.
4. Select New from the New Form dialog box.

   Form Designer appears with a new blank form.

New Command

Place a grid on the form using grid builder

1. Click the Grid button on the Form Controls toolbar.
2. Draw a grid on the form.

   A blank grid appears.
3. Click on the grid using the right mouse button.

   A pop-up menu appears.
4. Select Builder from the menu.

   The Grid Builder dialog box appears.

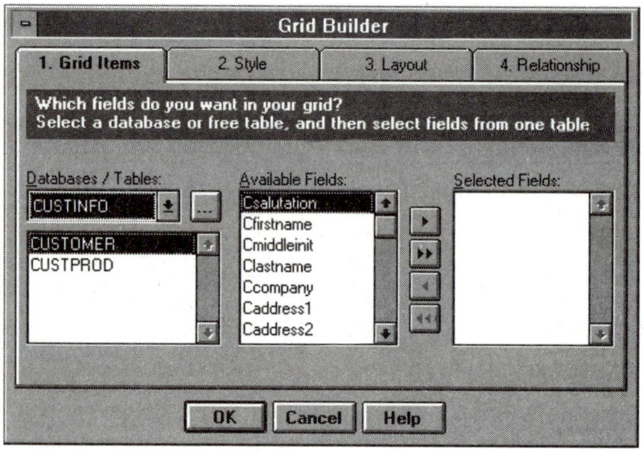

5 Choose Customer from the Database/Table column.

Select the fields and column headers for the new grid

1 From the list of fields under the Available Fields column, select ccustomerno.

2 Select the right arrow button.

The field ccustomerno moves to the Selected Fields column.

3 Repeat steps 1 and 2 for each of the following fields:
cfirstname
cmiddleinit
clastname
ccompany
caddress1
ccity
cstate
cpostalcode
chomephone

4 Click the OK button.

A form containing the newly-created grid with columns and headers appears.

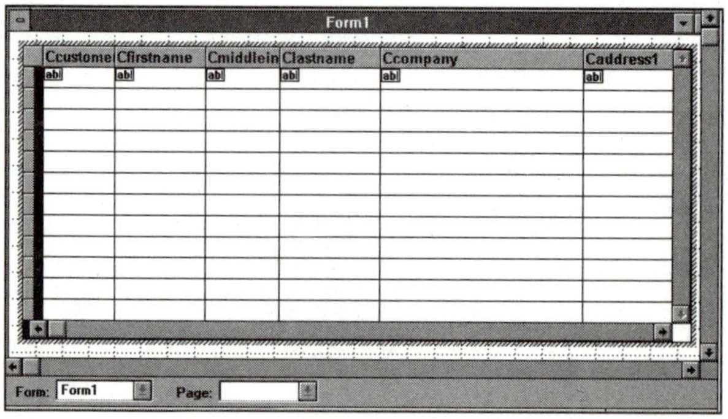

Save the form

1. Click File on the main menu.
2. Select Save.
3. Type **custmore** for the form name.
4. Set the drive and directory to c:\Litware\proj_05.
5. Select Save.
6. Close Form Designer.

One Step Further: Adding Combo Boxes and Option Groups

To further enhance the custdata form, you will add a combo box and an options group.

You will use the combo box to provide a listing of the proper two-digit postal code for state abbreviations. This box saves the CSR data entry time and ensures accurate state information. The CSR will scroll through the list to find and select the appropriate state abbreviation.

Add a combo box to the custdata form

1. Select the Document tab from Project Manager.
2. Select the custdata form.
3. Click the Modify button.
4. Click on the form using the right mouse button.
5. Select Properties from the shortcut menu.
6. Verify that Page1 is selected in the Object box.
7. Click the txtcstate text box on Page1 of the form.
   Press the delete key to delete this text box.

   You will place a combo box in the space you have just created.

Combo Box

8. On the Form Controls toolbar, click the Combo Box button.
9. Click and drag a combo box in the space left by the txtcstate text box.

   The combo box is now in place. You'll add properties to the combo box in Lesson 6.

   An option group provides an onscreen tool that allows the user to make selections without having to enter data. The option group that you will use contains the following titles: Mr., Mrs., and Ms.

Add an option group to the custdata form

1. Click the txtcsalutation text box on the custdata form. Press the delete key to delete this text box.

   You will place an option group box in the space you have just created.
2. On the Form Controls toolbar, click the Option Group button.

Option Group

3. Click and drag an Option Group box to replace the space left by the txtcsalutation text box.
4. Using the right mouse button, click the option text box.
5. Select Builder from the pop-up menu.

   The Option Group Builder appears

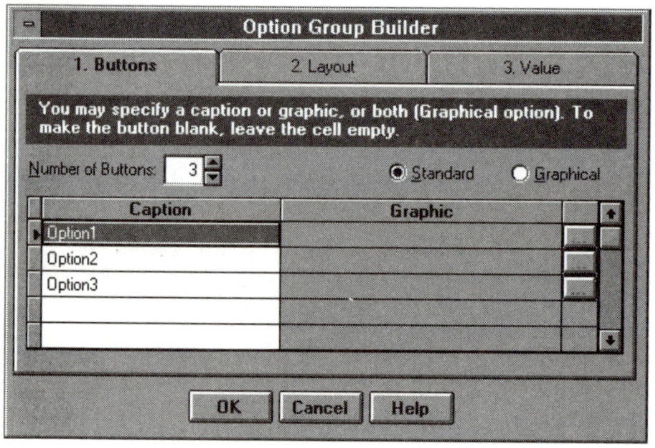

6. Click in the cell under Captions where Option1 is displayed, and type **Mr.** This changes the caption to Mr.
7. Change Option2 and Option3 to **Ms.** and **Mrs.** respectively.
8. Click the Layout tab.
9. Click the Horizontal option button.
10. Click the OK button.

    The custdata form appears.

Edit the option group

1. Using the right mouse button, click on the option group.
2. Select Edit from the popup menu.

   The option group is highlighted.
3. Click on the Ms. Option button and drag it closer to Mr. Do the same for Mrs.
4. Reposition and resize the Option Group box so that it matches the Figure below.

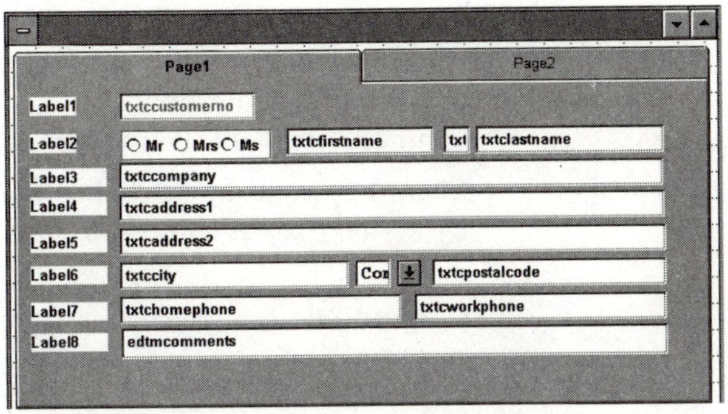

Save the form

1. Click File on the main menu.
2. Select Save.
3. Close Form Designer.
4. Close Visual FoxPro.

If you want to continue to the next lesson

1. Click File on the Menu bar.
2. Select Close.

If you want to quit Visual FoxPro for now

1. Click File on the Menu bar.
2. Select Exit.

Lesson Summary

To	Do This	Button
Create a new form	From the Project Manager, click the Documents tab and select Forms. Click the New button.	
Create a page frame	Click the Page Frame button on the Form Controls toolbar and drag a new page frame on to the Form Designer workspace.	
Add a text box	Click the Text Box button. Drag and drop a box.	

To	Do This	Button
Add a label	Click the Label button. Drag and drop a label box.	
Add a command	Click the Command Box button. Drag and drop a command box.	
Add a grid	Choose the Grid button. Drag and drop a grid.	

For online information about	From the Visual FoxPro Help Menu, choose Contents, select "Using Visual FoxPro," and then
Forms	Select the topic, "Using Forms"

For more information on	See in the *Microsoft Visual FoxPro Developer's Guide*
Forms	Chapter 9, "Creating Forms"

Preview of the Next Lesson

In this lesson, you created the custdata and custmore forms and added text, combo boxes, and an option group to the forms. In the next lesson, you will add functionality to these objects. You will work with form and control objects to determine properties, events, and methods, which will bring life to your database application.

Lesson

6

Setting Properties and Methods

Estimated time

60 min.

In this lesson you will learn how to:

- Assign behavior to objects on forms.
- Manipulate the appearance of a form.
- Use the Data Environment to set up the relationships between tables for a form.
- Design a form to handle events.
- Manage multiple pages in a form.
- Set the properties of screen controls.
- Change characteristics of controls and forms programmatically.

In this lesson, you will take the information you have learned so far to create a useful form. In Lesson 5 you designed a form using Form Designer; now you need to add functionality to the form by assigning behaviors and characteristics to the objects that make up the form.

Manipulating Form Properties

Forms in Microsoft Visual FoxPro 3 for Windows are objects with properties and methods. Data properties control the appearance and characteristics of the form. Methods control the behavior of the form when various events occur. In this lesson you will use Form Designer and the Data Environment to make the form work efficiently.

Start the lesson

1. Open Visual FoxPro.
2. From the File menu, select Open.
3. In the Drives and Directories lists, select c:\LITWARE\PROJ_06
4. Select LITWARE.PJX.
5. Click the OK button.

   The Project Manager displays the LitWare project.

Changing the Appearance of a Form

The quality team at LitWare has created system standards for the various forms so that users see a uniform interface on all LitWare forms. The CSRs must be able to read the forms easily and the application developers must be able to reproduce the screens for inclusion in the documentation. The quality team found that green and gray backgrounds are very readable and show up well when captured as a screen shot.
For a form requiring data entry, the standard screen background will be green; for pages on a page frame, such as the Customer/Product page, the background will be gray.

Load the custdata form

1. In Project Manager, click the Documents tab.
2. If Forms is not expanded, click the plus sign next to the word Forms.
3. Click the custdata form to select it.
4. Click the Modify button to open the form.

   The Form Designer loads the selected form.

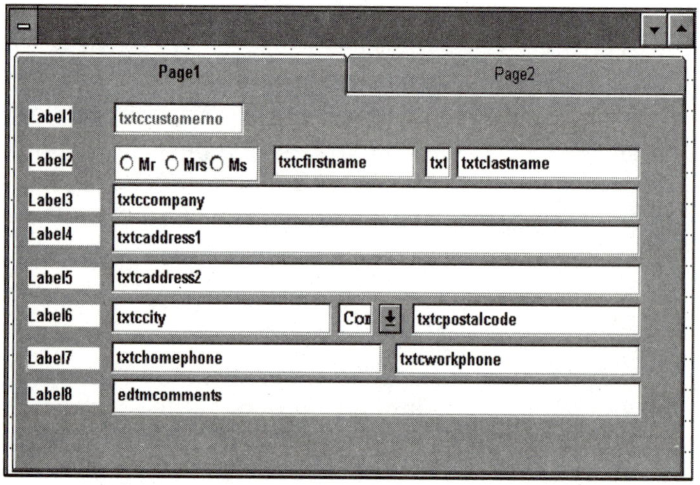

Set the background color for a form

In this exercise, you will set the background color of the Customer page to green, using the BackColor Property.

1. Make sure custdata appears in the Object box in the Properties window. If custdata does not appear in the Object box, click the scroll arrow to the right of the Object box, and select custdata in the drop-down list.
2. Click the BackColor property under the All or Layout tabs.
3. Double-click BackColor, or click on the ellipse (...) button.

Ellipse

   The Color Dialog box appears.

4. Click the green square on the bottom row of pre-defined colors to select green as the background color. The green square is fifth from the left.
5. Click OK to close the Color Dialog box.

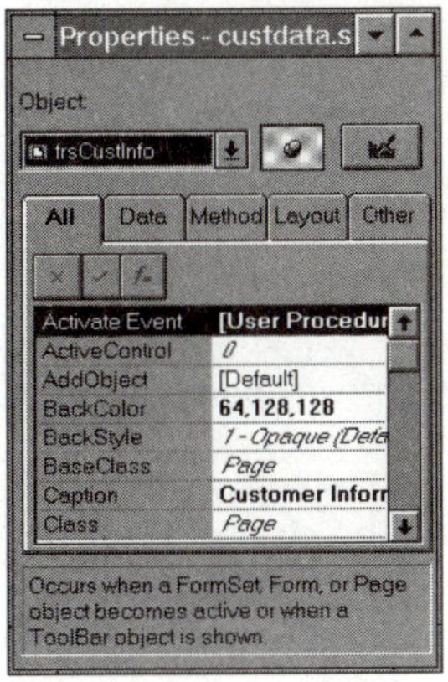

The property window shows the RGB numbers (64, 128, 128) for the selected color.

NOTE The RGB function is a way to set or determine the colors of an object. It accepts three arguments, each ranging from 0 to 255. The first sets the red, the second sets the green, and the third sets the blue proportions of the object. Hence RGB(255,0,0) means red, RGB(0,0,0) means black, and RGB(255,255,255) means white.

---

6. Click the Page2 tab to select the second page of the form. Make sure that frsProdInfo appears in the Object box in the Properties window.
7. Repeat steps 2-5 to choose gray for the background color of page 2 of the form. The gray square is one to the left of the green square. The RGB combination should be 128, 128, 128.

Set the size of a form

There are at least two ways to set the size of an object in the Form Designer: you can use the Properties window, or you can size the object directly. For multiple objects, you can use the Layout toolbar as well. Use the Properties window if you want control over the pixel size of an object; this is useful for matching the sizes of multiple objects, such as two pages. Use the mouse if you want to size the object directly, for example, if you want to set the size of a container relative to the objects it contains.

TIP You can use the Layout toolbar to align objects and set multiple objects to the same height, width, left alignment, right alignment, and so forth. If the Layout toolbar is not visible, select it from the View menu.

All methods and properties are also available on the All tab.

In this exercise, you will use the Properties window to set the size of the custdata form.

1. Make sure the custdata form appears in the Object box in the Properties window. If it is not showing, click the scroll arrow to the right of the Object box to display a drop-down list. You can select the custdata form from this list.
2. Select the Layout tab, and then click the Height property on this tab.
3. Type **454** and press Enter.

   The height of the form changes immediately in response to your input.
4. Repeat steps 2 and 3 to change the Width property of the form to 600.

TIP You can use the mouse to set the size of a form by clicking and dragging the border of the form to the position. Visual FoxPro will not warn you if the size of the form is too small for all the objects it contains, so take care to set the size appropriately.

Set the caption for a form or page

The Caption property defines the text that appears at the top of a form or page. The LitWare standard specifies that the company name must appear as the title of the form.

In this exercise, you'll set the caption for the form.

1. Make sure the Custdata form appears in the Object box in the Properties window. If it is not showing, click the scroll arrow to the right of the Object box to select the form from the drop-down list.
2. Click the Caption property on the Layout tab.
3. In the property text box, type **LitWare, Inc.** and press Enter.

   The title of the form changes immediately in response to your input.

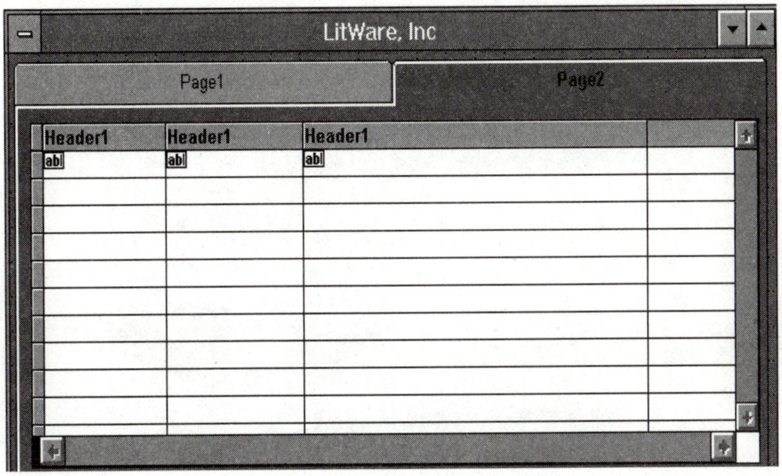

4 Repeat steps 2 and 3 to change the captions for the frscustinfo (Page1) and frsproducts (Page2) pages to Customer Information and Products Owned, respectively.

Setting the Data Environment

Visual FoxPro provides a simple way to automatically open and close tables used by a form and to set the relationships between those tables. This saves the developer from having to write code to accomplish the same task.

Open and close tables automatically

The custdata form displays customer information on the CustInfo page and a customer's product list with descriptions of each product on the ProdInfo page. Therefore, the form must use the Customer, Products, and CustProd tables.

In this exercise you will use the Data Environment to select the three tables named above and to make sure these tables automatically open and close with the custdata form.

1 Make sure the custdata form is open in the Forms Designer.

2 From the View menu, select Data Environment.

3 From the Data Environment menu, select Add.

A dialog box appears, allowing you to select a table or view from the open database. You can open a free table by clicking the **Other** button. Views will be discussed in Lesson 10.

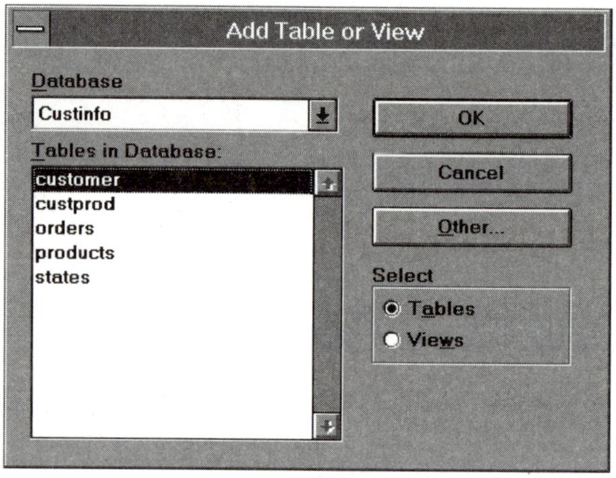

4 Select the customer table.

5 Click the OK button.

The Data Environment window displays the structure of the customer table.

6 Repeat steps 4 and 5 to select the custprod and products tables.

You'll notice that Visual FoxPro carries the relationship between the customer and custprod tables forward from the relationship defined in the database container.

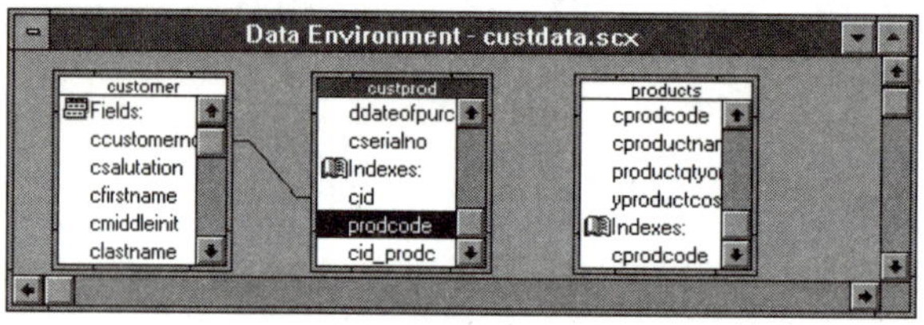

When tables are included in the Data Environment for a form, Visual FoxPro automatically opens and closes the tables when the form is run.

TIP To prevent the tables from being opened and closed automatically, set the AutoOpenTables and AutoCloseTables properties to .f. - False.

Setting Relationships between Tables

When you toured the sample application in Lesson 3, you saw that the grid on the ProdInfo form displays all products purchased by a specific customer. Since the layout of the grid is controlled entirely by the properties of the form, the grid, and the data environment, you do not need to write code to set up the grid.

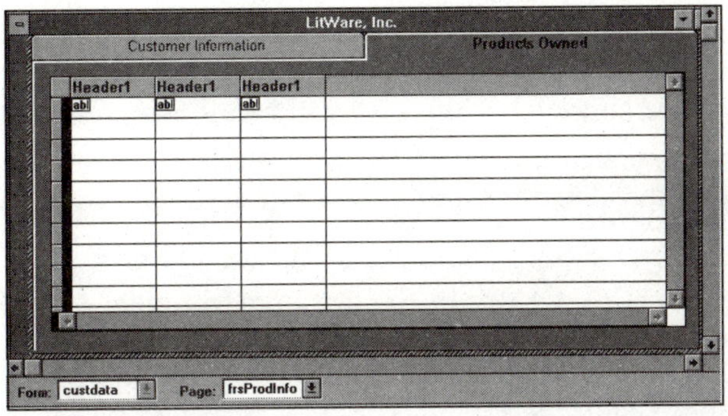

If you want the grid to display items for a specific customer, you must link the customer table to the custprod table. In order for the grid to display the proper description for the displayed product codes, you must make the records in the custprod table point to the appropriate record in the product table.

The Data Environment automatically assumes the link between the custprod and customer tables is the same as previously defined in the database container in Lesson 4. Because cid is the primary key field in the customer table, however, the database container sets up the customer as the target and custprod as the parent of the relationship.

Verify links and set relationships between tables

In this exercise, you'll verify the link between the custprod and customer tables using the Properties window. You will also delete existing relationships and create new relationships between tables as necessary.

1. From the View menu, select Data Environment.
2. In the Properties window, select Relation1 from the drop-down list in the Object box. You can also select Relation1 by clicking on the line connecting the custprod and customer tables.

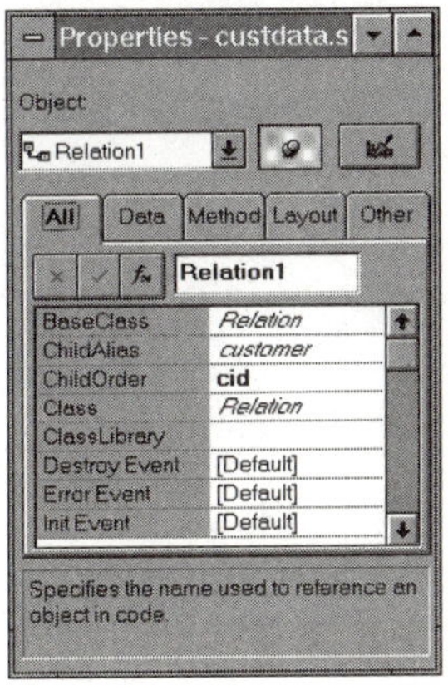

Notice that the ChildAlias property is customer and the ParentAlias property is custprod. Because the custprod *field* cid is linked to the customer *index* cid, these properties cannot be changed in the Properties window.

You must delete the existing relationship and create a new one with customer as the parent and custprod as the child in a one-to-many relationship.

NOTE Setting relationships in the Data Environment for a form affects the relationships for that form only. Deleting and setting new relationships in the Data Environment has no impact on the permanent relationships defined in the database container.

The grid automatically handles the one-to-many aspect of the customer to custprod relationship.

3 Press the Delete key.

4 Click and hold the customerno *field* (not the index) in the customer table.

You may want to resize the box to view more fields and indexes.

5 Drag the cursor to the cid index in the custprod table.

TIP If you drag to the cid field, Visual FoxPro automatically points to the cid index.

6 In the Properties window, notice that the ParentAlias and ChildAlias are now customer and custprod, respectively.

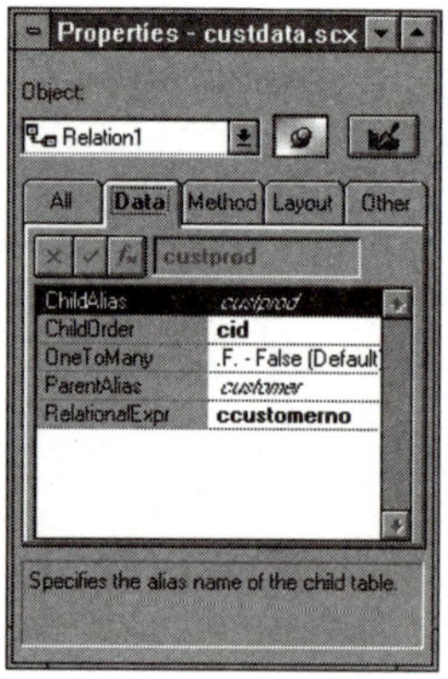

Create relationships between tables

Now you must create a relationship with the custprod table as the parent and the product table as the child, so that the product name associated with each product will appear on the grid.

1. In the **custprod** table, click and hold the **cproductcode** *field* (not the index).

   You may want to resize the box to view more fields and indexes.
2. Drag the cursor to the **cprodcode** index in the **products** table.

TIP If you drag the cursor to the product_code field, Visual FoxPro will automatically point to the pc index.

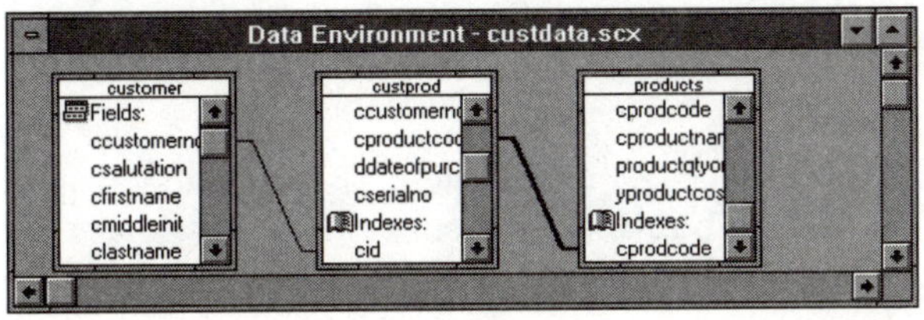

3. Close the Data Environment window.

   You have now learned how to create relationships in a form! Later you will use these relationships to populate the grid.

Manipulating Control Properties

Controls have events, methods, and properties, just as forms and pages do. A control is any object used to display or allow the user to enter information on the form. The events and methods associated with the controls can be used to initiate processes, validate input, and provide cues for the user.

Working with Controls

There are various controls available for use on a form, each with its own set of events and properties. On the custdata form, there are command buttons, grids, labels, combo boxes, option buttons, and text boxes.

Setting the properties and methods of command buttons

The custdata form has several command buttons: Add, Next, Previous, Order Form, and Close. Each has its own behavior and properties.

- The Add button allows the user to add a customer to the customer table.
- The Next and Previous buttons cause the record pointer in the customer table to move to the next or previous record.

- The Order Form button checks the current form from the screen and displays the Order Form.
- The Close button clears the current form from the screen and returns program control to the calling program.

Behaviors are defined in the method code for the relevant events. For these command buttons, only the Click event's method needs modification. When an object's properties or the container form of an object is referenced within a method, you must use a relative syntax referring to the container. You will use the syntax **THISFORM.Method()**, which will be discussed in more detail later in this lesson.

Set the click method of the Quit button

1. In the Properties window, select the cmdQuit command button from the Object drop-down list box.
2. Double-click the Click event under the All or Methods tab to display the Procedure Editor.
3. Type **Thisform.Release()** in the Methods editor to cause the current form to be released when this button is clicked.

   By default, the Release method of the form will cause the form to close and be released from memory.
4. Select Close from the file menu.

TIP Visual FoxPro allows the command RELEASE Thisform, which also causes the form to be released. However, the RELEASE command does not cause the Release method of the form to be executed. This is important if there is code in the Release method that should execute when the form is released. It is therefore good practice to always use the Thisform.Release() method.

Set the click method of the Add button

1. From the Object pull-down list in the Methods Editor, select the cmdAdd command button.

   The Click event should already be selected for editing.

TIP There are many ways to open the Procedure Editor for an object's methods. You can double-click on the object itself; double-click on the Method name in the Properties window; or, if the Methods editor is already open, select the desired object from the object pull-down in the Methods editor. To move from one method to another within an object, and from one object to another, use the Page Up and Page Down keys in the Methods editor.

---

2 Type **APPEND BLANK** in the Methods editor.

The APPEND BLANK command causes a blank record to be added to the current table.

Set the click method of the Next button

1 From the Object pull-down list in the Methods Editor, click the cmdNext command button.

The **Click** event should already be selected for editing.

2 Type the following in the Methods editor (text after double ampersands or after an asterisk at the beginning of a line is a comment and may be omitted):

```
*-- if there are no records in the table,
*-- the pointer is already at EOF() - past the last record in the
table,
*-- so, as a matter of good programming practice,
*-- test for that before attempting to move the record pointer.
IF NOT EOF()
 SKIP
ENDIF
*-- might be at End of File now, either because there are no records,
*-- or because the SKIP command moved the pointer past the last record.
IF EOF()
 *-- go to the last record in the file, and warn the user
 GO BOTTOM
 WAIT WINDOW "At  end of file!" NOWAIT
ENDIF
*--  execute the refresh method of the current form
*-- to have the form display contents of the current record
THISFORM.Refresh()
```

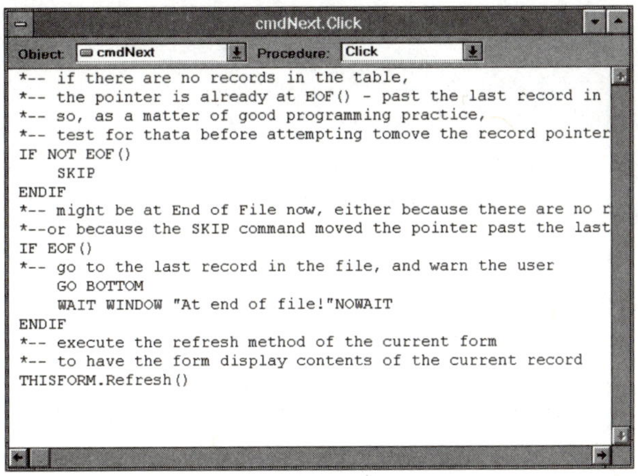

Set the Click Method of the Prev button

1. From the Object pull-down list in the Methods Editor, click the cmdPrev command button. The **Click** event should already be selected for editing.
2. In the Methods editor, type:

```
*-- test that pointer is not already at top of file
IF NOT BOF()
 SKIP -1
ENDIF
*-- might be at top of file now, either because there are no records,
*-- or because the SKIP -1 moved the pointer to the top of the table.
IF BOF()
 *-- go to the first record in the table, and warn the user
 GO TOP
 WAIT "Beginning of File Encountered..." WINDOW NOWAIT
ENDIF
*--  execute the refresh method of the current form
*-- to have the form display contents of the current record
THISFORM.Refresh()
```

3. Close the Methods editor.

You'll notice that there is no reference in the code to a specific table or form. These controls work just as well on any other single-table maintenance screen as they do here, with no code modification at all.

Assigning ToolTips to Command Buttons

Visual FoxPro displays ToolTips, or "balloon-style" Tips, when you pause the mouse cursor over an item. In developing this application, you will assign ToolTips to buttons to provide the user with additional information about how an item functions.

Assign ToolTips to command buttons

To enable ToolTips on a form, set the ShowTips property of the form to True; the default is False.

In this exercise, you'll add ToolTips to command buttons on the custdata form.

1. Open the Properties window if it is not already open.
2. From the drop-down list in the Object box, select the custdata form.
3. On the Layout Tab, double-click the ShowTips property and set it to .T. - true.
4. From the drop-down list in the Object box, select the cmdQuit command button.
5. Click the ToolTipText property on the All or Layout tabs.
6. Type **Close this form**

7 Repeat steps 4 through 6 to assign the following text to ToolTips:

For object:	Set the ToolTipText property to the value:
cmdAdd	Add a record
cmdNext	Move to next record
cmdPrev	Move to previous record
cmdOrder	Enter an order for this customer

Linking Tables and Grids

The grid object is a powerful and easy way to view multiple records at the same time. One of the functions of the customer information form is to display all products purchased by the currently selected customer. The grid object makes doing that as simple as a few mouse clicks. Remember, you've already set up table relationships for the grid with the Data Environment.

You created the three-column grid for displaying product information in Lesson 5. The grid displays the product code, description of the product, and date purchased for each item.

Link a table and a grid

In this exercise, you'll link the customer table and grid, using the custprod table as the source of data for the grid.

1 Open the Properties window if it is not already open.

2 From the drop-down list in the Object box, select the grdProdList grid object.

3 Click the LinkMaster property on the All or Data tab.

4 Type **Customer** to link the grid to the customer table.

5 Change the ReadOnly property to .t. - True.

This prevents the user from changing any information in the tables.

6 Set the RecordSource property to specify the custprod table as the default data source.

TIP If you're not sure which table you can use as a data source, double-click the property so that the source will cycle through the available tables. You can also select a table from the drop-down list box.

7 Set the RecordSourceType property to **1 - Alias** so that the grid control uses the open customer table as its data link.

TIP If you are not using the Data Environment and the table will not already be open when the form is run, set the RecordSourceProperty to 1 - Table. If you use Alias and the table is not already open, Visual FoxPro will generate an error.

Again, notice that you can double-click on the property to cycle through available choices.

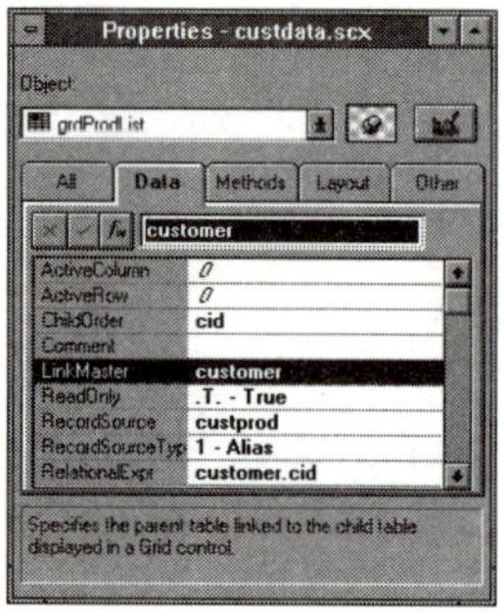

When you use the Data Environment, you can drag the table from the Data Environment (by clicking and dragging the title bar of the desired table) to the form to set up a default grid object containing a column for each field in the table.

TIP Since you set the relationship between the Customer and the Custprod tables in the Data Environment, it is not necessary to set it here using a property. Otherwise, you would set the RelationalExpr property of the Grid object to the linking field of the parent table—in this example, Customer.Cid.

The grid object is made up of several smaller objects, each with its own set of properties and methods. Columns, headers, text boxes, and other controls are some of the objects that may be contained in a grid.

Assign properties to objects in a grid

In this exercise, you will assign properties to the columns in the grid in order to display column headings and customer and product information.

1. Select the Column1 column object in the Properties window.
2. Set the ControlSource property on the All or Data tab to custprod.cproductcode.

   This sets the column to display the contents of the cproductcode field in the custprod table.
3. Set the name property on the Other tab to grcProdCode.
4. Select the first heading object.
5. Set the Caption property on the All or Layout tab to Product Code.
6. Set the name property on the All or Layout tab to grhProdCode.

7 Repeat steps 1 through 6 to assign the following properties:

Object	**Property**	**Value**
Column3	Name	grcProdName
	ControlSource	cproductname
Heading3	Name	grhProdName
	Caption	Description
Column2	Name	grcDatePurchased
	ControlSource	cdateofpurchase
Heading2	Name	grhDatePurchased
	Caption	Date of Purchase

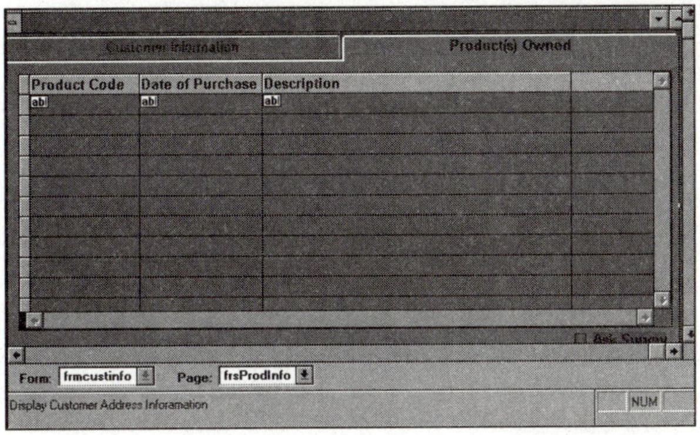

Defining Text Box and Label Properties

The user enters or views text in text boxes. Depending on how you define the control, input will contain information that goes to a table or a memory variable while text display will contain information that comes from a table or memory variable.

In the Customer Data form, all text boxes are bound to fields in the table. The CSR uses text boxes to enter customer information into the appropriate fields; labels provide the user with cues as to what information to enter into the text boxes. Additional information can be provided to the user using the StatusBarText property, which controls the text specified in the status bar at the bottom of the screen.

Set the StatusBarText property for text box fields

1. On the frsCustinfo page of the custdata form, select the txtCustomerno text box.
2. Select the StatusBarText property on the Layout or All tab.
3. Type **Customer's Identification Number** and press Enter.
4. Repeat steps 1 through 3 to assign the following properties:

Object	StatusBarText Property
txtcfirstname	Customer's First Name
txtcmiddleini	Customer's Middle Initial
txtclastname	Customer's Last Name
txtcaddress1	Address Line 1
txtcaddress2	Address Line 2
txtccity	City
combobox	State
txtcpostalcode	Zip Code
txtchomephone	Home Phone
txtcworkphone	Work Phone
edtmcomments	Comments

Some objects do not have a StatusBarText property. However, it is sometimes useful to give the user information about the function of those objects as well. You can use the MouseDown method and the SET MESSAGE command to create the text of the status bar for the page frame and its two pages. The MouseDown event of an object occurs when you click a mouse button down with the mouse cursor over the object. When the mouse button is clicked on the Tab of the individual pages, the MouseDown method of the page frame executes, and when the mouse is over the rest of the page, the MouseDown method of the active page of the page frame executes. Therefore, when the user holds down the mouse button over the Products Owned caption of the frsProdInfo page, the status bar will display "Display Products Owned by Customer," even if the mouse button is released over a different object.

NOTE The MouseDown event differs from the click event in that the MouseDown event fires when the mouse button is pressed down over an object. The MouseClick event fires when the mouse button is released after being pressed.

Set the text of the status bar for the page form and its two pages

1. Select the Custdata object in the Properties window.
2. Double-click MouseDown on the All Tab to open the Methods Editor.

   Notice that Visual FoxPro puts the following line in the Methods editor for you:

   ```
   LPARAMETERS nButton, nShift, nXCoord, nYCoord
   ```

   This is because the MouseDown event automatically passes those parameters to the method, so the method can determine which mouse button was clicked and where on the object it was clicked.
3. Type as the MouseDown method:

   ```
   *-- if on left side, say "Display Address Information",
   *-- otherwise say "Show Products Owned by Customer"
   IF nXCoord <= THIS.Left + (THIS.Width / 2 )
    SET MESSAGE TO ;
    "Display Customer Address Information"
   ELSE
    SET MESSAGE TO ;
    "Display Products Owned by Customer"
   ENDIF
   ```
4. Close the Methods Editor.
5. Repeat steps 1 through 4 to assign the following methods:

Object	**Type as the MouseDown method**
frsCustInfo	SET MESSAGE TO ; "Displaying Customer Address Information"
frsProdInfo	SET MESSAGE TO ; "Displaying Products Owned by Customer "

TIP You can assign StatusBarText in a method of an object as well, so you can set the StatusBarText property using the MouseDown (or any other) method. This might be useful in addition to ToolTips for providing information to the user.

Set the name and caption properties for the text boxes and their labels

1. On the frsCustInfo page of the CustInfo form, select the Label1 object next to the txtCustomerNo text box.
2. Select the Caption property on the Layout or All tab.

3. Type **Customer ID** and press Enter.
4. Select the Name property on the Other or All tab.
5. Type **lblCustId**
6. Repeat steps 1 through 5 to assign properties as follows:

Field	Property	Value
Label2	Caption	Name
	Name	lblcName
Label3	Caption	Address
	Name	lblcAdd1
Label4	Caption	Company
	Name	lblcCompany
Label5	Caption	City, State, Zip
	Name	lblCityStZip
Label6	Caption	Home Phone
	Name	lblchPhone
Label7	Caption	Work Phone
	Name	lblcwPhone
Label8	Caption	Comments
	Name	lblmComments

Changing Properties at Run Time

You can manipulate properties in the Properties window, or you can control them programmatically while the program is running.

The quality team at LitWare determined that to avoid confusion, the Add, Next, and Previous Command buttons should not be available when the user views the product information on the ProdInfo page; however, the buttons must be accessible from the CustInfo page. In order to accomplish this, you can set the Enabled property in the appropriate place in the form to control whether or not a mouse click on an object has any effect.

There are two ways to refer to object properties in a program: by direct reference in a program or the command window, and relative referencing to the object hierarchy within a method.

Direct referencing an object uses the syntax: [ObjectContainer.]Objectname.Property=<value>. This will be discussed further in the lesson on Classes.

Referencing Properties by Relative Object

It is often necessary to change the properties of an object by referring to it *relative* to the objects in which it exists. When you run a form, all the objects on the form are created from their definitions (set in the Forms and Class Designers). In order to change the properties of an object at run time, an object on a form (or in any container, such as a form set or grid) must be referred to relative to itself or its parent containers.

The simplest syntax for an object is: **THIS.property = value**. To refer to an object from its form container use the syntax: **THISFORM.object.property = value**, where *object* and *property* are replaced by the object and property names to be changed, and *value* is the new value assigned to the property.

NOTE THIS refers to the object whose method is being executed. THISFORM refers to the form containing this object. THISFORMSET refers to the form set containing the form, which contains this object. Though it takes some getting used to, the relative syntax is very helpful, especially since Visual FoxPro allows multiple instances of a form, or the same object to be on multiple forms. For example, a cmdClose button that closes the current form might appear on several different forms. Without relative referencing, it would be very difficult to distinguish one instance of the button from another.

Disable the cmdNext and cmdPrev buttons on the product information page

1. Open the Properties window.
2. From the Methods Editor or the drop-down list in the Object box, select the frsProdinfo page object.
3. Double-click on the Activate Event method on the Methods or All tab to open the Activate method for the prodinfo page.
4. Type the following commands to disable the Add, Next and Previous command buttons when the prodinfo page is activated:

```
THISFORM. cmdNext.Enabled = .f.
THISFORM. cmdPrev.Enabled = .f.
THISFORM. cmdAdd.Enabled = .f.
```

5. Close the Methods Editor.

Enable the cmdNext and cmdPrev buttons when the user selects the customer information page

1. Open the Properties window.
2. From the Object drop-down list box or Methods Editor, select the frscustinfo page object.
3. Double-click on the Activate Event method under the Methods or All tab to open the Activate method for the prodinfo page.
4. Type the following commands to enable the Add, Next, and Previous command buttons when the custinfo page is activated:

   ```
   THISFORM.cmdNext.Enabled = .t.
   THISFORM.cmdPrev.Enabled = .t.
   THISFORM.cmdAdd.Enabled = .t.
   ```

5. Close the Methods Editor.

TIP To make the button group invisible or visible based on the page being displayed, substitute the property **Visible** for **Enabled** in the above commands.

Generally, it is a good idea to use the relative syntax when reusing objects, since no parent objects need to be changed.

One Step Further: Setting the Properties for the Option Group

In the One Step Further section of Lesson 5, you added a combo box to allow CSRs to select a state from a list, and an option button group to allow CSRs to select a title (Mr., Mrs., or Ms.).

Now you'll set the properties of those objects to give them the desired functionality.

Set the properties of the Option Group

The CSR's selection in the Option Group should be stored in the cSalutation field of the customer table. The default value of the salutation should be blank, in case the CSR does not know the proper title for the customer.

1. Make sure the custdata form is loaded in the Forms Designer, with the page titled "Customer Information" visible.
2. Open the Properties window.
3. Select Option Group1 from the drop-down list in the Object box.
4. Set the ControlSource property (on the Data tab) to **customer.csalutation** to link the option group to the field in the table.

NOTE Because you are setting the ControlSource property of the button group, it will not be necessary to set the property of each button.

5 Type **.NULL.** in the Value property (under the Data tab).

Make sure to type the periods surrounding the word NULL.

6 Type **28** in the Height property (on the Layout tab).

7 Type **135** in the Width property (on the Layout tab).

Set the properties of the option buttons in the Option Group

Each of the buttons in the Option Group should have an appropriate caption and be initialized to 0, which Visual FoxPro interprets as meaning that the button is not selected.

1 Make sure the custdata form is open in the Form Designer.

2 From the Properties window, select the option button Option1.

3 On the All tab, set the properties of the Option1 button as follows:

Property	Value
Value	**0**
Height	**18**
Left	**5**
Top	**4**
Width	**44**

4 From the Properties window, select the option button Option2.

5 On the All tab, set the properties of the Option2 button as follows:

Property	Value
Value	**0**
Height	**18**
Left	**45**
Top	**4**
Width	**45**

6 From the Properties window, select the option button Option3.

7 On the All tab, set the properties of the Option3 button as follows:

Property	Value
Value	**0**
Height	**18**
Left	**90**
Top	**4**
Width	**41**

Set the properties of the Combo box

The Combo box should allow the CSR to select a state based on a states table, prompted by the state abbreviation and name. The state abbreviation for each customer is stored in the cState field of the customer table. The combo box font should be a non-proportional one so that the columns of the combo box line up properly.

1. Make sure the custdata form is open in the Form Designer.
2. Open the Properties window if it is not already open.
3. Select Combo1 from the drop-down list in the Object box.
4. On the All tab, set the properties of the Combo1 box as follows:

Property	Value
ControlSource	**customer.cstate**
RowSourceType	**2-Alias**
RowSource	**State**
ColumnCount	**2**
FontName	**Courier New**
StatusBarText	**Select a State**

5. Close the Form Designer.

   Visual FoxPro displays a dialog box asking if you want to save the changes to Form Designer custdata.scx.
6. Click Yes.

If you want to continue to the next lesson

1. Click File on the Menu bar
2. Select Close.

If you want to quit Visual FoxPro for now

1. Click File on the Menu bar.
2. Select Exit.

Lesson Summary

In this lesson you learned how to modify the appearance and behavior of various type of objects. Forms, pages, and controls have elements in common that you can manipulate during development as well as while the program is running.

To	Do This
Open a form	Open the Project Manager. Click the Forms tab. Click the desired form, and then click Modify.

To	Do This
Open the Properties window	Select View from the Visual FoxPro menu, and then click Properties.
Open the Code window	Select View from the Visual FoxPro menu, and then click Code.
Open the Dataenvironment window	Select View from the FoxPro menu and then click Data Environment. *or* Using the right mouse button, click on the form to open a shortcut menu, and then select Data Environment.
Select an object in a form	Open the form and click on the desired object. *or* Select the object from the Object box in the Properties window. *or* Select the object from the Object box in the Code window.
Change an object's property	Select the object, open the Properties window. click the property. Type the desired value, and then press ENTER.
Change an object's method code	Select the object. open the Properties window, and then double-click the method. *or* Open the code window, select the desired method from the drop-down list in the Object box, and then type the desired code.

For online information about	From the Visual FoxPro Help Menu, choose Contents, select "Using Visual FoxPro," and then
Properties	Select the topic, "Properties"
Methods	Select the topic, "Methods"
Controls	Select the topic, "Controls"

For more information on	See in the *Microsoft Visual FoxPro Developer's Guide*
Properties	Chapter 9, "Creating Forms"
Methods	Chapter 9, "Creating Forms"
Controls	Chapter 11, "Using Controls"

Preview of the Next Lesson

In Lesson 7, you will learn how to create classes so you can avoid manipulating object properties and methods on an object-by-object basis, and you will learn how to create objects that can be reused on multiple forms. Classes allow you to define "blueprints," make changes to blueprints, and see your changes reflected in objects created from those blueprints.

Lesson

7

Using Classes

Estimated time

60 min.

In this lesson you will learn how to:

- Create your own classes from Visual FoxPro's base classes.
- Save an object as a new class.
- Create new objects from your own classes.
- Modify class properties.

Classes serve as the reusable "blueprints" from which you can create all objects in Microsoft Visual FoxPro 3 for Windows. Classes and objects are very similar, but not the same. A class describes the functionality of an object; an object created from the class executes the described functionality in an application. In Lesson 5, the form and control objects you used to build the custdata form were created from Visual FoxPro's built-in base classes.

You can use Visual FoxPro's base classes to create custom classes that more precisely match your development needs. By creating your own classes, you can save and reuse code and properties to create any number of ready-made objects for use in your applications.

In this lesson, you will prepare for future development at LitWare by creating new classes for commonly used objects. You will also create objects from your new classes to build the Custfind form, which will be used by LitWare Customer Service Representatives (CSRs) to locate records when customers call.

Start the lesson

1. Open Visual FoxPro.
2. From the File Menu, select Open.
3. In the Directories list box, select c:\LITWARE\PROJ_07.
4. Select litware.pjx.
5. Click the OK button.

The Project Manager displays the LitWare project.

Creating Your Own Classes

Visual FoxPro's base classes allow you to create a wide variety of objects including forms, command buttons, and grids quickly and efficiently. You can use Visual FoxPro's base classes to create objects to use in your application as a foundation for your own classes.

Visual FoxPro allows you to create your own classes by *subclassing* base classes, or new classes, and by saving existing objects as new classes. Both methods allow you to take advantage of development you have already done to complete future applications or new pieces of existing applications more quickly.

Subclassing Visual FoxPro's Base Classes

Subclassing creates new classes that retain, or *inherit*, the properties of the parent class. Subclassing allows you to generate classes for specific development purposes by making modifications to existing classes and saving the modifications as a new class.

For example, if a customer requests that a particular font be used for all the labels on forms in an application, you can subclass Visual FoxPro's label base class, set the Font property to the desired font, and save the modified class as a subclass. When you begin development of the application, you can use the new label subclass to create all the label objects in the application. Each object created from your new label subclass will bear the customer's font choice. If the customer later changes their mind about the font to use, you can change the Font property in the subclass and all occurrences of the label object will reflect that change.

Create the litFormSet class

While you are creating the current LitWare application, it is a good idea to start saving some of your work so that you can use it in future LitWare applications as well as the current one. In this exercise, you'll create a new formset subclass for LitWare form objects, and store it in a file where other classes for the LitWare application will be stored as well.

Formsets allow you to add forms to the application with all of the standard properties predefined. This makes it possible to work with multiple forms as a group. If you wish to add a toolbar to all of the forms in your application, as you will do in Lesson 8, you can just add it to the formset and it will be included on all of the forms that use the formset.

1. In the Project Manager, click the Classes tab.

New button

2. Click the New button.

   The New Class dialog box appears.

3. Type **litFormSet** in the Class Name text box.
4. Select Formset from the Based On drop-down list box.

   By definition, subclasses must be based on an existing class. In this case, you will base the litFormSet on Visual FoxPro's formset base class. Once you have created subclasses of your own, you can base new classes on subclasses that you have already created.

5. Type **c:\litware\proj_07\litware** in the Store In text box.

   The Store In text box requires you to enter the name of a *class library*. A class library is a container for organizing classes. To work with classes in the Visual Class Designer, the classes must be stored in a class library. Visual FoxPro allows you to create a new class library each time you create a subclass, or to store the subclass in an existing class library. In this exercise, you have indicated that you will store the new litFormSet class in the LitWare class library. Since it does not already exist, Visual FoxPro will create the file LITWARE.VCX.

> **NOTE** For each new class library, Visual FoxPro creates a .VCT and .VCX file. A .VCX file is a standard Visual FoxPro table of data that stores information about the classes contained in the library; the .VCT file is the associated memo file.

   In practice, you might have two or more Class Libraries, one for generic objects and routines pertaining to all applications or clients, and a more specific one to conform to the standards and needs of a particular application.

6. Click the OK button.

   The Class Designer appears. Notice that the Class Designer looks almost exactly like the Form Designer. Because you indicated in the New Class dialog box that the new class is to be based on Visual FoxPro's formset base class, the Class Designer shows information relevant to form sets.

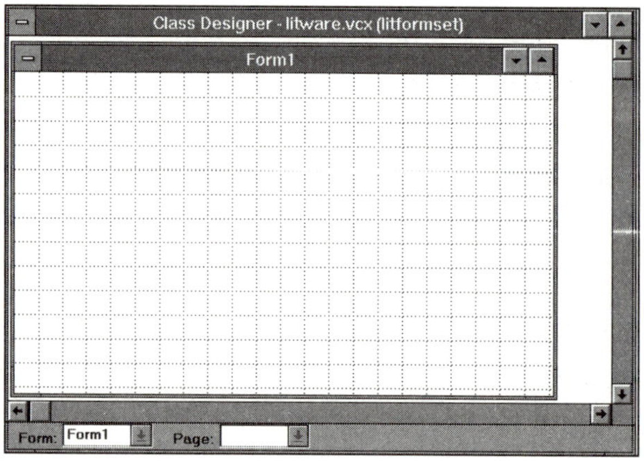

Set litFormSet class properties

The litFormSet class should be generic enough to serve as the starting point for any form used in any application developed for LitWare, Inc. Most forms used in applications developed for LitWare, Inc. will have the same Height, Width, BackColor, and Caption property settings. In this exercise, you will define default property settings for LitWare form objects. Recall from Lesson 6 that the LitWare standard is to have the company name as the title for forms. The background for the form will be green, the caption will be **LitWare, Inc.**, and the dimensions will be 300 by 550 pixels.

1 Open the Properties window, if it is not displayed already.

   You can display the Properties window when using the Form or Class Designer by choosing Properties from the View menu.

2 From the Object drop-down list box in the Properties window, select Form1.

3 Set properties for Form1 using the settings below:

Property	**Setting**
Name	litForm
BackColor	Green (64,128,128)
Caption	LitWare, Inc.
ScaleMode	3-Pixels
Height	300
Width	550

4 Save the class.

5 Close the Class Designer.

Create the litCommand class

Creating all command buttons from the same class helps to standardize the "look and feel" of forms within applications, and across applications within a company.

1. In the Project Manager, click the Classes tab.
2. Click the New button.

   The New Class dialog box appears.
3. Type **litCommand** in the Class Name text box.
4. Select Command Button from the Based On drop-down list box.

   The LitWare class library is already selected as the class library file.
5. Click the OK button.

   The Class Designer appears and displays the Command Button class.

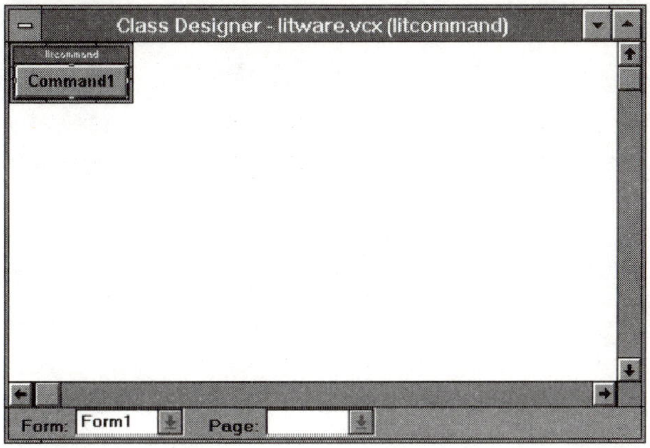

Set litCommand class properties

The LitWare standard command button size is 30 pixels high and 90 pixels wide; caption text appears in 9 point Courier New. If the command button's caption is too long to fit in the command button's width, the second option is for the button to be 150 pixels wide.

1. Display the Properties window.
2. Select Class Info on the Class menu.

   The Class Information dialog box appears.

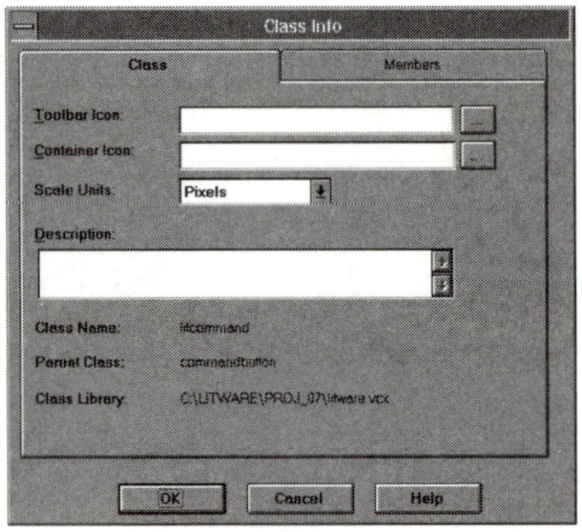

3 Set the Scale Units to Pixels.

4 Click OK.

5 Set the command button's properties using the settings below.

Property	**Setting**
Height	30
Width	90
FontName	Courier New
FontSize	9 (point)

6 Save the class.

7 Close the Class Designer.

TIP Visual FoxPro will not allow you to close the Class Designer if you are in the process of setting a property. In order to close the Class Designer, you must first accept property settings by clicking the Accept button in the Properties window or by pressing the Enter key.

Subclassing Your Own Classes

Any class can be subclassed, including classes you have created yourself. Each subclass created from any existing class inherits all the property settings and methods of the class from which it was created—the *parent* class.

Once you begin to subclass your own classes, a *class hierarchy* begins to form, in which parent classes rank above their related subclasses. In a class hierarchy, the principle of inheritance means that property and method modifications made to a parent class carry through to the related subclasses. This provides the ability to modify entire groups of classes by modifying a single parent class. For example, if you detect a bug in a parent class, the fix you make in the parent class will be implemented automatically in each subclass created from that parent.

If you have overridden—changed—any of the properties or methods in the subclass, changes made to those properties or methods in the parent class will not affect the subclass.

Create a new class for Close buttons

Now that you have created a generic command button class that standardizes button appearance, you can use it to begin creating command button subclasses with unique methods for Click events.

1. In the Project Manager, click the Classes tab.
2. Click the New button.

   The New Class dialog box appears.
3. Type **litCmdClose** in the Class Name text box.

Dialog

4. Click the Dialog button next to the Based On drop-down list box.

   The Open dialog box appears. You will base the litCmdClose class on your own litCommand class so that the new Close button class inherits the Height, Width, and FontSize properties of the parent class.

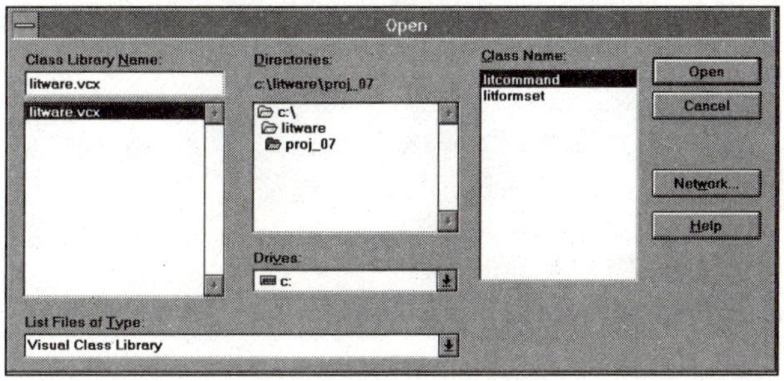

5. Select LITWARE.VCX from the Class Library Name list box.

   A list of classes in the LitWare class library appears in the Class Name list box.
6. Select litCommand from the list of classes.
7. Click the Open button.

   The From line in the New Class dialog box displays the path for LITWARE.VCX.
8. Click the OK button.

   The Class Designer appears with the properties you entered for the litCommand class. You can now assign the properties specific to the litCmdClose class.
9. Set the properties and methods below using the settings to the right.

Property/Method	**Setting**
Caption	Close
StatusBarText	Close this window
ForeColor	Red (255,0,0)
Click Event	THISFORM.Release()

NOTE If the AutoRelease property of the Form Set is set to true, when the Release method of the last form in a form set is executed, the form set is released as well.

10 Save the class.

11 Close the Class Designer.

Creating a Class from an Object

Visual FoxPro also allows you to create a class from any existing object or set of objects. For example, if you have already created a grid in the Form Designer that perfectly meets the requirements of your application, you can save it as a class and use it again. You can save controls, forms, form sets, and any combination of objects as a class. This allows you to work with a particular object until you are satisfied with its functionality, and then you can save it as a class.

Save standard customer information as a class

Almost every form that handles customer-related data will need to display the customer name and ID number. If you save the controls that display customer name and ID number as a class, you will make it easy to add the controls to new forms at LitWare, Inc.

1. In the Project Manager, click the Documents tab.
2. Click the plus sign next to Forms to expand the category.
3. Select custdata.
4. Click the Modify button.

   The Form Designer opens and displays the custdata form. The form looks like the following illustration.

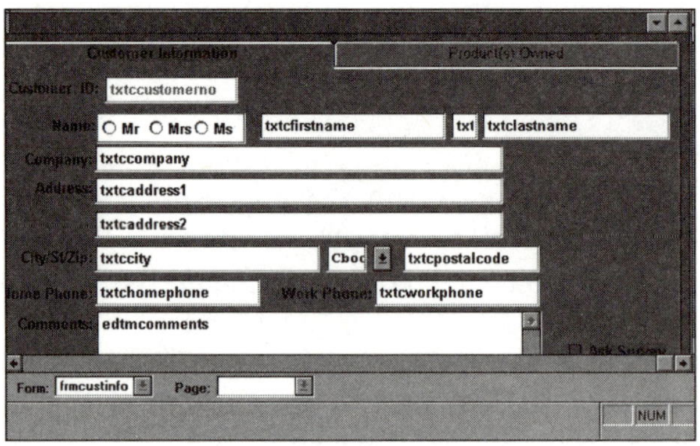

5 In the Properties window, select txtCustomerno from the Object drop-down list box.

Handles appear around the txtCustomerno text box, indicating that it is selected.

6 Shift-click the Customer ID label, Name label, and the three name text boxes to select them as well.

NOTE Shift-clicking an item allows you to select or deselect an item without affecting other selected items. Clicking an item without holding down shift deselects any previous selections.

---

7 From the File menu, select Save As Class.

The Save Class dialog box appears.

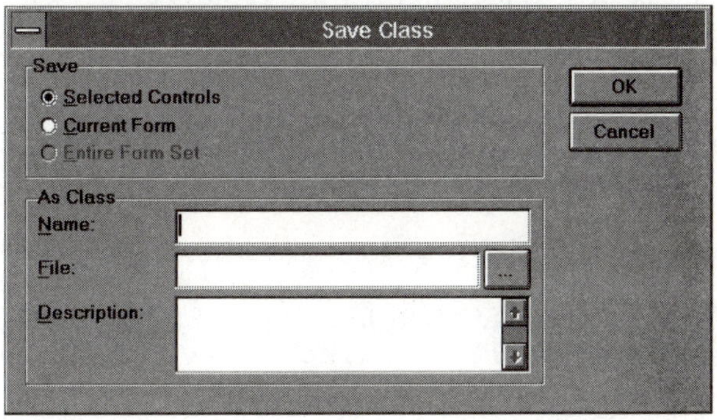

The Save Class dialog box allows you to specify whether you are saving a form or selected controls as a class and allows you to select a class library to which to add the new class.

8 Select Selected Controls as the Save option.

9 In the Class Name text box, type **litCustHead**

10 In the File text box, type **C:\Litware|proj_07\LitWare**

The file referred to in this option is the class library file.

11 In the Description text box, type **Customer header text boxes and labels**

12 Click the OK button.

Visual FoxPro saves the new class to the LitWare class library.

13 Close the Form Designer.

Setting Up Visual FoxPro to Use Your Classes

In Lesson 5, you used the Form Designer to create new form and control objects from Visual FoxPro's base classes. Once you have defined your own classes, Visual FoxPro makes it easy to use them for creating new objects.

Visual FoxPro provides several methods for creating objects from your own classes. You can:

- Use your own classes as default classes for all new forms and form sets.
- Drag a control class from the Classes page of Project Manager and drop it onto a form to create the control object.
- Register your own class libraries to access your control classes directly from the Form Controls toolbar in the Form Designer.
- Create objects from classes programmatically using the CREATEOBJECT() function.

Each method enhances your effort to develop custom applications quickly by creating objects based on your own classes.

Making Your Forms Class the Default

By default, each time you create a new form Visual FoxPro creates the new form object from its own form base class. However, as noted above, you can easily set up your own form and formset classes as the default classes. Once you have set your forms class as the default, each new form you create will possess the properties of the forms class you defined.

Set the litFormSet class as the default

In this exercise, you will make the new litFormSet class the default form set class.

1. From the Tools menu, select Options.

   The Options dialog box appears.

   The Options dialog box provides you with a wide variety of settings for customizing your Visual FoxPro environment.

2. Click the Forms tab.

   The Forms page appears.

3. In the Template Classes section of the Forms page, click the Formset check box.

   The Formset Template dialog box appears.

4. From the Class Library Name list box, select LITWARE.VCX.

   A list of the classes contained in the LitWare class library appears in the Class Name list box.

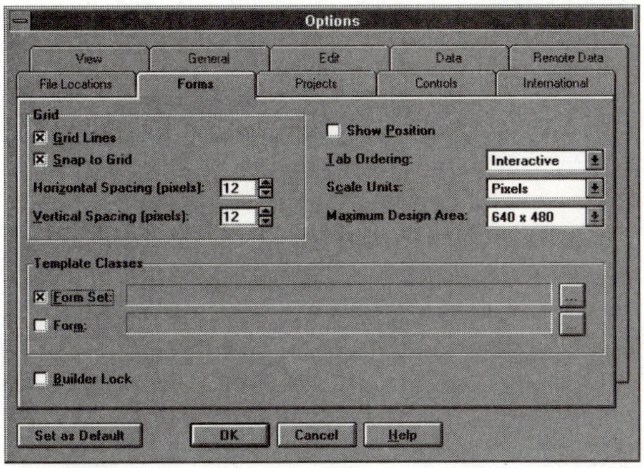

WARNING If you double-click on the class library name, Visual FoxPro will select the first class in the list and close the selection dialog box. If the selected class is not a form, this will generate an error. To reopen the Class Selector screen, click the ellipse box on the Formset line.

5. Select litFormSet from the Class Name list box.
6. Click the OK button.

   LitFormSet appears as the default formset class.

Registering Class Libraries

The Form Controls toolbar gives you easy access to each of Visual FoxPro's control base classes. Registering your own class libraries in a project allows you to add your own class buttons to the Form Controls toolbar. Once you have registered your own class library, you can point and click to create objects based on your own classes.

Register the LitWare class library

Work on the LitWare application will go much more quickly if you can create classes from the LitWare class library directly from the Form Controls toolbar.

1. Open the Options dialog box, if it is not displayed already.
2. Click the Controls tab.

   The Control page appears.

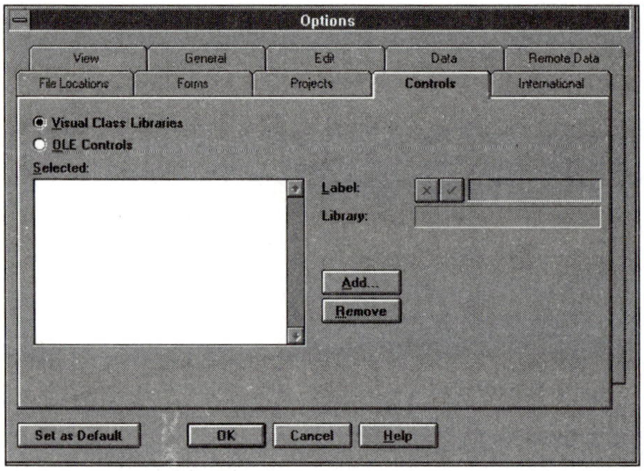

3 Click the Visual Class Libraries Option button at the top of the page.

4 Click the Add button.

The Open dialog box appears.

5 Select LITWARE.VCX from the File Name list box to register the classes contained in the LitWare class library.

6 Click the Open button.

LitWare appears in the Selected list box.

7 Click the OK button to close the Options dialog box.

Clicking the Set As Default button in the Options dialog box would make the current settings the defaults for every Visual FoxPro session.

Creating Objects From Your Own Classes

Now that you have created your own classes and configured Visual FoxPro to use your classes as defaults for new forms and controls, you can take advantage of the power provided by classes to quickly create objects with properties that meet your development needs.

In the following exercises, you will use new classes to begin building the custfind form. In the LitWare application, CSRs will use the custfind form to enter the name and customer ID number of callers. Once the data has been entered into the form, the user can click the Search button to locate the matching customer record.

Start building the custfind form

The first step in creating the custfind form is to create a new form object.

1 From the Project Manager, select the Documents tab.

2 Select Forms.

3 Click New.

The New Form dialog box appears, allowing you to use a FormWizard or create a New Form.

4 Click the New Form button.

The Form Designer appears. Notice that the new form has all the characteristics of the litFormSet class that you defined earlier.

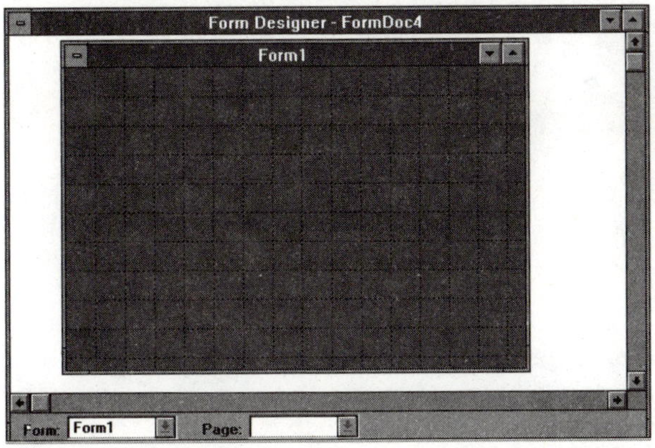

5 Save the form as CUSTFIND.SCX in the PROJ_07 directory.

Add customer information text boxes and labels

The controls you saved as the litCustHead class can be used by LitWare reps to identify customers by name and customer ID number in the custfind form. In the exercise below, you will include the litCustHead class on the custfind form.

1 Make sure the custfind form is showing in the Form Designer.

2 Click the Project Manager to select it.

3 Click the Classes tab.

4 Click the plus sign next to LitWare to expand the class library.

5 Drag the litCustHead class from the Project Manager onto the new form. Place the object in the upper-left corner of the form.

The object appears on the form. Notice that there is now an object named LitCustHead1 on the form, listed in the Properties window.

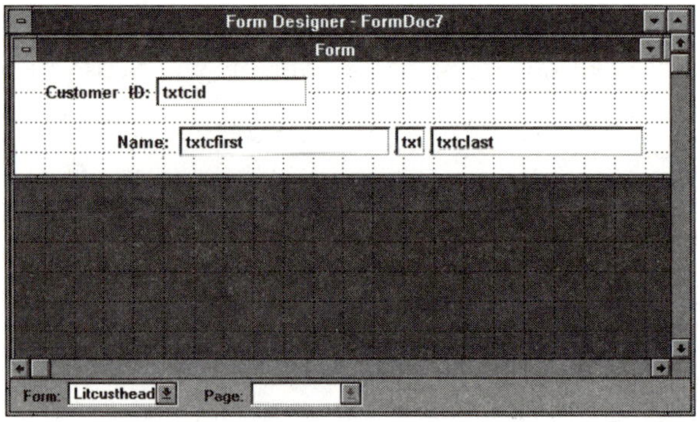

6 Set the BackColor property of the litCustHead object to green (64,128,128) to match the rest of the form.

TIP You can also set the BackColor property of an object to Transparent, and the color of the form will show through the object. For maximum reusability, set the BackColor to Transparent in the class definition, so the object will be transparent on all forms in which it is used.

---

7 Resize the border so that all the controls in the group are visible.

You can set the BorderWidth property for the class for maximum reusability.

8 Set the BorderWidth property for object to 0.

This prevents the border around the object grouping from showing, and makes it invisible to the user that these objects are grouped together as a result of being saved as a class.

Add a Close button

Many forms in the LitWare application will have a Close button that allows the user to close the form. In this exercise, you will add your own Close button to the custfind form directly from the Form Controls toolbar.

View Classes

1 In the Form Controls tool bar, click the View Classes button.

A drop-down menu of available class libraries appears.

2 Select LitWare.

The toolbar changes to show classes in the LitWare class library.

3 Click the litCmdClose button.

TIP If the class icons are too small to read, take advantage of Visual FoxPro's ToolTips by pointing to the icon until Visual FoxPro identifies the button with a small yellow label.

---

4 Click the form.

Place the cross hair two grid squares below the text box for middle initial.

Visual FoxPro places the litCmdClose button at the selected location.

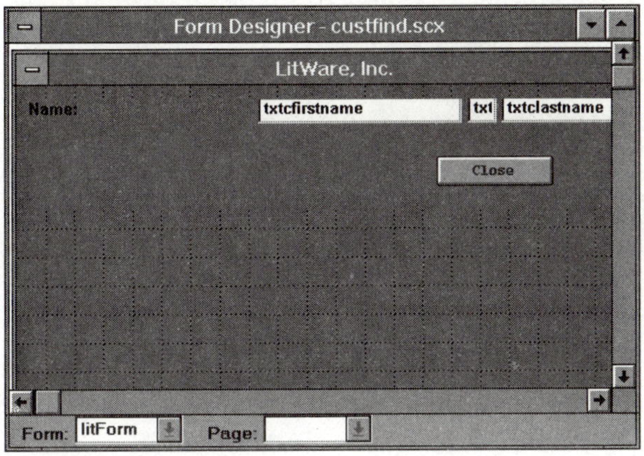

Add a Search button

Once the customer service rep has typed the name or customer ID number into the text boxes contained in the litCustHead object, the rep will click the Search button to find the matching customer record.

1 In the Form Controls toolbar, click the litCommand button.

2 Click the cross hair two grid squares below the txtfirst label in the first name text box.

Visual FoxPro places a new command button at the selected location.

3 Set the Caption property to "Search."

4 Resize the form window to eliminate unused space.

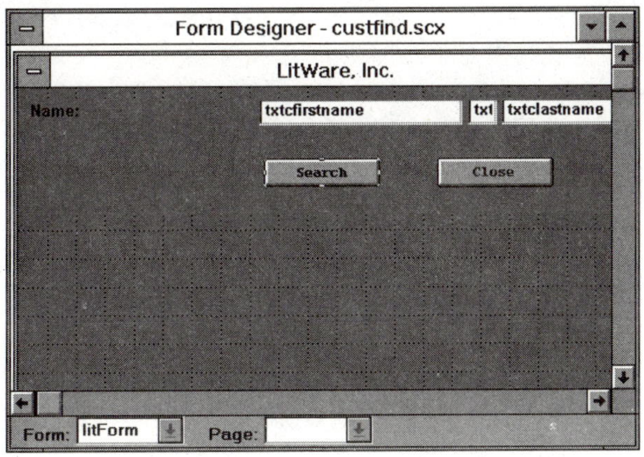

Run the form

Before you begin to modify object properties for the custfind form, you will want to see how it functions first. There are several ways to run a form: from the command window by typing DO FORM <formname> <enter>; from the Program pull-down menu by selecting DO and then selecting file type Form; or from the Project Manager by highlighting the form and then clicking Run.

You can also run the form from the Form Designer:

1 With the Form Designer still open, select Run from the Form menu.

TIP You can also click on the form with the right mouse button and select Run from the shortcut menu that appears. Or you can click the Run button on the system toolbar to run the form.

If you have made changes since the last time the form was saved, a message appears asking if you want to save your changes.

2 Click Yes to save your changes.

The custfind form appears. Notice that the text boxes contain customer data but that they are disabled; information cannot be entered. You will modify properties of the litCustHead class to activate the text boxes in the next section.

3 Click the Close button.

The custfind form closes, and the Project Manager window becomes the active window.

Modifying Class Properties

In addition to allowing you to quickly create ready-made objects, classes also allow you to control objects' behavior after the classes have been created. When you modify the properties of a particular class, the same properties are inherited by every object created from the class. This allows you to modify entire groups of objects by modifying the class from which the objects were created.

Object properties that have been set manually, however, will not be overridden by changes made to the parent class. This ensures that objects in which you have customized properties for a particular purpose will not be altered.

In the following exercises, you will modify properties of the classes used to create the custfind form to change the behavior of the form's objects.

Modify the litCmdClose command button

In your observation of LitWare employees using the prototype, you noticed that many of them accidentally close forms when attempting to perform other routine tasks. Therefore, the Close button should display a warning message before actually closing the form to make sure that the user does not close the application in error.

1 In the Project Manager, select the litCmdClose class from the Classes page.

2 Click the Modify button.

The Class Designer appears for the litCmdClose class.

3 In the Properties window, select the Click Event from the Methods page.

4 Double-click the Click Event line.

The Methods Editor appears and displays the code that you typed earlier in the lesson to release the form.

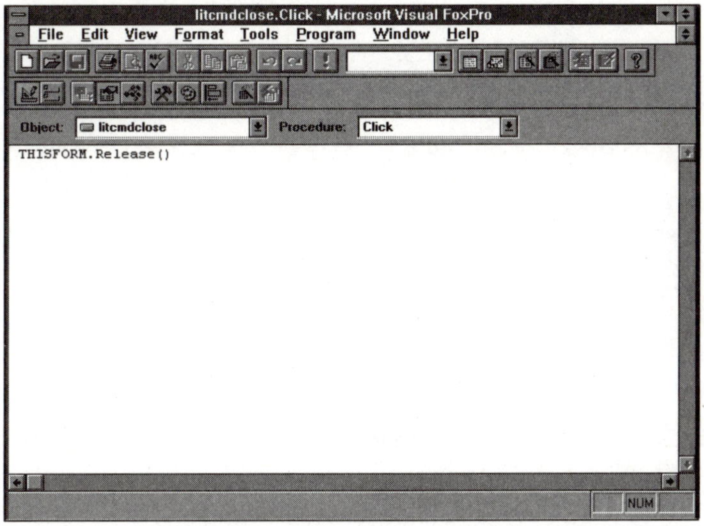

5 Before the existing line, type the code below:

```
lnClose = MESSAGEBOX("Do you really want to close this form?", 4+32)
IF lnClose = 6  && user said Yes
```

6 After the existing line, type

```
ENDIF
```

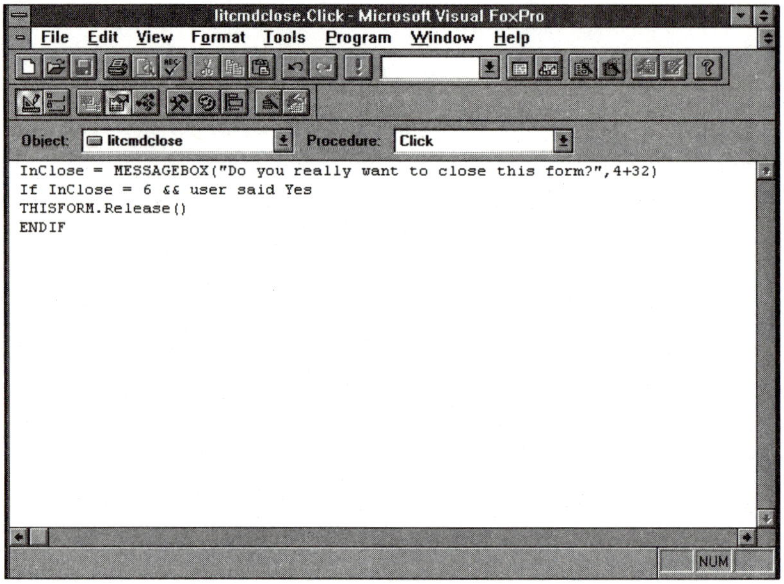

7 Close the Procedure Editor.

8 Save changes to the class.

The modifications you made to the Click Event property have now been saved to the class, and will apply to any objects created from the class. Any existing or future subclasses created from the litCmdClose class will also inherit the change.

9 Close the Class Designer.

Run the form

In this exercise you will run the custfind form again to see the effects of the class properties you changed.

1 In the Project Manager, select the custfind form.

2 Click the Run button.

The custfind form appears.

3 Click the Close button to close the form.

A message dialog box appears and displays the message you typed into the method code for the Close button.

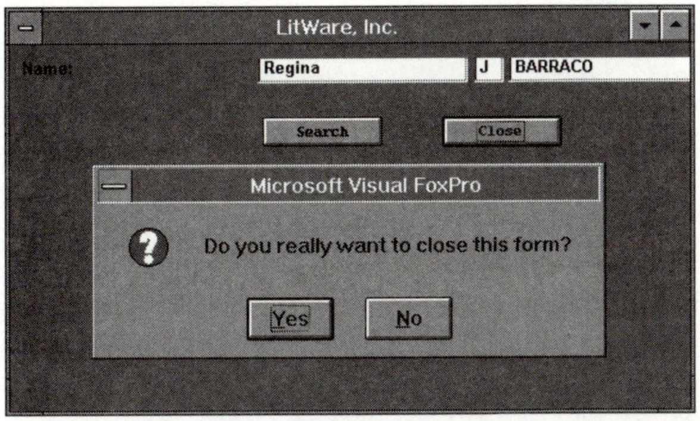

4 Click Yes to close the form.

The custfind form closes.

Changing Class Properties at Runtime

Changing class properties when the application is running allows you to override the default properties of a class without updating any other object, even those created from the same class, or affecting the properties of the class itself. It also allows you to use one set of properties when you are designing a form, and another set when the form is running, as illustrated in the next exercise.

Set the position properties

All instances of the litFormSet class should initially appear in a particular position on the screen, 10 pixels down and 10 pixels to the right of the top and left of the screen. You can position the form in the Class Designer by dragging it to the desired position or setting the Top and Left properties. However, you may not be able to leave the form at the desired position during development, since those properties, when changed in the Property window, affect the item in the Class Designer as well. This might obscure other windows you need to see, like the Properties window or Forms Controls Window. Setting the Top and Left properties at run time will help you avoid these problems.

1 Open the Class Designer for the litFormSet class.

2 Select litform in the Object drop-down list box.

3 From the Methods Tab, select the Load event in the Properties window.

4 Double-click on the Load Event line.

The Methods Editor appears.

5 In the Methods Editor, type the following code.

```
THIS.Top=10
THIS.Left=10
```

6 Close the Methods Editor.

7 Save changes to the class.

8 Close the Class Designer.

9 Run the form.

Notice that the form is now positioned as you specified, regardless of its position in the Class Designer during development.

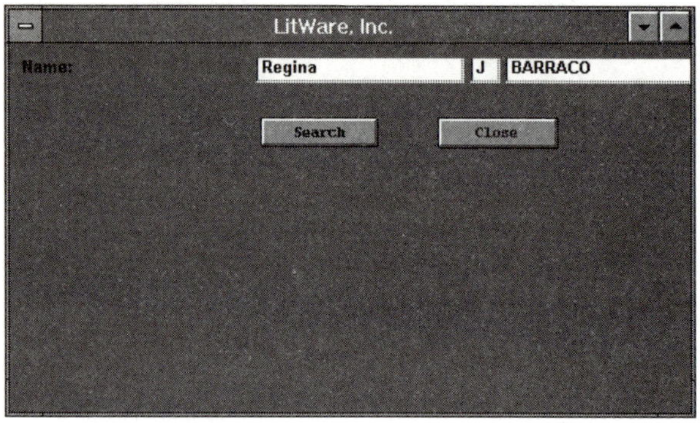

10 Close the form.

One Step Further: Creating a New Class From an Existing Class

The LitWare application needs a way to maintain the list of products in inventory. The inventory information is stored in the products table, but you have not yet created a file maintenance function for that table. The form you create for maintaining the inventory table will have other uses as well, possibly including a link to an inventory screen for checking item availability. The product maintenance form will use the same command buttons for navigation as the custdata form, so it makes sense to create a class from those buttons.

Create a class from existing buttons

1 Open the custdata form in the Forms Designer.

2 Hold down the shift key, and click the Add, Next, and Previous command buttons.

All three buttons are selected.

3 From the File menu, select Save As Class.

The Save Class dialog appears.

4 Save the class with the following information:

Save	Selected Controls
Name	LitNavButtons
File	LitWare
Description	Navigation buttons for file maintenance forms.

5 Click OK.

6 Close the custdata form.

Since you did not make any changes to the form, it is not necessary for you to save it.

NOTE The command buttons on the custdata form you selected to save as a class do not become instances of that class, so any changes you make to the new subclass will not affect those buttons on the custdata form.

Modify the new LitNavButtons class in the Class Designer

Before you use the new class on a form, you will set properties of the class so you don't have to change those properties on each form. You will also add another class to this one so that every form that uses the command buttons you selected above will also use the Close button class you defined earlier in this lesson.

1 Open the Class Designer for the LitNavButtons class.

2 Display the Properties window.

3 Set the following properties:

Object	**Property**	**Value**
LitNavButtons	BackStyle	0 - Transparent
	Height	35
	Width	415
CmdAdd	Height	30
	Width	90
	Left	0
	Top	0
CmdNext	Height	30
	Width	90
	Left	108
	Top	0
CmdBack1	Height	30
	Width	90
	Left	216
	Top	0

4 Use the Form Controls toolbar to add the litCmdClose button.

5 Set the following properties for the Close button:

Height	30
Width	90
Left	324
Top	0

6 Close the Class Designer, and save your changes.

Create a new form using the new class

Now you will create the new form for product file maintenance. You will use the subclass you created earlier in this lesson

1 From the Project Manager, select the Documents tab.

2 Select Forms.

3 Click New.

The New Form dialog box appears, allowing you to use a FormWizard or create a New Form.

4 Click the New Form button.

The Forms Designer appears.

5 Select Data Environment from the View menu.

6 Select Add from the Data Environment menu.

7 Select products table from the Add Table or View window.

8 Click OK.

9 Click and drag all the fields in the products table from the Data Environment to the form.

10 Arrange the fields on the form and add the following labels to the form.

Label	**Next to Field**
Product Code	Text1
Product Name	Text2
Quantity	Text3
Cost	Text4

11 On the Form Controls toolbar, click the View Classes button.

A menu of available classes appears.

12 If LitWare is not available, select Add, and add the LitWare class library.

LitNav

13 Select the LitNavButtons class

14 Add the class to the form.

The form should look like this:

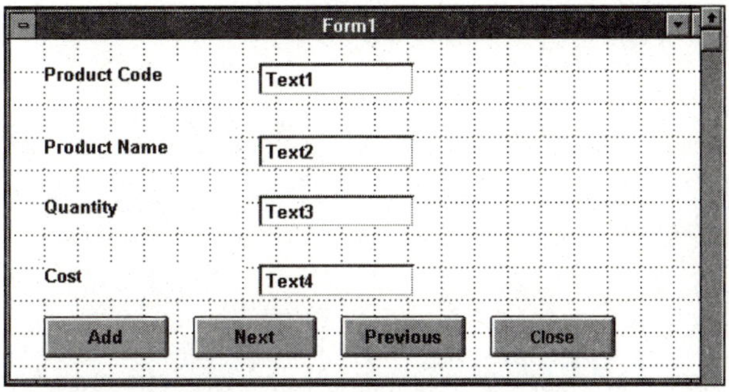

15 Close the form, and save it as Prdmaint.scx.

If you want to continue to the next lesson

1. Click File on the Menu bar
2. Select Close.

If you want to quit Visual FoxPro for now

1. Click File on the Menu bar.
2. Select Exit.

Lesson Summary

To	Do This
Create a class library	Create the new class library by saving a class to it. *or* Use the CREATE CLASSLIB <libname> command.
Create a new class	Use the CREATE CLASS <classname> AS <parentclass> command.
Create a class from existing objects	Select the objects you want to save as a class (open a form or formset, and then click on the desired objects). Click to save the current Form, Formset, or selected objects. Enter the class name, base class, and class library in which to save the class.
Use a class as a base for forms	From the Tools menu, select Options. Select the Forms tab. Click Form in the Template Classes box. Select the desired class library. Select the desired form class.

To	Do This
Register a class for use by a form	From the Tools menu, select Options. Select the Controls tab. Select the Visual Class Libraries button Click Add. Select the desired Class Library.
Use a user-defined class to create an object	Open or create the desired form. In the Forms Control tool bar, click the View Classes icon. Select the desired class library. If it is not an option, select Add to register the class library. Select the desired class.

For online information on	From the Visual FoxPro Help Menu, choose Contents, select "Using Visual FoxPro," and then
Using Classes	Select the topic, "Forms" or "Designing Classes"

For more information on	See in the *Microsoft Visual FoxPro Developer's Guide*
Using Classes	Chapter 10, "Designing Classes"

Preview of the Next Lesson

In the next lesson, you will give users the tools they need to navigate the LitWare application by adding a menu system and toolbar to the project. You will create a menu system with multiple menu options, submenus, and hot keys, and also code menu option results. In the LitWare toolbar, you will specify bitmaps to use for button faces and attach the toolbar to a form set.

Lesson

8

Adding Menus and Toolbars

Estimated time
45 min.

In this lesson you will learn how to:

- Define the levels of your menu system.
- Customize your menu for easy use.
- Generate a menu program.
- Create a new toolbar class.
- Add a toolbar object to a form set.

All applications must provide a way for the user to access the system's features. In the LitWare application, Customer Service Representatives (CSRs) must be able to bring up the customer lookup screen so they can enter data and perform other system maintenance functions. LitWare managers must be able to select reports without needing to type commands in the command window, or having to know the types of files Microsoft Visual FoxPro 3 for Windows uses for generating reports.

Menus and toolbars provide an easy way to navigate through an application and access its features. As a standard method for a user to interact with software applications, the functionality of a menu bar contributes greatly to the user's overall impression of the software. A good menu system can support the user by having options organized into submenus, allowing the user to use "hot-keys" to access frequently-used system operations, and letting the user know which options are available for selection.

LitWare CSRs will use a menu bar to open forms, get help, run queries and reports, and quit the application. You can create your own menu system by using Visual FoxPro's built-in menu tools to define customized menu and submenu options.

Using Visual FoxPro's toolbar base class, you can also create your own toolbar class with buttons for common tasks. In this lesson, you will take advantage of this feature, and from your new toolbar subclass, you will create a toolbar object and add it to a form set in the LitWare application.

Start the lesson

1 Open Visual FoxPro.
2 From the File menu, select Open.
3 In the Drives and Directories lists, select c:\litware\proj_08.
4 Select litware.pjx
5 Click the OK button.

The Project Manager displays the LitWare project.

Creating a New Menu System

Creating a menu system is a process that involves several distinct steps. First you must define menu and submenu options. Then you must add functionality to menu options. Finally you must generate the menu program.

To help you build menus quickly, you can use the Visual FoxPro Menu Designer. The Menu Designer allows you to define the structure and functionality of your menu system by providing easy-to-use dialog boxes and drop-down lists that you can use to create and modify your menu system.

Defining Menu Options

Menus present the enduser with a list of options to initiate an activity. Some menu items display submenus, or additional options, when the user selects the menu item. Before you develop a menu for any application, you need to determine what choices the end user will be able to make, how those choices relate to each other, and which menu options "belong" to other menu options. In the following exercises, you will create a main system menu with several system level, main options. Each main option will contain at least one submenu option.

Create a new menu

LitWare CSRs will perform a variety of tasks that are not necessarily available from the forms used in the LitWare application. For example, they may need to print a form, access Help files, run queries or reports, or quit the application. You will provide access to these tasks by creating the menu system below.

1 In the Project Manager, click the Other tab.

The Other page appears, displaying the Menus, Text, and Other files categories.

2 From the list of categories, select Menus.

New

3 Click the New button.

TIP If the Project Manager is docked or collapsed, the New button will not be visible. You can click the right mouse button to bring up the context-sensitive menu, and select New from there.

The Menu Designer appears with the first text box in the Prompt column selected. You'll notice that the Menu Level box on the right side of the Menu Designer says "Menu Bar." Options typed at this level will appear in the system menu bar at the top of the screen.

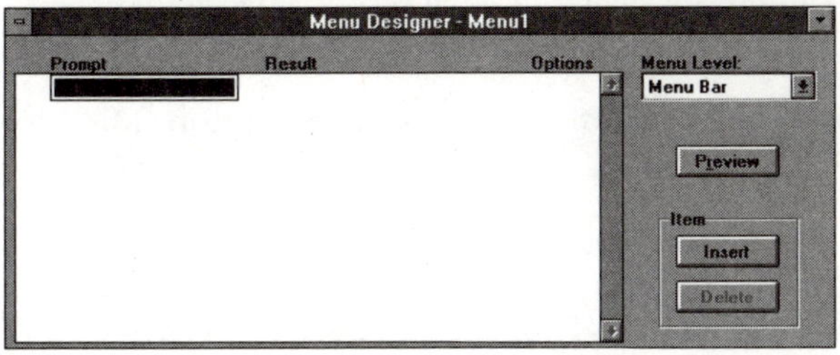

TIP You can also select the Menu option on the system menu. There is a Quick Menu option under the menu option. This option creates a copy of the basic Visual FoxPro system menu, and is useful for creating quick menus that you can customize, or for examining how the system menu works.

Specify menu bar options

If you've used other Windows applications, you're familiar with the "standard" menu bar. The File option is usually first, followed by Edit, and then menu options specific to each application. Below you will create the options for the LitWare menu to conform to the Windows standard.

1 Type **File** in the first Prompt text box.

By default, Submenu is selected in the Result column for each new Menu Bar option. Since no submenus have been created, Visual FoxPro provides the Create button. You will create submenu options in the next section.

2 Click the empty Prompt text box under File and type **Edit**

3 Repeat step 2 to add Programs, Window, Utilities and Output as the remaining Menu Bar options.

The Menu Designer looks like the following illustration.

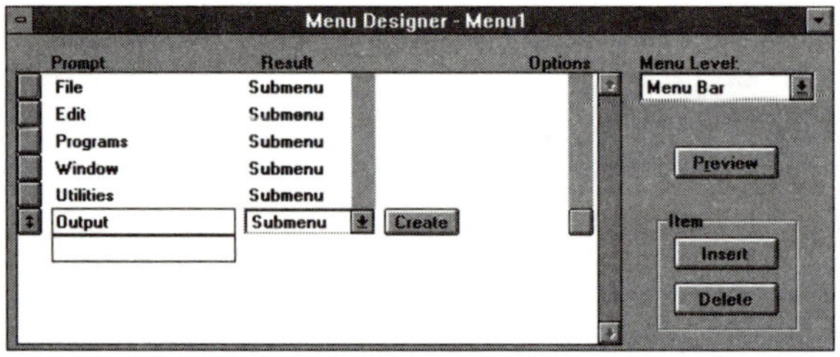

4 Save the menu by selecting Save on the File menu.

5 Assign the menu the name LitWare.

Visual FoxPro automatically adds the extension .MNX to menu files.

NOTE Menu files (.MNXs) are tables, just as form files (.SCXs) and class libraries (.VCXs) are tables. There is a corresponding memo file for each with the extension .MNT for menus, .SCT for forms, and .VCT for class libraries.

Specify submenu options

Commands to close the current form, quit the LitWare application, and access Help files should appear on the File menu. Edit provides standard Windows editing functions, such as Copy, Cut, and Paste. Window, another standard Windows option, allows the user to select an open window, or cycle through open windows within an application. The Program menu provides access to user functions, such as looking up a caller. Options under Output allow the user to run queries and reports. You will fill in Utilities options after the LitWare application has had a chance to be used in the field.

In the following procedure, you'll define the menu options for the File menu bar.

1 In the Menu Designer, select the File menu bar option.

2 Click the scroll arrow to the right of the Result box for the File prompt, and select Submenu from the drop-down list if it is not selected already.

3 Click the Create button to the right of the Result box in the first line.

File appears in the Menu Level drop-down list. Prompts typed at this level will appear when the user selects the File menu on the menu bar.

When the user opens the File menu from the LitWare application menu bar, the Close form, Quit, and Help options should appear.

4 Click the first Prompt text box and type **Close form**

5 Click the second Prompt text box and type **Quit**

6 Click the third Prompt text box and type **Help**

Define the menu options for the other menu bars

1. Select Menu Bar from the drop-down list in the Menu Level box.

   The Menu Designer displays Menu Bar options.

2. Repeat steps 1 through 6 in the preceding procedure to create the submenus for the Programs, Edit, and Output Menu Bar options. Use the submenu prompts below.

Main Menu Option	Submenu Options
Edit	Undo Redo Cut Copy Paste
Programs	Handle a call
Output	Run a Query Run a Report

   Most options at the Menu Bar level will display submenus when the user selects the option.

3. Select Menu Bar from the Menu Level drop-down list.
4. Save the menu by selecting Save on the File menu.

Defining Results of Menu Selections

The next step in building your menu system is to assign results to each submenu option. Visual FoxPro's Menu Designer provides several options for assigning results.

Use the Quick Menu to get the names of the bars.

Command Executes a one-line Visual FoxPro command. Use the command option to call a program, form, or function in the application.

Procedure Executes multiple Visual FoxPro commands. Use the procedure option to save, set up, and restore any necessary environment settings before and after calling programs or forms, or to initialize variables used by called programs.

Submenu Provides the user with further choices.

Bar# Allows you to use the built-in functionality of system bars provided with Visual FoxPro.

Assign a procedure to the Quit menu option

The Quit option should quickly quit the LitWare application, but display a warning in case the user has mistakenly selected the command. You can assign a procedure to the Quit command that allows users to change their minds before quitting.

1. Select the Quit submenu option of the File menu.
2. From the Results drop-down list for the Quit prompt, select Procedure.
3. Click the Create button.

   The Procedure Editor window appears.
4. Type the following code.

```
*-- call the Messagebox function with the Yes and No options
*-- to allow the user to confirm Quitting
*-- if the user selects Yes, Messagebox will return 6
IF MESSAGEBOX("Are you sure you want to leave the Application?", 4+32,
"LitWare Application")  = 6
 *-- close data here
 CLOSE DATABASE
 *-- clear the wait state
 CLEAR EVENTS
ENDIF
```

The CLEAR EVENTS command is used to clear the wait state that the READ EVENTS command puts in place. READ EVENTS causes Visual FoxPro to wait for user input, and also removes the command window while the application is running. This command is necessary for Visual FoxPro applications running without the full version of Visual FoxPro; that is, applications compiled and running from the Professional version of Visual FoxPro. If READ EVENTS is not used, there is no wait state, and the application will immediately close with no user input. This is obviously not a desirable occurrence, so READ EVENTS is used as part of the menu. Placement of the command will be discussed later in this lesson.

TIP If the same code can be called from multiple places in the application, make the procedure a separate program or put it in one of your procedure files. Then you can call it with a single command from multiple places, including the menu, in the format **DO quitproc**.

5. Close the Procedure Editor window.
6. From the Menu Level drop-down list, select Menu Bar.

   The Menu Designer displays the Menu Bar level prompts.

Assign a procedure to the Close menu option

Use the Menu Level drop-down list to move to upper level menus. Move to lower level menus by selecting Edit from that menu line.

1 Repeat steps 1-5 above to assign the following procedure to the Close command on the File menu.

Type the following code.

```
*-- test if there is a parent container to the current form
IF TYPE( "_SCREEN.Activeform.Parent") <> 'U'
*-- there is a formset; execute its release method,
*-- by referring to it as the parent of the current active form
 _SCREEN.Activeform.Parent.Release()
ELSE
 *-- there is no formset, just release the active form
 _SCREEN.Activeform.Release()
ENDIF
```

2 Close the procedure editor.

NOTE This will cause the Release method of the active formset (if there is one) or form to execute. Later, you will use the Menu Designer to make this menu item inaccessible if there is no active form.

Assign a command to the program option

Assigning commands to menu options is similar to assigning a procedures to a menu option.

1 Select Menu Bar from the Menu Level drop-down list, if it is not already selected.

2 Select the Programs menu bar option.

3 Click the Edit button to the right of the Results box for the Programs menu option.

The Menu Designer displays the Submenu level of the Programs menu option.

4 Select Command from the drop-down list in the Results box for the Handle a call prompt.

5 Press the Tab key to move to the next text box in the line.

6 Type DO FORM CustFind

7 Save the menu by selecting Save on the File menu.

Assign a bar # procedure to the Edit and Window options

Bar # procedures are predefined procedures for common tasks such as undo, redo, cut and paste.

1. Select Menu Bar from the Menu Level drop-down list, if it is not already selected.
2. Select the Edit menu bar option.
3. Click the Edit button to the right of the Results box for the Edit menu option.

   The Menu Designer displays the Submenu level of the Edit menu option.
4. Select Bar # from the drop-down list in the Results box for the Undo prompt.
5. Press the Tab key to move to the next text box in the line.
6. Type **_med_undo**
7. Repeat steps 1-6 above to assign the following bar # options.

Menu	**Option**	**Result**	**Type**
Edit	Redo	Bar #	_med_redo
	Cut	Bar #	_med_cut
	Copy	Bar #	_med_copy
	Paste	Bar #	_med_paste
Window	Cycle	Bar #	_mwi_rotate

8. Save the menu by selecting Save on the File menu.

Preview the menu

You can preview what the menu will look like without actually running it. Previewing the menu does not execute the menu, but it allows you to see what the menu will look like and which commands, procedures, or bars will be executed as a result of a menu selection.

Preview

1. Click the Preview button.

   The system menu changes to reflect the menu you designed, and the preview box appears.

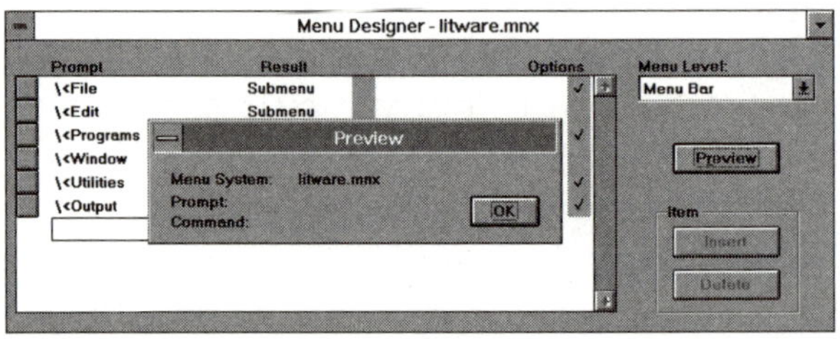

2. Click Programs on the menu bar.

   The Handle a Call option appears.

3 Click Handle a Call.

The Preview box shows the result (the prompt and the command that would be executed) of your selection.

4 Click OK in the Preview box to close it.

Making Your Menu System Easy to Use

Beyond basic functionality, most menu systems in today's Windows applications include features that make them easier to use. Among the most common of these features are:

- "Hot-keys" to access menu commands from the keyboard.
- Disabling–graying out–commands that are unavailable to the user due to some condition in the application.
- Displaying menu item descriptions in the status bar to further explain menu options.

Assign hot keys to menu items

In Windows applications, you can use hot keys to bypass menus. Hot keys that represent a main menu selection use the Alt key plus a highlighted letter. Submenu selections use the Ctrl key plus a letter as a shortcut. As LitWare reps gain experience using the LitWare application, they will probably want to use hot key combinations to select frequently-used submenu options, rather than navigate menus with the mouse or keyboard.

In addition to setting the hot keys for each menu bar option, you also need to display the hot key combinations in the menu, so that the user will know that they are available.

In this exercise, you'll set the hot key for the Quit option to Ctrl-Q.

1 From the Menu Level drop-down list, select Menu Bar if it is not already selected.

2 Select the File menu bar prompt.

3 Click the Edit button for the File prompt.

The Menu Designer changes to display submenu prompts for the File menu.

4 Select the Quit prompt.

5 Click the Options button.

The Prompt Options dialog box appears.

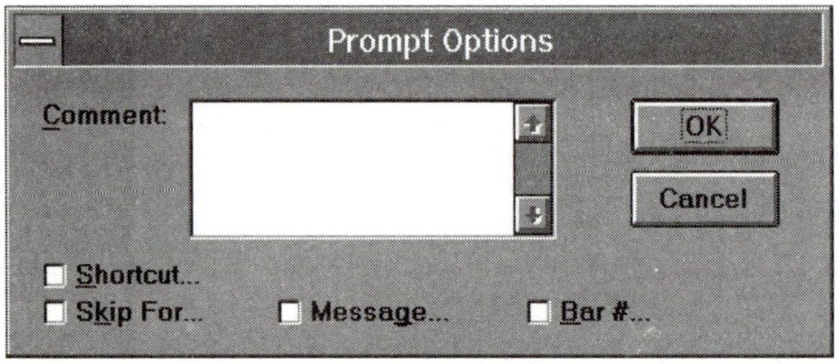

6 Click the Shortcut check box.

The shortcut Key Definition dialog box appears.

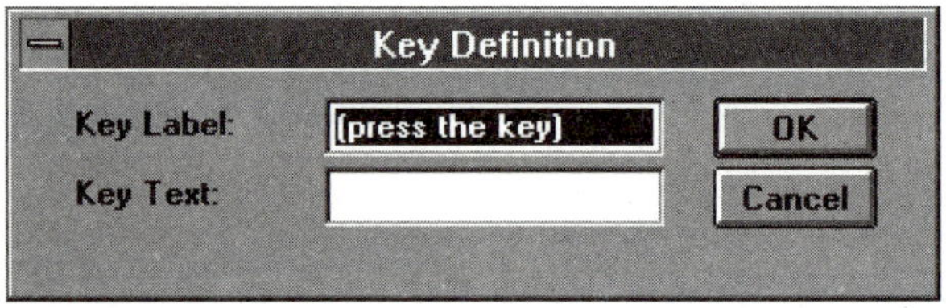

7 Press Ctrl+Q.

The key combination appears in the Key Label Box.

8 Tab to the Key Text box.

WARNING If you press keys other than Tab to advance to the next Key Text box, the Key Definition dialog box will accept those keys as the desired hot key.

---

9 In the Key Text box, type **^Q**

The "^" character is used to indicate the Control key.

10 Click OK.

The Key Definition dialog box disappears.

11 Click OK in the Prompt Options dialog box.

NOTE For items listed on the main menu bar, the key text is not displayed; it is displayed for sub-menu items only.

The Visual FoxPro system bars have their own "standard" shortcut keys. Those standards are reflected in the keys set.

Use the "\<" combination to tell Visual FoxPro to underline the letter that follows. You can place this key combination before any one of the letters in the text of the prompt. In the absence of the \<, Visual FoxPro underlines the first character by default.

12 Change the prompt to \<**Quit** from Quit.

TIP Although it is not necessary to put the \< key sequence before the first letter because Visual FoxPro automatically sets it to the default if none is specified, it makes future menu maintenance easier, and is therefore a good practice.

13 Repeat steps 1 - 11 to assign hot keys to other menu options:

Menu	**Option**	**Hot Key**	**Key Text**
Edit	Undo	Ctrl-U	^U
	Redo	Ctrl-R	^R
	Cut	Ctrl-X	^X
	Copy	Ctrl-C	^C
	Paste	Ctrl-V	^V
Program	Handle a Call	Ctrl-H	^H
Window	Cycle	Ctrl-F1	^F1

Define menu messages

Use messages to explain each menu option as it is highlighted. Remember that users can highlight a menu choice using the keyboard or mouse before selecting it, and the message will appear in the system bar at the bottom of the screen.

1 Display the submenu prompts for the File menu bar option.

2 Select the Quit prompt.

3 Click the Options button.

The Prompt Options dialog box appears.

4 Click the Message check box.

The Expression Builder appears.

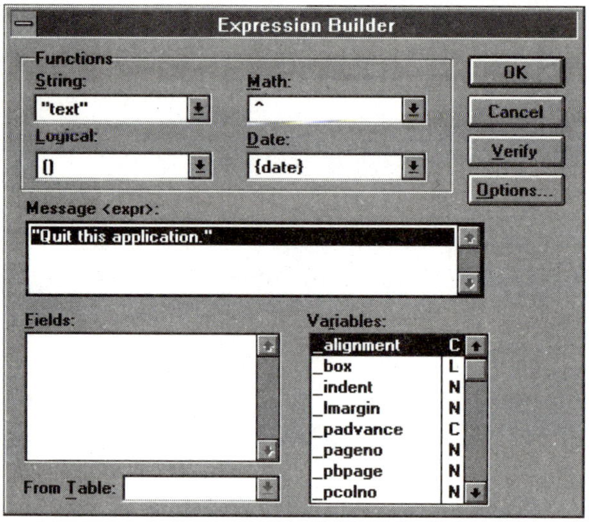

5. Type (including quotes): **"Quit this application"**
6. Click the OK button to close the Expression Builder.

   The Prompt Options dialog box appears.
7. Click the OK button to close the Options dialog.

Disabling Menu Options

Not all options of the menu should be available at all times to all users. For example, it does not make sense to allow the user to select the "Close form" option if there is no form open. For security reasons, not all users might have access to all menu items. However, allowing the user to encounter situations in which the expected result does not occur can undermine user's confidence, or worse yet, suggest to the user that the software is unreliable or prone to malfunction.

Visual FoxPro allows you to disable unavailable options. The SKIP FOR clause of the menu builder disables menu options based on the value returned by the SKIP FOR expression, and grays out those options so that the user knows they are not available.

Disable the Quit option

In this exercise, you'll disable the Quit option if there is an active form, by checking for the existence of an active form on the screen. The user will not be able to quit the application while a form is active.

1. Display the submenu prompts for the File menu bar option.
2. Click the Options button for the Quit prompt.
3. Click the Skip For check box.

   The Expression Builder dialog box appears.

4 In the Expression Box, type:

```
TYPE("_SCREEN.Activeform") = "O"
```

5 Click the OK button.

The Prompt Options dialog box appears.

6 Click the OK button.

The Menu Designer appears.

NOTE The Activeform property of the _SCREEN memory variable contains a reference to an active form on the screen. If there is no active form on the screen, the variable type of the property will be "U"—undefined. If there is an active form on the screen, the TYPE function will return "O"—object. Therefore, this setting will not allow the user to select Quit if there is a form on the screen.

Disable the Close option

Conversely, the Close option of the file menu should be available only if there is a form on the screen.

1 Click the Options button for the Close Form prompt.

2 Click the Skip For check box.

The Expression Builder dialog box appears.

3 In the Expression Box, type:

```
TYPE("_SCREEN.Activeform") <> "O"
```

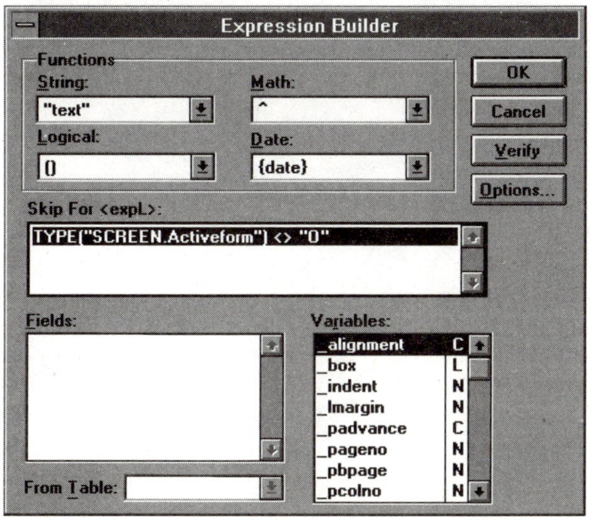

4 Click OK.

The Prompt Options dialog box appears.

5 Click OK.

The Menu Designer appears.

Creating Default Procedures for Menu Options Not Available at Installation Time

The LitWare upgrade products have already been announced and are available, so the application needs to be on line as soon as possible. Since the application will be used for customer lookup and order processing without completed menu systems and reports, you might have to wait until later to complete the menu. However, it is considered poor practice to have nothing happen in response to a user selection. Rather than omit the menu options from the menu at this point, you can tell the user that the selected option is not available yet.

Create a message for an unassigned menu bar item

In this exercise, you'll create a general message for an unassigned menu bar item.

1 From the View menu on the Visual FoxPro menu bar, select General Options.

The General Options dialog box appears.

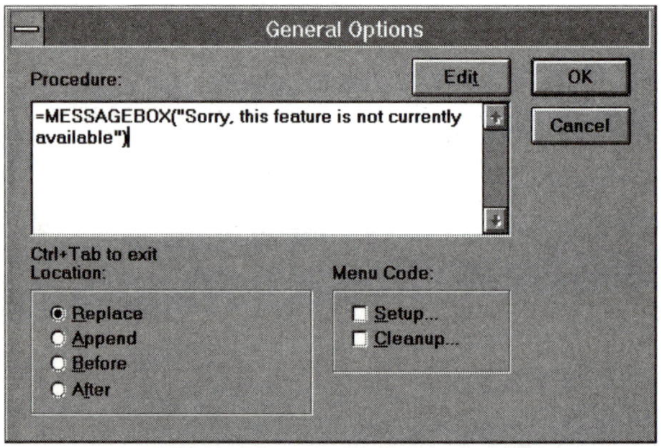

2 In the Procedure text box, type

```
=MESSAGEBOX("Sorry, this feature is not currently available")
```

3 Click the OK button to close the General Options dialog box.

Display a message for the items on the Output menu

The Procedure of a menu or of a particular menu level is executed when no result is assigned to a menu option. Since no result has yet been assigned to any of the options on the Output menu, the user selecting those options will cause the below procedure to be executed.

1. Select Menu Bar from the drop-down list in the Menu Level box.
2. In the Output prompt line, click the Edit button.

   Prompts for the Output menu appear.
3. From the View menu on the Visual FoxPro menu bar, select Menu Options.

   The Menu Options dialog box appears.
4. In the Procedure box, type

   ```
   =MESSAGEBOX("Sorry, Output options are under construction.")
   ```
5. Click the OK button to close the Menu Option dialog box.

   The Menu Designer appears.

Replace the system menu

1. Make sure the Menu Designer is open and that the LitWare menu is selected.
2. From the View menu on the Visual FoxPro menu bar, select General Options.
3. Make sure that the default location says replace.

NOTE the default Location is Replace; this option will cause your menu to be used instead of the currently defined system menu. Other choices are ***Append***, which will add the new menu to the existing system menu, and ***Before*** and ***After***, which will allow you to designate where on an existing menu Visual FoxPro should place the new menu.

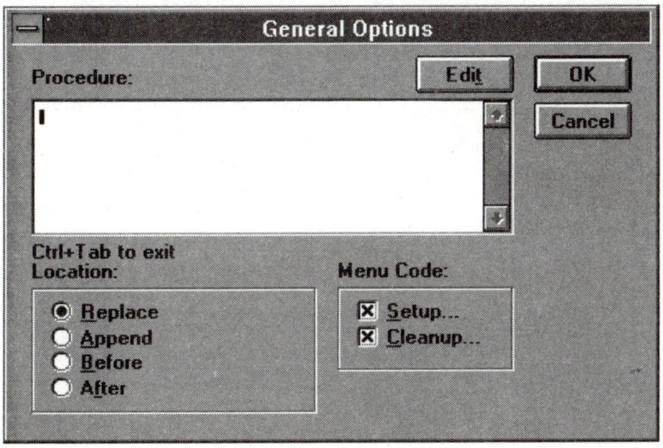

4 Click OK to close the General Options box and replace the system menu with the LitWare menu.

Use break lines to group menu options

You can make your menu more visually appealing by grouping options by function on a submenu. You can see examples of break lines in use on any of the Visual FoxPro system submenus. In this exercise, you will separate the Quit option from the other two options on the File submenu by using a break line.

1 Click the Edit box on the File line in the Menu Designer.

The menu level changes to File.

You will put the break line before the Quit prompt.

2 Click the Quit prompt.

3 Click the Insert button.

The default prompt New Item appears above Quit.

4 At the prompt type \-.

This combination tells Visual FoxPro to create a break line. You cannot select the break line, so the result column is irrelevant.

Enter the setup and cleanup code

It is good practice to save the settings of the system before changing them. For example, the application should not run with TALK1 set on, so there should be code to turn it off before the application begins execution. Before the setting is changed, though, you want to make sure that you set it back when the user is finished. The system menu and environment settings should return to original states after the user clicks Quit—when the CLEAR EVENTS code executes. You need to reset TALK to its original value.

NOTE the setting of TALK controls whether the results of operations are echoed to the screen. For example, with TALK set to ON, the command x=0 will result in the number 0 being displayed in the active window or on the screen. Since it disrupts the screen, most operations in an application should be done with TALK OFF. Much development and testing, however, may be done with TALK set ON, since it is useful to the developer to see the results of operations, so TALK may be ON when an application is started.

---

1 From the View menu in the Visual FoxPro menu bar, select General Options.

The General Options dialog box appears.

2 Click Cleanup and Setup.

The editor for the Cleanup and Setup code opens behind the General Options dialog box.

3 Click the OK button to close the General Options dialog box.

4 In the Setup Code edit window, type the following code.

```
IF SET("TALK") = "ON"
  SET TALK OFF
  glOldTalk = .t.
ELSE
  glOldTalk = .f.
ENDIF
*-- save the current setting of the system menu
PUSH MENU _MSYSMENU
```

Before presenting the user with the menu, any other code to be executed such as opening any system information tables (which might contain the location of data files) would also be placed here.

5 Close the Setup Code Editor window.

6 In the editor for the Cleanup Code type the following code.

```
*-- wait for user input
READ EVENTS
*-- the following code executes after CLEAR EVENTS
*-- restore the system menu to its previous setting
POP MENU _MSYSMENU
*-- if talk was on before, turn it back on
IF glOldTalk
 SET TALK ON
ENDIF
```

7 Close the Cleanup Code editor.

Generate the source code

Visual FoxPro automatically generates a menu program file (.MPR) when an application is built from a project. You can generate the menu program manually to test the menu without building the application.

1 From the Menu on the Visual FoxPro menu bar, select Generate.

A dialog box appears asking if you want to save changes to the menu.

2 Click the Yes button.

The Generate Menu dialog box appears. Notice that the Output File is, (by default), the name of the menu with an **.MPR** extension. There is usually no reason to change the default extension. The .MPR is a Visual FoxPro executable program, just like a .PRG.

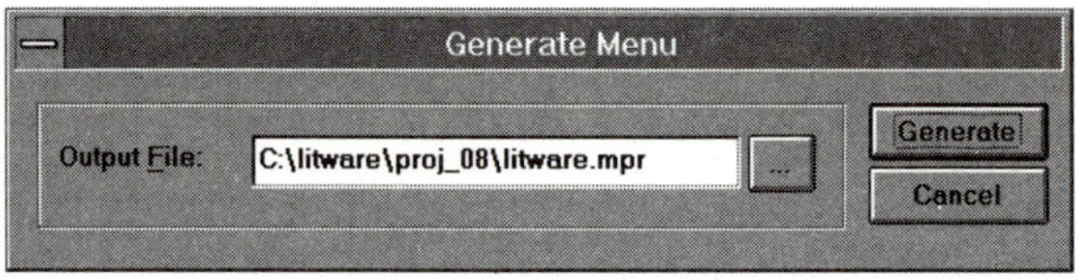

3 Click the Generate button.

The Visual FoxPro menu generator generates the code.

4 Close the Menu Designer.

Running a Menu

To run your menu in an application, use the Menu Designer to generate a menu program (.MPR). Menu programs are written in standard FoxPro code, and may be viewed or modified in any text editor.

The Menu Designer generates menu program code using the information you have entered about menu options and results. Because a menu program is a standard FoxPro program, there may be tasks that you will want to complete before presenting the user with the menu, or after the menu has executed. For example, in order to tell Visual FoxPro to execute its event handling, the command READ EVENTS should be in the cleanup code of the menu (which executes after the menu has been defined). READ EVENTS, as explained previously, causes Visual FoxPro to wait for user input.

NOTE Modifying code generated by the Menu Designer is *not* recommended, since each time a menu program is generated, the modified code will be overwritten.

Run your new menu (from the Project Manager)

1 Select LitWare on Menus from the Other page.

2 Click Run.

The menu changes to the LitWare menu; you can run your screen from the menu.

3 Select Quit from the File submenu.

The Visual FoxPro system menu returns.

Creating Custom Toolbars

In any application, toolbars provide the user with one-button shortcuts for frequently performed tasks. Toolbars combine elements of menus and forms to give the user a visual way to select options. Although command buttons are the most frequently used controls for a toolbar, you may use any control object on a toolbar.

It is also a good idea to have menu options for most or all of the toolbar functions. This allows users to use either keyboard shortcut keys (assigned in the menu builder) or the menu to access frequently-used functions.

Defining a Toolbar Class

Before you can implement a toolbar, you must define a class for it, just as you defined classes for forms and controls in Lesson 7. Visual FoxPro provides a Toolbar base class that you can use to define your custom toolbar class.

Define the toolbar class

1. Click the Classes tab in the Project Manager.
2. Click New.

   The New Class dialog box appears.

   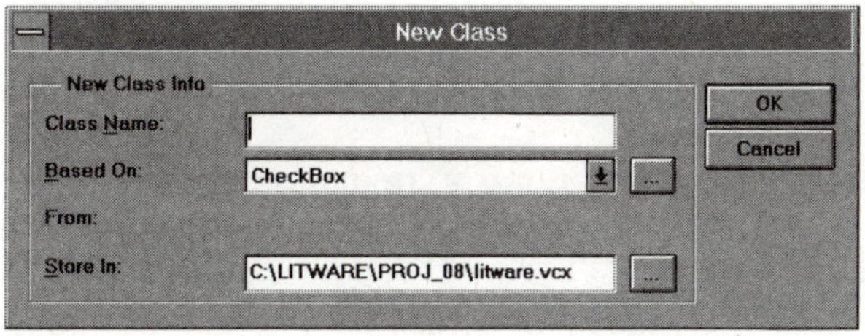

   Just as you did in Lesson 6, prefix the new class name with **lit**, and then save the class in Litware.vcx.
3. Type **litToolbar** as the Class Name.
4. Select Toolbar as the Based On class.
5. Type **LitWare** as the Store In library.
6. Click OK.

   The Class Designer appears.

Defining Toolbar Properties

Now you must assign appearance and behavior to the toolbar. You will place three command buttons on the toolbar, which will perform the tasks of printing the current form, closing the current form, and invoking help.

Assign controls to the toolbar

1. Make sure the Form Controls toolbar is visible.
2. Click the command button icon.
3. Move the mouse pointer to the left margin of the Class Designer.

   The mouse pointer changes to a cross hair.

Command

4 Click the desired spot.

The command button appears.

5 Add two more command buttons to the toolbar.

Defining Actions and Appearance

You must assign appropriate icons and actions to each of the three command buttons on the toolbar; you can also use tooltips to help the user. The first button will print the current form, the second will close the current form, and the third will display Visual FoxPro Help.

Assign properties to the first command button

1 Click the first command button, or select command1 from the Object drop-down list box in the Properties Window.

2 On the Layout tab in the Properties Window, select the Picture property.

3 Double-click the property line or click the selector [...] button to display the file locator.

4 Locate and select the WZPRINT.BMP file in the wizards\wizbmp subdirectory of your main Visual FoxPro directory.

5 Click OK

The icon on the command button changes immediately to display the print icon.

6 On the Layout tab in the Properties Window, select the ToolTipText property.

7 Type **Print this form**

8 On the Methods tab in the Properties Window, select the Click event.

9 Double-click the Click event to display the Methods editor.

The button should call the Print method for the active form. Get the form's name by using the _SCREEN memory variable's Activeform property.

10 Type **_SCREEN.Activeform.Print()** in the Methods editor.

11 Close the Methods Editor.

12 Type litToolCmdPrint in the Name property.

Use the same steps to assign the following properties and methods to the other two command buttons in the toolbar.

Button print:

Property/Method	Value
Name	litToolCmdClose
Cancel	.t. - true
Click Event	**THISFORMSET.Release()**
Picture	wizards\wizbmps\wzclose.bmp
ToolTipText	**Close this Form Set**

Help:

Name	litToolCmdHelp
Click Event	HELP
Picture	VFP\samples\controls\help.bmp
ToolTipText	**Visual FoxPro Help**

Once context-sensitive help is in place in your application, you can change the ToolTipText property.

13 Close the class, and save your changes.

Using the Toolbar in a Formset

Before you can use a toolbar, you must add it to a formset or use code to create the toolbar object from the class. The toolbar does not get added directly to a form; Visual FoxPro manipulates the toolbar object as it does a Form object.

The toolbar will be added to the Custdata form created in Lessons 5 and 6.

Add the toolbar to a formset using the Form Designer

1 Open the Custdata form from the Project Manager.

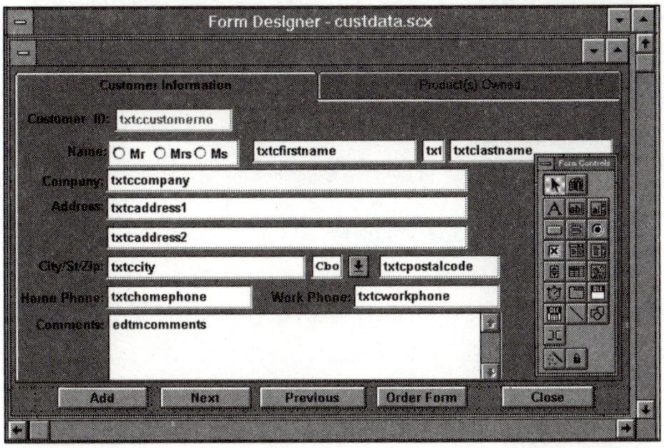

Classes

LitToolBar

2 Click the View Classes button on the Form Controls toolbar.

The Classes menu appears.

3 If **LitWare** does not appear on the menu, click the Add button to select it.

4 Click the button for the litToolBar class.

5 Click on the form just above the Customer Information caption.

If you are adding the toolbar to a form not in a formset, Visual FoxPro warns you that a form set object is required before you can add a Form.

6 Click Yes to create a Formset.

The litToolBar object appears on the form. You may resize the form and position the toolbar as you wish; also, both forms are movable at run time.

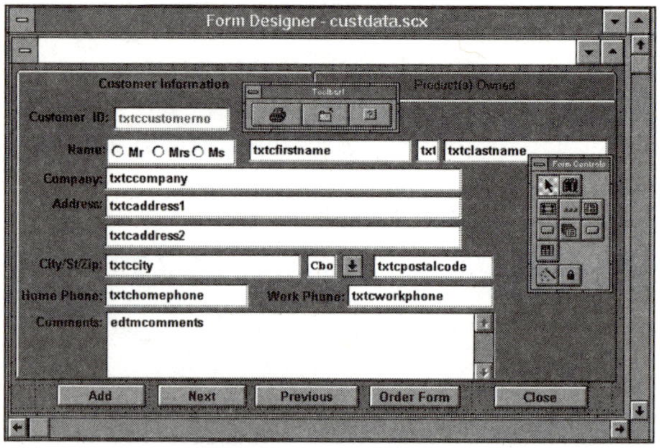

Add the toolbar to a formset using code

1 Make sure the form is in a formset.

If the form is not in a formset, you can create a formset for the form while the form is open by selecting Create Formset on the Form menu.

2 In the Formset's **Init** event method, type:

```
SET CLASSLIB TO LitWare ADDITIVE
loToolBar=CREATEOBJECT("littoolbar")
loToolBar.show()
```

One Step Further: Adding Combo Boxes to the Toolbar

When viewing information in a form, it is helpful to allow the user to view records in various sequences. For example, a CSR viewing the Customer Information (custdata) form might want to move through the records in customer ID order or customer name order. Recall from Lesson 4 that indexes maintain the order of a table, and there may be multiple indexes for a table. You can allow the CSR to select the order of the table with a combo box that will present the user with a list of indexes.

Add a combo box to the toolbar

1. Open the litToolBar class in the Class Designer.

Combo Box

2. Add a combo box to the toolbar.
3. Set the properties of the combo box:

Property	Value
Height	27
Left	115
ToolTipText	Select an order to view the data
Top	4
Width	216
Name	KeyList

Set functionality of the combo box

The combo box needs to list the index tags available for the table selected in a form, and when the user selects the order from the combo box, it must set the order of the table to that index tag.

Below you will use the toolbar's Init Event method to populate the list.

1. In the Init Event for litToolBar, type the following code:

```
lnKeyCtr = 1
*-- for each tag of the table, add it to the list
DO WHILE NOT EMPTY( TAG( lnKeyCtr ) )
 *-- exclude the Deleted tag from the list
 IF TAG(lnKeyCtr) <> 'DELETED'
       *-- the AddListItem method adds to the combo box list
       THISFORM.KeyList.AddListItem( KEY( lnKeyCtr ),lnKeyCtr )
 ENDIF
 lnKeyCtr = lnKeyCtr + 1
ENDDO
IF lnKeyCtr = 1
 *-- there's only 1 tag, don't allow selection
 THISFORM.KeyList.DISABLE
ELSE
 *-- assign the initial value to the combo box
 THISFORM.KeyList.Value = 1
ENDIF
```

2. In the Click event of KeyList, type the following code:

```
*-- use the IndexToItemId method to get the number of the selection
lnId = THIS.IndexToItemId( THIS.Value )
*-- verify a valid selection
IF lnId <> 0
 SET ORDER TO (TAG( lnId ))
```

```
 *-- notify the user of the success
 WAIT WINDOW "Order set to tag " + TAG( lnId ) NOWAIT
ELSE
 WAIT WINDOW "Invalid Selection Made..." NOWAIT
ENDIF
```

3. Close and save the litToolBar class.

If you want to continue to the next lesson.

1. Click File on the Menu bar.
2. Select Close.

If you want to quit Visual FoxPro for now

1. Click File on the Menu bar.
2. Select Exit.

Lesson Summary

To	Do This
Create a menu	Open the Project Manager, select Other, select Menus, and then click New, or In the command window, type **CREATE MENU**
Define results of a menu selection	In the Menu Designer, select Submenu, Command, Procedure, or Select Bar # (Pad Name) from the Results drop-down list box. Then build the submenu, write the command, code the procedure, or enter the system Bar#.
Highlight a hot key	Put \< before the key that you want to highlight for a menu item.
Assign a hot key	For the desired menu prompt, click the Options box, and then click Shortcut. Press the desired key combination.
Disable a menu option	For the menu prompt, click the Options box, and then click Skip For. Enter a logical expression that when true will cause the menu option to be disabled.

To	Do This
Create a default procedure	From the system menu, select View, and then General Options or Menu Options. In the Procedures box, type the code that should execute if no result is defined for a menu selection.
Create a toolbar	Create a class from the Toolbar base class. Add objects and properties just as you did for classes and forms.
Use a toolbar	Attach the toolbar to a form set using the Forms Designer or code in the Form Sets Init method.

For online information about	From the Visual FoxPro Help Menu, choose Contents, select "Using Visual FoxPro," and then
Menus	Select the topic, "Designing Menus"
Toolbars	Select the topic, "Creating Custom Toolbars"

For more information on	See in the *Microsoft Visual FoxPro Developer's Guide*
Menus	Chapter 12, "Designing Menus"
Toolbars	Chapter 13, "Creating Custom Toolbars"

Preview of the Next Lesson

In the next lesson, you will learn how to program for simultaneous access by multiple users. How to open tables exclusively and shared, lock; tables, records, and table headers. Use data sessions, data buffering and transaction processing.

Lesson

9

Programming for Shared Access

Estimated time
60 min.

In this lesson you will learn how to:

- Control simultaneous access to data.
- Open tables exclusively and shared.
- Lock tables, records, and table headers.
- Use data sessions.
- Use data buffering.
- Manipulate records in a data buffer.
- Manage conflicts between users attempting to access the same data.
- Use transaction processing.

The Customer Service Representatives (CSRs) at the LitWare, Inc., Help Desk answer phones and take orders from customers. When a customer calls, the CSR opens the Customer Information form and enters the customer's name; the LitWare application searches for and returns customer information. The CSR types in the order that the customer places. Before the application saves the order, it first verifies that sufficient stock exists for all items on the order. Orders are entered throughout the day, but are not shipped until after business hours. When the CSR enters an order, the application updates the allocated quantity for the ordered item. When the item is shipped, the line on the order is marked as shipped, and the inventory file is updated for allocated and on-hand quantity. Because it is likely that more than one CSR will be entering an order at any time, and multiple CSRs will be accessing customer information simultaneously, the application must handle any attempts by multiple CSRs to access or update information in the various tables. This lesson discusses how to program for simultaneous access by multiple users.

Start the lesson

1. Open Visual FoxPro.
2. From the File menu, select Open.
3. In the Drives and Directories lists, select c:\litware\proj_09.
4. Select litware.pjx.
5. Click the OK button. The Project Manager displays the LitWare project.

Controlling Data Access

Because several CSRs will be searching for customers and entering orders simultaneously, the tables used by the LitWare application must be accessible to all representatives at the same time. Also, it is possible that two or more CSRs may try to access and update the information at the same time, so it is important that updates and queries are done based only on the most current information. The application must provide efficient ways to use and share data among users, restrict access to data when necessary, and resolve any data access conflicts between users so that no user intervention is required.

The following questions need to be answered for this application before you can determine access requirements:

- Who will be accessing the data?
- Will the users update data or only view it?
- What subset of the table will the user manipulate: individual records, sets of records, or only new records.
- How likely is it that multiple users will attempt to access and update the same information?

The answers to these questions will determine the type of access the Litware application and its components will provide.

Setting Access Types

There are two basic types of data access in a database application: exclusive and shared. When you set access to a table as exclusive, only one user can access the table at a time. To program a table to be opened exclusively, you can use the EXCLUSIVE keyword of the USE command, or you can have the program issue the SET EXCLUSIVE ON command before it opens tables. To make the default mode of operation exclusive, you can also include the line EXCLUSIVE=ON in your CONFIG.FPW file.

The following two code samples show how you can program the Customer table to be opened exclusively:

```
Sample 1:
SET EXCLUSIVE ON
USE Customer
Sample 2:
USE Customer EXCLUSIVE
```

TIP Issuing a SET EXCLUSIVE command has no effect on tables that are already open. If a table has already been opened for shared access, issuing SET EXCLUSIVE ON will not change the status of that open table, only of tables opened after that point. If tables are already open for shared access, and a particular function of the application requires that they be opened in exclusive mode, the application should close the tables before it issues the SET EXCLUSIVE ON command, and then reopen the tables.

One of the benefits of exclusive use is improved speed on a network. Since a file opened for exclusive use cannot be opened by other users, it is not necessary to code record or file locks (discussed later in this lesson). Locking files and records creates traffic over a network, so eliminating the need for locks reduces network traffic and speeds data processing. Obviously, for most operations exclusive use should be implemented sparingly, since only one user at a time will be able to access each table in the application.

Create a program to reindex tables

An important component of any well-designed application is a program to reindex tables, because index files can be damaged (for example, when a workstation is turned off while files are open or being updated—indexes might be damaged when Visual FoxPro has updated the table but not the index file). There can also be an option in the program to permanently remove deleted records from the table ("pack" the table). These programs require tables to be used exclusively.

TIP Indexes are "pointers" to records in a table, maintained in a separate file (CDX or IDX—for a discussion of indexes, see Lesson 4). If an index is damaged or out-of-date, the pointers in the index file may point to incorrect or nonexistent records in the table, or not point to new or changed records. Reindexing updates the pointers in the index tables. There are two commands to rebuild the index files: REINDEX, and INDEX ON. The REINDEX command examines information in the index file header, and rebuilds the index based on that information. The INDEX ON command (in the form **INDEX ON <expression> TAG <tagname>**) builds the index from scratch, without regard to existing information in the index file header. The preferred method of rebuilding indexes is the INDEX ON command, since it is possible that the header information in the index file is also damaged, and the REINDEX command will not address that problem.

---

1. Click the Code tab in the Project Manager.
2. Click the Program icon.
3. Click New.

   An empty Program Editor window appears.

4. Type the following code:

```
*-- This is a generic program to recreate existing indexes
*-- for every table in the current directory.
*-- It doesn't consider databases,
*-- or it assumes that the necessary database is open
*-- so it can access the tables in it.
*-- Close any open tables
CLOSE TABLES
*-- make sure SAFETY is OFF,
*-- but first save its current setting
LOCAL lcOldSafety
STORE SET("SAFETY") TO lcOldSafety
SET SAFETY OFF
*-- create an array of dbf files in this directory
lnDBFCount = ADIR( laDbfList, "*.DBF")
*-- for each table in the list, open it
FOR lnDBFNo = 1 TO lnDbfCount
  *-- the file name is in column 1 of the array
  *-- put the table name in a variable for code readability,
  STORE laDbfList[ lnDbfNo, 1] TO lcDbfName
  *-- open the table exclusively
  *-- it can  be opened with name substitution, since the name
  *-- of the table is contained in the variable "lcDbfName"
  USE ( lcDBFName ) EXCLUSIVE
  *-- for each index tag for this table, recreate it
  *-- by using the name and expression of the tag
  PRIVATE lcTagName, lcTagExpr, lnTagNo
  STORE TAG( 1 ) TO lcTagName
  STORE KEY( 1 ) TO lcTagExpr
```

```
     STORE 1 TO lnTagNo
     DO WHILE NOT EMPTY( lcTagName )
            *-- keep the user informed of progress
            WAIT WINDOW "Indexing " + lcDbfName + " " + ;
            LTRIM( STR( RECCOUNT() ) ) + ;
            " Records, Tag " + lcTagName NOWAIT
            *-- recreate the index
            *-- use macro expansion, since the tag name and expression
            *-- are stored in memory variables
            INDEX ON &lcTagExpr TAG &lcTagName
            STORE lnTagNo + 1 TO lnTagNo
            STORE TAG( lnTagNo ) TO lcTagName
            STORE KEY( lnTagNo ) TO lcTagExpr
     ENDDO
     WAIT CLEAR
     *-- close the table
     USE
     *-- do the next table in the list
     *-- advance the counter for the array
    ENDFOR
    *-- reset safety to its old setting
    *-- necessary only if setting has changed
    IF lcOldSafety <> "OFF"
     SET SAFETY ON
    ENDIF
```

5 Save the program as IndexDbf.prg.

6 Close the program.

NOTE You can now return to the menu you developed in Lesson 8 and assign the command **DO Indexdbf** to the Reindex option of the utility menu.

Shared Access to Data Tables

The default mode of opening tables is shared. Shared access allows multiple users to open tables simultaneously to view the data, and possibly to update it. To open tables for shared access, set EXCLUSIVE OFF before opening tables. If EXCLUSIVE is set on, you can open a table for shared access by using the SHARED keyword of the USE command.

The following two code samples show how you can program the customer table for shared access.

```
Sample 1:
SET EXCLUSIVE OFF
USE Customer
Sample 2:
USE Customer SHARED
```

When a table is opened for shared access, any table or record to be updated must be locked before the update is performed. Alternatively, to avoid multiple lock attempts, updates may be performed initially on a buffered copy of the data, and then the contents of the buffer can be written to the table on disk.

Locking Data

Since multiple users may attempt to update the same information at the same time and Visual FoxPro saves the contents of whole records at a time, it is important to ensure all users update only the most current data.

For example, if two users are editing the same customer record at the same time, and one changes the address and saves those changes, and then the other changes the credit limit and saves those changes, the second set of changes will, by default, overwrite the first user's changes. Such an occurrence can be prevented with locking.

Visual FoxPro allows you to prevent other users from updating the data by locking records and tables. Locks do not prevent other users from accessing and viewing data, only from updating the data.

Record locks are most appropriate for operations that update only a single record in a table, such as a standard single-record REPLACE command or editing a record in a form. Procedures that update multiple records with a single command, such as REPLACE...FOR..., require the entire table to be locked. Still other commands that append a single record to the table require only the table header to be locked.

Using Automatic Locking

Many Visual FoxPro commands attempt to implement the appropriate type of lock before executing the command. A list of commands that automatically lock records and tables appears in Chapter 19 of the Visual FoxPro Developer's Guide.

In some cases, automatic (also called implicit) record locking is unavoidable. The BROWSE, CHANGE, EDIT, and MODIFY MEMO commands automatically attempt to lock the current record and any related records when the user tries to edit the record, unless the file is already locked.

When you use implicit record locking, record locks are released when the user moves to another record or activates another window, even if MULTILOCKS is ON.

NOTE SET MULTILOCKS enables or disables multiple records being locked by the same user simultaneously. If SET MULTILOCKS is ON, the user can manually lock multiple records in the same table at the same time, and multiple individual records in a table can be locked without locking the entire table.

NOTE A table lock prevents other users from locking records in a table, and a record lock prevents other users from locking the table. However, two users may lock different records in a table. For example, if User A has locked record number one in the customer table, User B will not be able to lock record one until User A releases that lock. However, User B can lock record two (or any other record not locked by another user). If User A has locked the Customer table, other users will not be able to lock the Customer table, nor any of the records in the Customer table. Similarly, if User A has a lock on any record in the Customer table, no other user will be able to lock the Customer table.

Using a Manual Record Lock

The RLOCK() and LOCK() functions attempt to lock the current record, and return .t. - True if the lock was successful, or .f. - False if the lock failed. To release a manual record lock, use the UNLOCK command, or close the table. The manual record lock is useful for performing single record updates, as the following code sample illustrates:

```
IF RLOCK()
 REPLACE nCreditLimit WITH m.NewCreditLimit
ELSE
 WAIT WINDOW "Could not lock record. Try again later!"
ENDIF
```

Using a Manual Table Lock

The FLOCK() function attempts to lock the current table, and returns .t. - True if the attempt was successful, or .f. - False if the attempt failed. Table locks are used for scoped REPLACE commands (FOR, WHILE, etc.), or to ensure that the current operation is performed on the most current data, even if the operation itself performs no updates, as in the case of reports.

NOTE The REPLACE command updates a field in a table with a value, a memory variable, a constant, or the contents of another field. By default, it operates on the current record. You can use keywords to perform the update on the entire table (ALL), only certain records (FOR <condition> or WHILE <condition>) or all records from the current one to the last one (REST).

For example, an inventory on-hand report is a snapshot of the inventory at a particular point in time. You may not want the on-hand field of the inventory table to be adjusted while the report is running, so you would lock the file before running the report

```
DO WHILE NOT  FLOCK()
 *-- waiting for the table to be locked
ENDDO
*-- run the report
*-- unlock the table
UNLOCK
```

Using a Table Header Lock

When you add a single record to a table with the APPEND BLANK, APPEND FROM ARRAY, or INSERT INTO (SQL, not the old xBase INSERT) commands, you need to lock only the table header. To manually lock the table header, use the RLOCK(0) function.

Write code to add a record to the Customer table

1. From the Project Manager, open the custdata form.
2. Select the cmdadd object in properties.
3. Open the Click event method, by double clicking on it.
4. Type the following code:

```
SELECT Customer
IF RLOCK(0)
 APPEND BLANK
ELSE
  = MESSAGEBOX( "Could not lock table header; Record not added. Try
again later!" )
ENDIF
```

5. Close the Procedure Editor.

Using Data Sessions

Visual FoxPro provides data sessions to allow each user on a network and each instance of a form or form set to manipulate data independently. Each data session is a separate data environment for a form or form set; the session tracks open tables, relations, indexes, and record pointers.

Because forms using data sessions are completely independent of each other, changes made to data or record pointers in one instance of a form are not instantly reflected in other active instances of the same form. Locks set in those forms are in place for only that instance of the form.

DataSession set to 1 (no data sessions) is the Visual FoxPro default for forms.

Changes made to data in forms that don't use data sessions are immediately reflected in other instances of that form.

To enable multiple data sessions for a form, set the DataSession property to 2, either in the Properties window or in code. To disable multiple data sessions and have changes made in one instance of a form reflected in all instances of the form, set the DataSession property to 1.

If you are not using data sessions for a form, however, keep in mind that you must code for maintaining record pointers and selecting areas for each instance of a form, or restrict the user to running only one copy of a form at a time.

Protecting Original Data with Data Buffering

Using buffering for record and table edits allows you to protect the original data from editing by other users. Buffered data resides in local memory or a temporary disk location managed by Visual FoxPro. Users can then continue to access the original data, but when one user attempts to save changes from the buffer to the live table, Visual FoxPro verifies that no other user has changed the data, and the copy to be saved is still the most current copy of the data. If other users have changed the data, Visual FoxPro provides tools to determine the changes and resolve conflicts.

Choosing a Buffering Method

The types of buffering correspond to the types of record locks available in Visual FoxPro: table buffering is recommended when multiple records will be updated in a single operation; and record buffering is useful when a single record will be edited at a time. Depending on the operation of the application, you must also choose between optimistic buffering and pessimistic buffering. The buffering property is set with the CURSORSETPROP function, using the following values.

Value	Enables
1 (default)	No buffering
2	Pessimistic record buffering
3	Optimistic record buffering
4	Pessimistic table buffering
5	Optimistic table buffering

All lock types are released upon successful execution of the TABLEUPDATE() function.

Set the Customer Data form to use optimistic buffering

Optimistic buffering should be used when you can safely assume that only one user at a time will attempt to change any given record. It minimizes the time that the record or table is locked, because it attempts the lock only when the data is saved to the table.

In the LitWare application, you will use optimistic record buffering for the custdata form, because it is highly unlikely that two or more users will attempt to edit the same customer record at the same time.

Objects on forms and form sets default to record buffering, except for grids, which use table buffering.

1. From the Project Manager, open the custdata form.
2. On the All or Data tabs in the Properties Window, select BufferMode.
3. Set the BufferMode property to 2 - Optimistic.

NOTE You can override the default record buffering for a form or form set by changing the property BufferModeOverride in the Data Environment for the desired table or cursor.

4 Close the custdata form and save the changes.

Optimistic record locks wait until the user moves the record pointer (as with the SKIP command) or the application issues the TABLEUPDATE() function before attempting to lock the record. If the lock is successful, Visual FoxPro then verifies that the record hasn't been updated by anyone else by comparing the original (pre-edit) values in the buffer to the values in the record in the live table. If the record hasn't been updated by anyone else (the values in the pre-edit buffer are the same as the values in the live table), Visual FoxPro updates the live record from the buffer. If the record has been updated by another user, FoxPro generates an error (if the update attempt was caused by movement of the record pointer), or the TABLEUPDATE() function returns .F. - False. In any event, the record lock is then released immediately.

Set the Customer Order form to use pessimistic buffering

Pessimistic buffering deals with the likelihood that a second user will attempt to change the record or table while a user is editing it, and prevents other users from doing so by locking the table or record as soon as the first user begins editing. The drawback to this method is its rigidity; it maximizes the length of the lock on the record or table and while it is locked, no one else can lock or update this record or table. In addition, pessimistic record buffering increases network traffic, because every time the user moves to a new record, the lock on the current record must be released, and the new record must be locked.

In the LitWare application, you will use pessimistic buffering on the Customer Order form, because it is possible that multiple users will enter orders for, or attempt to update the same item at the same time, causing a conflict.

Remember that the default behavior for grids is table buffering.

1 From the Project Manager, open the custordr form.
2 On the Data tab in the Properties Window, select BufferMode.
3 Set the BufferMode property to 1 - Pessimistic Buffering.
4 Save the changes.

Manipulating Records in a Table Buffer

When you enable table buffering, changes made to the table are written to the buffer, not to the disk file. Changes are written to the disk file when the application executes the TABLEUPDATE() function. Until that point, the application can cancel any changes with the TABLEREVERT() function.

The LitWare application uses an order form to take customer orders. Since items are entered onto the order form in a grid, and the form uses pessimistic buffering, orders are not written to the live data until the application executes the TABLEUPDATE() function.

Appending Records

When records are added to a buffered table, Visual FoxPro assigns the new records sequentially negative record numbers to distinguish them from existing records, and to make it clear that they are buffered —not yet added to the live table. So the first record added is -1, the second -2. Records are added to the buffer the same way they are added directly to a table, with the APPEND BLANK or INSERT INTO commands.

Add the Add Item button to the Customer Order form

1. Select Classes in the Project Manager.
2. Drag the litCommand button onto the form—3 squares in and half a square below the grid—to create a new command button.
3. Assign the new command button the following properties:

   Name: cmdAdd

   Caption: Add Item
4. Type the following code for the Click method:

   ```
   m.cId = customer.cid
   INSERT INTO Orders FROM MEMVAR
   THISFORM.grdProdList.SetFocus()
   ```

   This code adds a record to the Orders table, with the cId field filled in from the memory variable m.cId, which was initialized from the cId field of the current record in the Customer field. After adding the record to the Orders table, the method gives the focus to the grid—makes it the active object—so the user can enter the information for the new line.
5. Close the Click Method window.

Deleting Records

You can delete records from the buffered table, just as you can from a table you are manipulating directly. However, if you use the DELETE command to delete an appended record from the buffer, its record number becomes invalid; you must remove the record from the buffer with the TABLEREVERT() function.

Therefore, if you know the record to be deleted has just been added (because the record number is negative, or you are working in the record buffer only,) the DELETE command is not necessary to remove records appended to a buffer; you can remove the records with TABLEREVERT().

Since all new orders append records to the buffer, and the order form does not pertain to records that already exist in the order table, you can assign a method to the Delete button that uses TABLEREVERT() to remove those records.

Add the Delete Item button to the Customer Order form

1. Select Classes in the Project Manager.
2. Drag the litCommand button onto the form—1 1/2 squares to the right of the Add Item button—to create a new command button.
3. Assign the new command button the following properties:

Name:	cmdDelete
Caption:	Delete Item

4. Type the following code for the Click method:

```
=TABLEREVERT( .f. )
THISFORM.Refresh()
```

NOTE The .f. parameter passed to TABLEREVERT indicates that the function should restore the original state of the current record only. You can also restore the original record state if you call the TABLEREVERT function with no parameters. In this case, the record did not originally exist, so it is removed. A parameter of .t. passed to TABLEREVERT would mean to undo all changes to the entire buffer; clear all appended records and undo all edits.

5. Close the Method editor.

Writing or Discarding the Updates

Once the CSR has made all the desired changes to the order, he or she will either save or cancel the order. If there is insufficient stock for a line item on the order, the user may choose to delete the line or cancel the entire order, but the form will not allow the order to be saved if there is insufficient on-hand quantity for any of the lines.

Add a Save command button to the Customer Order form

1. Select Classes in the Project Manager.
2. Drag the litCommand button onto the form—1 1/2 squares to the right of the Delete Item button—to create a new command button.
3. Assign the new command button the following properties:

Name:	cmdSave
Caption:	Save Order

4. Type the following code for the Click method:

```
= TABLEUPDATE( .t. )
THISFORM.Release()
```

The form looks like the following form:

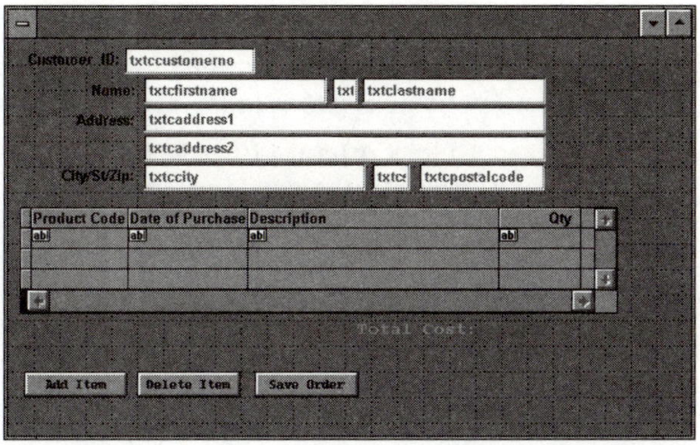

NOTE The .t. passed as the first parameter of TABLEUPDATE indicates that the function should save all changes to the buffer. A parameter of .f. (or no parameters) passed to TABLEUPDATE would mean to write only the current record in the buffer to the live table.

TABLEUPDATE accepts a second parameter to indicate whether or not the update should be forced. The default, .f. (false), indicates not to force the update over another user's changes. A second parameter of .t. (true) would force the update to be made, even if another user had changed values in the record. Though there are circumstances under which an update should be forced, this option should be used with care.

5 Close the Click Method window.

6 Close the custordr form.

Add a Cancel command button to the Customer Order form

1 Select Classes in the Project Manager.

2 Drag the litCommand button onto the form—1 1/2 squares to the right of the Save Order button—to create a new command button.

3 Assign the new command button the following properties:

Name:	cmdCancel
Caption:	Cancel Order

4 Type the following code for the Click method:

```
= TABLEREVERT( .t. )
THISFORM.Release()
```

5 Close the Click Method window.

Managing Conflicts with an Error Handler

What happens when two users attempt to access the same record or lock the same table? For example, what if two users attempt to enter orders for the same item at the same time? While unlikely, it is possible. The system needs to isolate and deal with the possibility.

When a file, file header, or record lock attempt fails, Visual FoxPro generates an error. Visual FoxPro gives you the ability to trap errors and handle them as they occur, with the ON ERROR command.

One of the first things an application should do is trap any errors so that users are not faced with the "Cancel, Ignore" choice. The ON ERROR command is invoked when an error occurs in Visual FoxPro and gives the developer the ability to gracefully handle foreseeable and unforeseeable situations. The syntax for ON ERROR is: ON ERROR [command]. Called with no command option, ON ERROR returns error handling to Visual FoxPro's own error handler.

Set up the error handler for the LitWare application

1. From the Project Manager, open the Litware menu, from the Other tab.
2. Select General Options from the View menu.

   The General Options window appears.

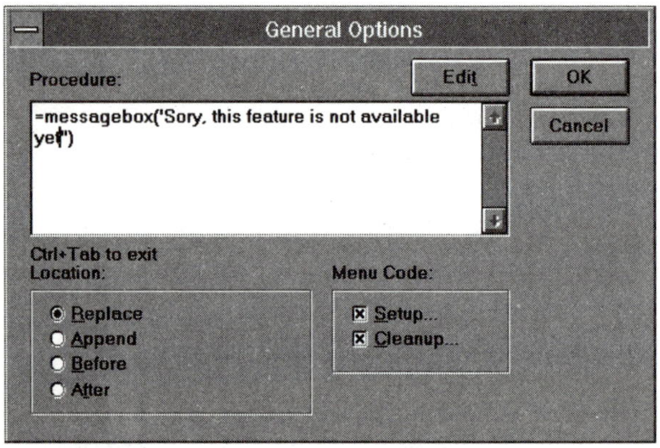

3. Click Setup.

   The existing setup code appears.

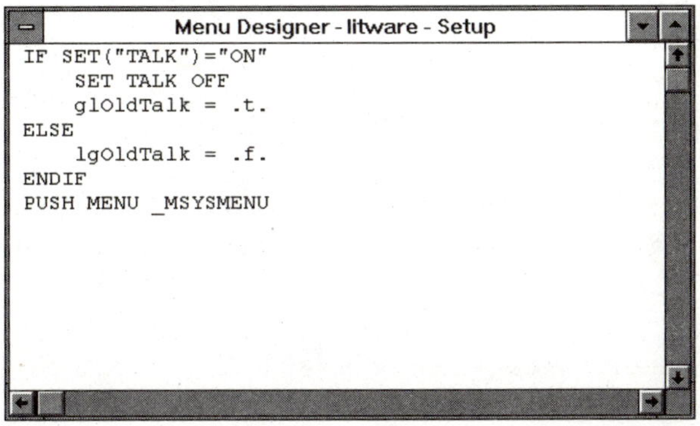

4 Click OK to close the General Options window.

5 Add the following line to the bottom of the Setup Code window:

```
ON ERROR DO err_hnd WITH ERROR(), MESSAGE()
```

6 Close the Setup Code window.

7 Save and close the Menu Designer.

Write the err_hnd program to handle locking conflicts

1 Click the Code tab in the Project Manager.

2 Click the Program icon.

3 Click New.

An empty Program Editor window appears.

4 Type the following code:

```
*-- simple program to trap and deal with errors
PARAMETERS tnErrorNum, tcErrorMsg
*-- deal with the individual errors
DO CASE
CASE tnErrorNum = 108
 *-- could not lock file
 =MESSAGEBOX( "Could Not Lock File; Already Locked by Another User")
CASE tnErrorNum = 109
 *-- could not lock record
 =MESSAGEBOX( "Could Not Lock Record; Already Locked by Another
User")
OTHERWISE
 *-- other errors need to be handled separately
 =MESSAGEBOX( tcErrorMsg )
ENDCASE
RETURN
```

5 Save the program as ERR_HND.PRG, and then close it.

Use SET REPROCESS to handle lock attempts

The **SET REPROCESS** command tells Visual FoxPro how to handle failed lock attempts: there are three general settings of SET REPROCESS.

SET REPROCESS TO AUTOMATIC This setting tells Visual FoxPro to continue to attempt the lock indefinitely, until the user presses Escape or the lock is successful. If the user presses Escape and there is an ON ERROR error handler active, the error handler is called.

SET REPROCESS TO -1 This setting tells Visual FoxPro to attempt the lock in definitely until it is successful. It cannot be interrupted by Escape, and the error handler is not called, since the lock cannot fail.

SET REPROCESS TO n [SECONDS] This setting tells Visual FoxPro to retry the lock a maximum of n times or seconds, until it is successful or the user presses Escape. If there is an ON ERROR routine active, it is called if the first lock attempt fails, and the lock is not then automatically retried. If n is 0, Visual FoxPro will try indefinitely, until the lock is successful or Escape is pressed. (SET REPROCESS TO -2 is equivalent to SET REPROCESS TO AUTOMATIC).

Notice that SET REPROCESS TO AUTOMATIC is the only option that automatically reattempts a failed lock indefinitely while still allowing the active ON ERROR procedure to be invoked, so if your application uses an error handler to handle locking conflicts, you probably want to use SET REPROCESS TO AUTOMATIC.

Below you will set the REPROCESS option in the Save button of the Customer Order Form.

1. From the Project Manager, open the custordr form.
2. Select the Save Order command button.
3. In the Click method for the Save Order button, insert the following line as the first line:

```
SET REPROCESS TO AUTOMATIC
```

The Click method now looks as follows:

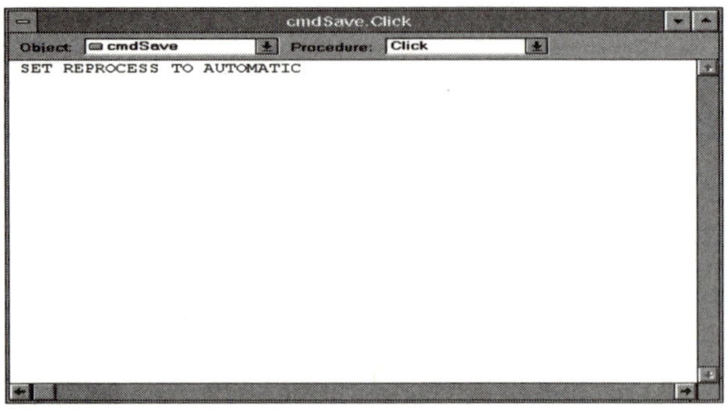

4. Close the Click Method window.

Using Transaction Handling

As mentioned before, the LitWare order form should not allow the user to save an order that has any line for which there is not sufficient stock on hand. The system increments the allocated field in the Products table for an item as each new line is entered. If the order can't be saved because there is no stock available, you must remove the effects of the order.

Use the BEGIN TRANSACTION, END TRANSACTION, and ROLLBACK commands to begin and end transactions, and to reverse the updates.

Put code for transaction handling in the Save button of the Customer Order form

1. Select the Save Order Command button.
2. Replace the code for the Click method with the following:

```
*-- turn on pessimistic table buffering for the products table,
because we're updating
*-- multiple records, and want to prevent other users from updating
the same
*-- records we are.
=CURSORSETPROP('Buffering', 4, 'products')
SELECT custprod
LOCAL llAllOk
STORE .t. TO llAllOk
BEGIN TRANSACTION
 SEEK m.OrderNum
 SCAN WHILE OrderNum = m.OrderNum
        SELECT products
        SEEK custprod.prod_id
        REPLACE Allocated WITH Allocated + custprod.QtyOrd
        *-- if allocated is higher than on hand, fail transaction
        IF Allocated > OnHand
               STORE .f. TO llAllOk
        EXIT
        SELECT custprod
 ENDSCAN
 *-- if everything ok to this point, update live tables
 IF llAllOk
        *-- update the live custprod table; the whole table, don't
        force update
        llAllOk = TABLEUPDATE( .t., .f., "CUSTPROD")
 ENDIF
 IF llAllOk
        *-- update the live products table
        llAllOk = TABLEUPDATE( .t., .f., "PRODUCTS")
 ENDIF
 *-- if anything is not ok, roll back the transaction,
```

```
  *-- otherwise, save it by ending it.
  IF NOT llAllOk
       ROLLBACK
       *-- at this point, notify the user that the update failed
       =MESSAGEBOX "Order Could Not be Saved."
  ENDIF
END TRANSACTION
THISFORM. Release()
```

3 Close the Click Method window.

4 Close the Customer Order form and save changes.

One Step Further: Determining the Effects of Buffering

Visual FoxPro allows you to run multiple instances of a form with no special coding. You can run multiple instances of a form the same way you run a single instance of a form—by selecting and running the form multiple times from the Project Manager, or typing **DO FORM <formname>** in the command window.

To see the effects of running with and without buffering, run multiple sessions of the custdata form, with and without buffering enabled.

Set the custdata form to use no buffering

First, make sure that the form set does not use buffering. Also, because the form has not been set up to use data sessions, you will change the AutoCloseTables property of the Data Environment to false, so when you close the first instance of the form, the other open copies of the form can still access the customer table.

1 Open the custdata form in the Forms Designer.

2 Open the Data Environment.

For more details on how to open the Data Environment, see Lesson 6.

3 Set the AutoCloseTables property to .f. - false.

4 Close the Data Environment.

5 Select the form set frmcustinfo in properties.

6 Set the BufferMode property to 0 - No Buffering.

TIP You can click the right mouse button on a property to access the shortcut menu for that property. The shortcut menu allows you to reset the property to its default value or access help for the property.

---

7 Save your changes to the custdata form and close it.

Run the custdata form multiple times with no buffering

1. Run the custdata form from Program Manager.

   For more details on how to run a form from Program Manager, see Lesson 6.
2. Click and drag the title bar of the form to the right of the screen.
3. Run a second instance of the custdata form from Program Manager.

   Notice that both copies of the form display the same information.
4. Make a change to the information on the second copy of the form: in the second address line, type **Apt. 1A**
5. Click on the first instance of the form.

   Notice that the change you made in the second copy of the form is reflected in the first copy; since the form set is not using buffering, the two copies are linked to the same data in the table on the disk.
6. Close both copies of the form.

Set the custdata form to use buffering

Now you will see the effects of using data buffering on running multiple copies of a form.

1. Open the custdata form in the Forms Designer.
2. Set the BufferMode property to 1 - Pessimistic.

   To use buffering, each instance of the form must have its own data session, so set the form to use data sessions.
3. Set the DataSession property to 2 - Private Data Session.
4. Save your changes to the custdata form and close it.

Run the custdata form multiple times with buffering

1. Run the custdata form from Program Manager.
2. Click and drag the title bar of the form to the right of the screen.
3. Run a second instance of the custdata form from Program Manager.

   Notice that both copies of the form display the same information.
4. Make a change to the information on the second copy of the form: in the company line, type **ABC Company**
5. Click on the first instance of the form.

   Notice that the change you made in the second copy of the form is not reflected in the first copy; since the form set is using buffering, the updated record has not been written to the table on the disk. To force the change to be written to disk, move the record pointer.

6. Click the second copy of the form, where you made the change to the company field.
7. Click Next to move the record pointer.

   The form reflects the data in the record.
8. Click the first copy of the form.

   Notice that the company field is now filled in with the data you entered in the second copy of the form. When the record pointer moved, the changes were written to the disk.
9. Close both copies of the form.

If you want to continue to the next lesson

1. Click File on the Menu bar.
2. Select Close.

If you want to quit Visual FoxPro for now

1. From the Visual FoxPro main screen, click File on the Menu bar.
2. Select Exit.

Lesson Summary

In this lesson you learned how to manage shared access to tables, and deal with conflicts when multiple users attempt to update the same data at the same time.

To	Do This
Open a table exclusively	Use the EXCLUSIVE keyword of the USE command. *or* Issue the SET EXCLUSIVE ON command before opening the table.
Open a table shared	Use the SHARED keyword of the USE command. *or* Issue the SET EXCLUSIVE OFF command before opening the table.
Lock a table	Use the FLOCK() function.
Lock a record	Use the LOCK() or RLOCK() functions.
Lock a table header	Use the RLOCK(0) function.
Enable or disable data sessions	Set the DataSessions property of the form or form set.

To	Do This
Use data buffering	Set the BufferMode property of the form or form set. *or* Set the BufferModeOverride property of the Data Environment for a particular table in a form or form set.
Save buffered records	Use the TABLEUPDATE() function.
Remove a newly added record from a buffer	Use the TABLEREVERT(.f.) function.
Undo changes to a record in a buffer	Use the TABLEREVERT(.f.) function.
Undo all changes to a record buffer	Use the TABLEREVERT(.t.) function.
Use transaction processing	Use the BEGIN TRANSACTION, END TRANSACTION, and ROLLBACK commands.

For online information about	From the Visual FoxPro Help Menu, choose Contents, select "Using Visual FoxPro," and then
Shared Access	Type **Shared Access** and select "Show Topics"

For more information on	See the *Microsoft Visual FoxPro Developer's Guide*
Shared Access	Chapter 19, "Programming for Shared Access"

Preview of the Next Lesson

In the next lesson, you will learn how to use queries to turn your data into useful information, and to present the user with a transparent way of considering multiple tables as one. You will create a query, add tables to the query, select the fields for the query, and run the query to select only matching information. Using views, you can define relationships between tables and view a cursor (a temporary table), which consists of the data in the two tables linked together as you defined.

Part

2

Review & Practice

You will review and practice how to:

- Create a new database table.
- Set field properties.
- Create indexes and relationships.
- Build a new form
- Add control objects
- Create a new class
- Connect forms and controls with data sources
- Enter method code for controls
- Modify a menu bar

Now that you have learned the skills necessary to work with tables, forms, menus and toolbars, this review and practice will give you the opportunity to use these skills. You will create a new table, and relate the table to the customer table. You will design a form to manipulate data in the new table and add control objects; you will also name objects, and classes, and set properties. The form will then be connected to the appropriate data sources. The menu will be modified to use this new form.

Scenario

Trace DelRio, manager of the customer service department at LitWare, has asked you to design a customer feedback survey to be given to each incoming caller. The survey should be brief, and LitWare CSRs should be able to read survey questions easily and enter caller responses quickly. The CSR will record the survey answers in a table for regular analysis.

Step 1: Create a New Table

1. Open the LitWare directory, open the P2Review subdirectory, and then open the litware project.
2. Create a new table called Survey, using the following fields:

Name	Type	Width	Comment
SID	C	5	Customer ID#
Q1	L	1	Satisfied with service
Q2	L	1	Mailing list indicator
Q3	L	1	Drawing for prize
Q4	C	200	Comments and suggestions
SDate	DT	8	Date and Time field

3. Set Q4 to all null values.
4. Set SID to verify value between 10000 - 50000.
5. Index survey table on SID.
6. Relate survey SID to Customer Table CID.

For more information on	See
Creating a new table	Lesson 4
Setting properties and indexing tables	Lesson 4

Step 2: Create a New Form

To enter data in the survey table, you will create a new form called Survey. Use the Form Designer to create the following form.

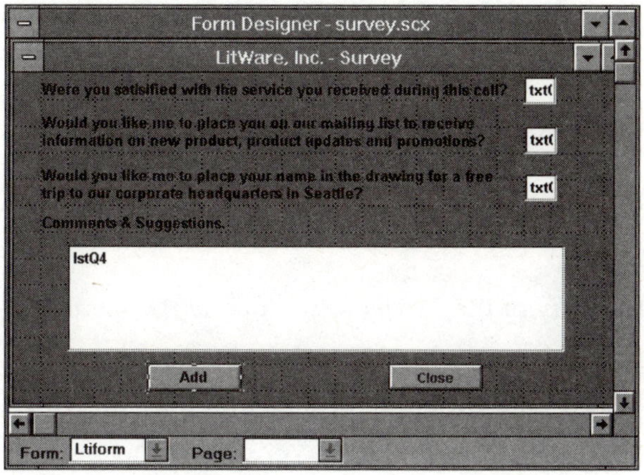

1 From the Project Manager, add the LitCustHead class onto the new form.

2 Create a label that says, "Were you satisfied with the service you received during this call?"

3 Create a text field to accept a Y or N.

4 Create a label that says, "Would you like me to place you on our mailing list to receive information on new products, product updates, and promotions?"

5 Create a text field to accept a Y or N.

6 Create a label that says, "Would you like me to place your name in the drawing for a free trip to our corporate headquarters in Seattle?"

7 Create a text field to accept a Y or N.

8 Create a label that says "Comments & Suggestions."

9 Create a text field to accept 200 characters.

10 Create a command button to add the information to the table.

11 Create a command button to quit the form.

12 Connect the form to the data sources.

13 Add the method to activate the add with a double click.

14 Add the method to activate the quit with a double click.

For more information on	See
Designing forms	Lesson 5
Setting data and method properties	Lesson 6
Using classes	Lesson 7

Step 3: Modify the Menu

To allow for quick entry of the survey form, modify the menu bar so that the form can be displayed.

1. Select menus on the Other tab in the Project Manager
2. Edit the programs menu to add survey as a submenu.
3. Assign the command DO form Survey to the survey option of the programs submenu.
4. Assign the Hotkey CTRL S to run the survey.

For more information on	See
Menus	Lesson 8

If you want to continue to the next lesson

1. Click File on the Menu bar.
2. Select Close.

If you want to quit Visual FoxPro for now

1. Click File on the Menu bar.
2. Select Exit.

Part

3

Utilizing the LitWare Application

Lesson

10

Creating Queries

Estimated time

60 min.

In this lesson you will learn how to:

- Create a query.
- Add tables.
- Select fields.
- Order and group query results.
- Run a query.
- Update a remote table using a view.

Queries are tools for searching tables and retrieving data. They provide answers to questions based on information contained in tables. You ask questions and then build queries to find the answers. The information found can then be output to a designated format.

In this lesson you will discover how to use Query Designer in Microsoft Visual FoxPro 3 for Windows, a graphical object-oriented organizational tool designed to save time and improve the accuracy of queries. You will learn how to create and work with queries based on tables and data utilized by LitWare. You will also send the results of the query to the screen, a text file, or to a browse window.

Queries organize information and provide subsets of data for review or information for reports. In this lesson, you will search the LitWare customer, custprod and products tables to create the queries and direct the output results. The output can include browse windows, tables, reports, and text files. LitWare is interested in producing queries that will answer the following questions:

- Which customers own which products?
- When did the customer purchase the product?

Start the lesson

1. Open Visual FoxPro.
2. From the File menu, select Open.
3. In the Drives and Directories lists, select c:\litware\proj_10.
4. Select litware.pjx.
5. Click the OK button. The project Manager displays the LitWare project.

Using Query Designer

Query Designer, like other designers you have used, provides tools to create and run queries rapidly and easily.

Open the Query Designer

1. Click the Data Tab on the Project Manager.
2. Click Queries.
3. Click the New button.

   The New Query window appears.
4. Click the New Query button.

   The Add Table or View window appears, listing tables available for use in the query, which is a list of all the tables in the LitWare project. You will be using the customer, custprod, and product tables in this lesson.

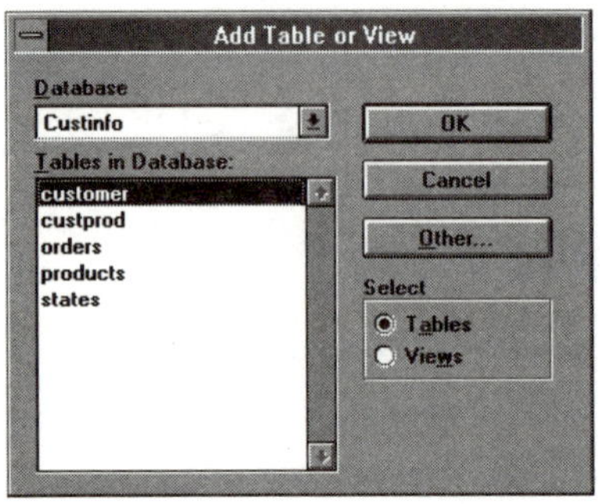

5 If the custinfo database does not appear in the Database text box, scroll to find it, and then click the custinfo database to select it.

6 In the Tables list, click the customer table.

7 Click the OK button.

The Query Designer toolbar may open with the New Query.

The table appears in the top pane of the Query Designer.

The Query Designer appears with the customer table displayed.

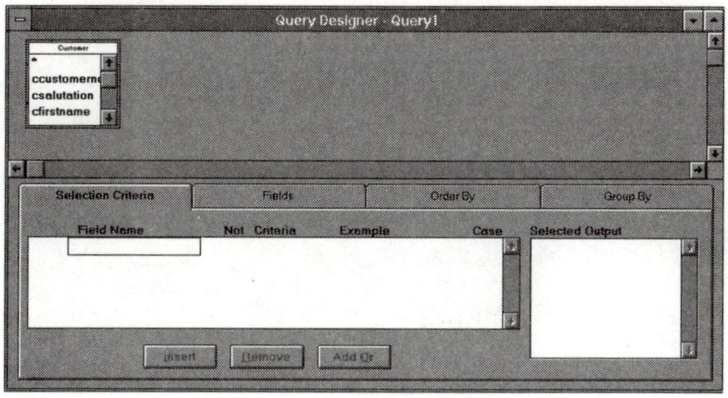

Open the Query Designer toolbar

1 On the View menu, click toolbars.

The toolbars window appears.

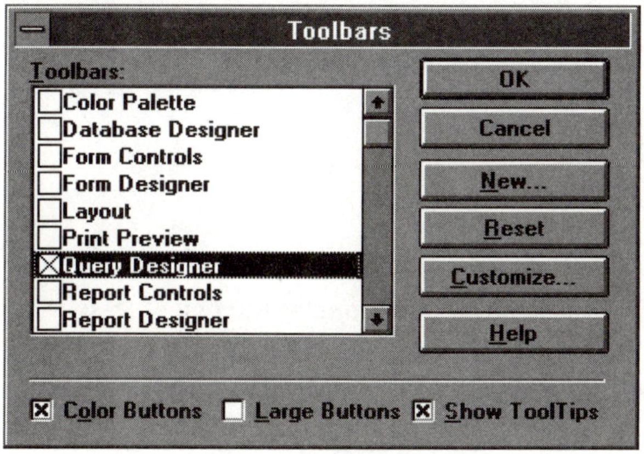

2 Click the checkbox next to Query Designer.

3 Click the OK button.

The Query Designer toolbar appears.

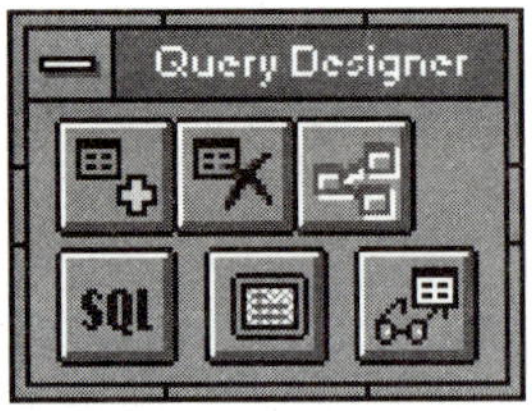

Adding Tables

In order to build the queries required to provide the answers to the LitWare questions, you must first add the custprod and products tables to the Query Designer. These tables contain information required for the query.

Add the custprod table

Add Table

1 Click the Add Table button.

TIP You can use the right mouse button to click on the top pane of the Query Designer, and then select Add Table from the shortcut menu.

The Add Table or View dialog box appears.

2 Select the custprod table.

3 Click the OK button.

Add the products table

1 Click the Add Table button.

The Add Table or View dialog box appears.

2 Select the products table.

3 Click the OK button.

The tables appear in the top pane of the Query Designer with the relationship lines in view.

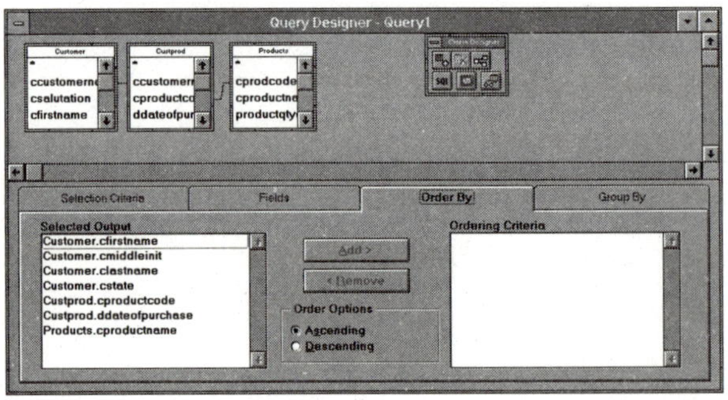

The lower half of the pane contains the tools for selecting and ordering your query. You'll see tabs labeled Selection Criteria, Fields, Order By, and Group By.

These criteria were established when you added the tables. The links established for the tables are listed under Selection Criteria:

```
Customer.ccustomerno   equal   Custprod.ccustomerno

Products.cprodcode     equal   Custprod.cproductcode
```

These data relationships provide the links between the tables that determine which products are owned by LitWare customers. The ccustomerno (customer number) is linked between the customer and products tables. The product links come from the cprodcode (product code number) on the products and custprod tables. The combination of the two links forms a data pathway that allows the data to be queried, and then displayed as a list of products owned by the LitWare customers.

Adding Fields

Before you can run a query, you must select and add the fields from the tables that you want to include in the results. In many cases you may want to include all of the fields. In other cases, you may want to select only the fields that will be included in a report. In this exercise, you will select fields that will be included in a report for LitWare. This report will answer the question "Which customers own which products?"

Add a field

1. Click the Fields tab.

   A list of available fields appears.

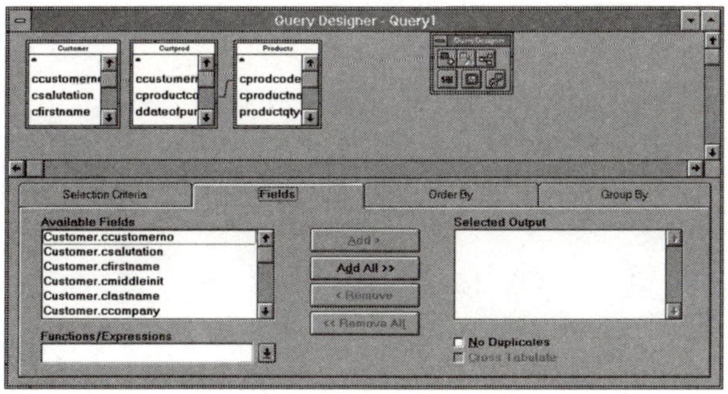

2 While holding down the Control Key, click on the field names to use in the query.

Customer.cfirstname
Customer.cmiddleinit
Customer.clastname
Customer.cstate
Custprod.cproductcode
Products.cproductname
Custprod.dateofpurchase

3 When the fields are selected, release the Control Key.

4 Click the Add button. The selected fields appear in Selected Output.

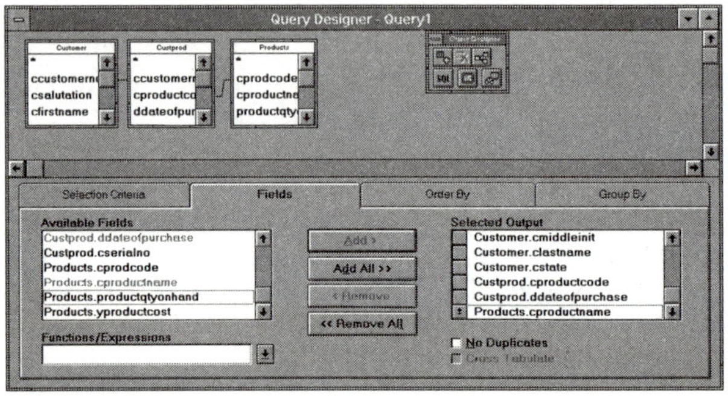

Ordering Query Results

Now that you have built the query to search and retrieve the data, you need to order the output. Ordering refers to the way the records or rows will be sorted when they appear in the output. For LitWare, Inc., the records will be sorted by customer last name and customer first name.

Set the order

1 Click the Order By tab.

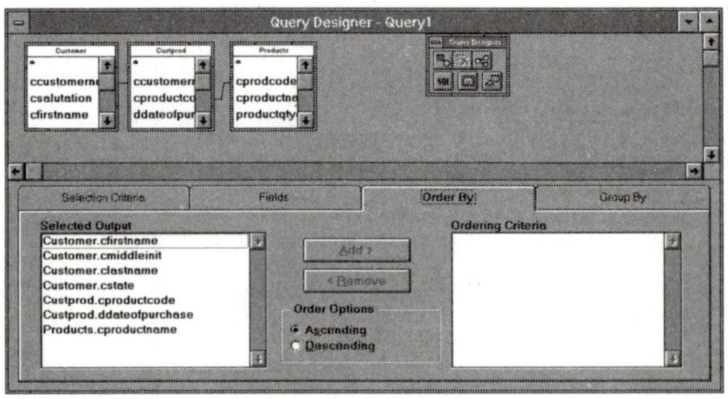

Note that the fields available for selection are the fields you selected previously.

2 While holding down the Control Key, click Customer.clastname and Customer.cfirstname.

3 Release the Control Key.

4 Click the Add button.

5 If the Customer.clastname field is not listed before Customer.cfirstname, click and drag the button in front of the field name to place it above Customer.cfirstname.

6 Click the Ascending check box to set the order.

Ascending order lists the customers alphabetically by last name, beginning with A.

Group a query

The next step in the query development process is grouping similar records so that you can perform calculations, do statistical analysis, and examine groups of data. LitWare wants to determine how their products are selling in each state, so the grouping in this exercise will be by state.

1 Click the Group By tab.

To group the LitWare query you must select the fields that will be used in the grouping output.

2 Click the customer.cstate field.

3 Click the Add button.

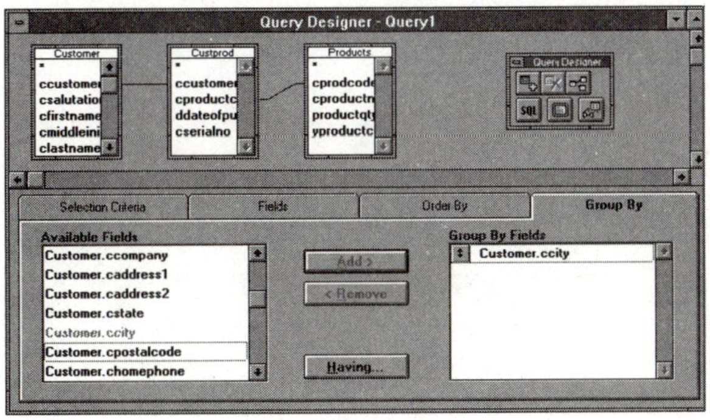

The query development is now complete. You will need to run a query in order to view the results. Before you run the query you will save it.

Save a query

Once you save a query, you can run or modify the query from the Project Manager.

1. On the File menu, click Save.
2. Type **customer** to name the query.
3. Set the drive and directory path to c:\litware\proj_10.
4. Click the Save button.

   The Query Designer now reads Query Designer - customer.

Determining Output Format and Running a Query

Now that you have created the query, you need to determine the output format. You choose Run Query to activate the search and retrieval function, which results in the generation of the query. When you have finished building the query, saving the query, and specifying the output, you can then run the query. Remember that the output format selected in the query is the one that is saved and used when you run the query format.

Query Destination

➤ On the Query Designer toolbar, click the Query Destination button.

The Query Destination window appears.

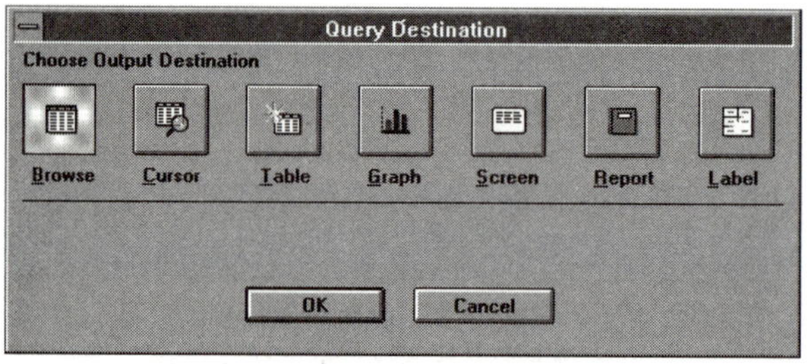

Your query output destination options are:

Browse	Results appear in a browse window.
Cursor	Saves results in a cursor. The cursor is a read-only table that is not saved when you exit the project.
Table	Saves and displays the results as a table.
Graph	Makes results available for use with Microsoft Graph (not active in this project).
Screen	Displays results in the main Visual FoxPro window or in the currently active output window.
Report	Sends output to a selected report file.
Label	Sends output to an existing label file (no label files were created in the LitWare project). A label file is a text file that holds the output of a table in label format.

Browse a query

On the Query Designer toolbar, click the Query Destination button.

1. In the Query Destination dialog box, click the Browse button.
2. Click the OK button.
3. From the Query menu, select Run Query.

   The Query Browse window appears.

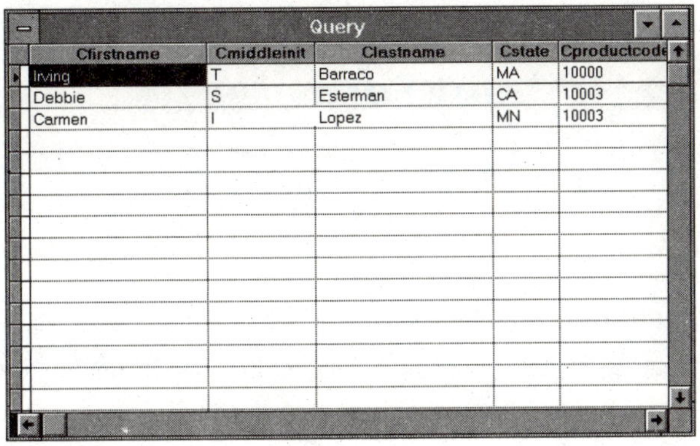

NOTE The states are listed in alphabetical order and customers are listed in alphabetical order within the states as specified by the LitWare query requirements.

4. Close the Query Browse window.

Create a temporary results read-only table

1. On the Query Designer toolbar, click the Query Destination button.
2. In the Query Destination dialog box, click the Cursor button.
3. In the Cursor Name text box, type **custcursor** to name the cursor.
4. Click the OK button.
5. From the Query menu, select Run Query.
6. From the View menu, select Browse custcursor.

   The Custcursor Browse window appears.

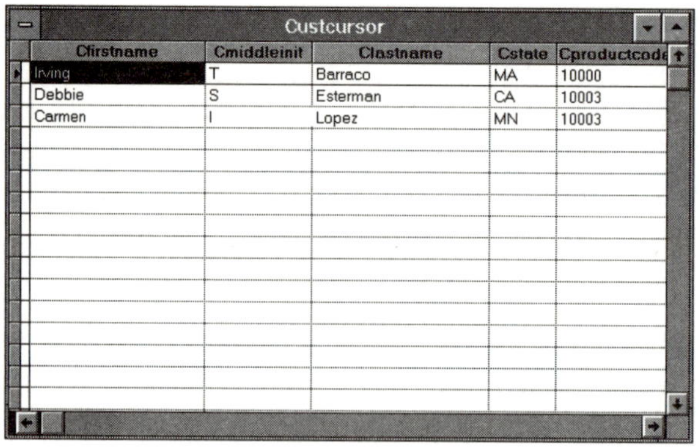

7 Close the Custcursor Browse window.

Create a results table

1 On the Query Designer toolbar, click the Query Destination button.

2 In the Query Destination dialog box, click the Table button.

3 Type **custquer** for the table name.

4 Click the OK button.

5 From the Query menu, select Run Query.

6 From the View menu, select Browse custquer.

The custquer Browse window appears.

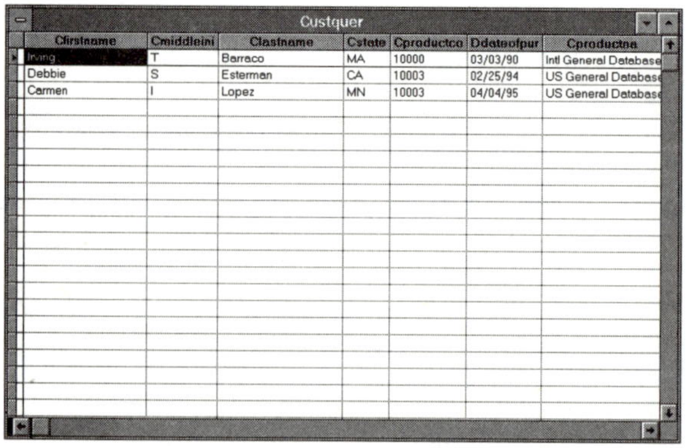

7 Close the custquer Browse window.

Display your results on the active output screen

1 On the Query Designer toolbar, click the Query Destination button.

2 In the Query Destination dialog box, click the Screen button.

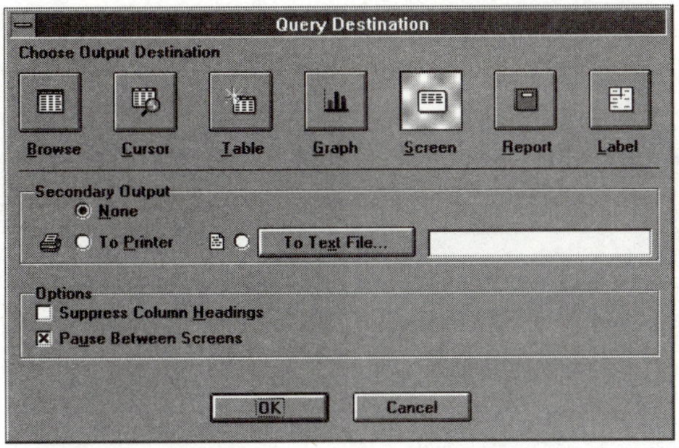

3 Click the OK button.

4 From the Query menu, select Run Query.

The query will be displayed in the Visual FoxPro window or the current active window. To view the Visual FoxPro window, minimize the Query Designer window and close the Project Manager.

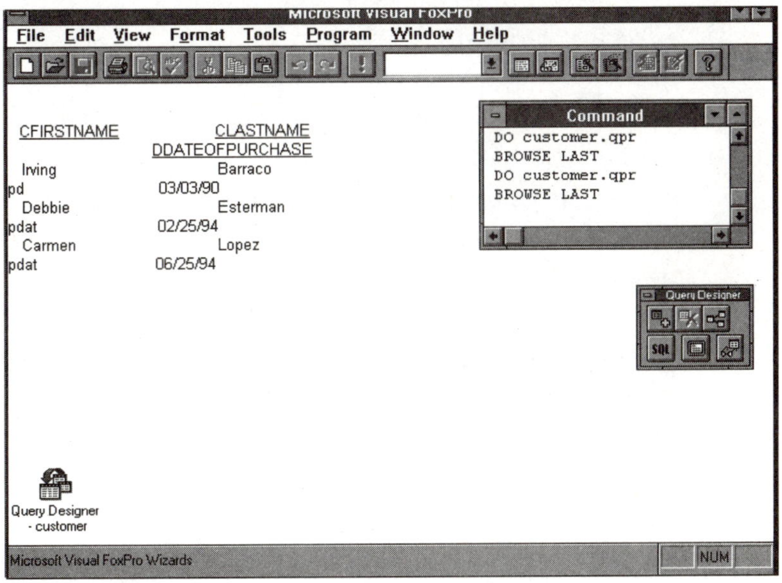

5 Close the screen output by typing **clear** in the Command window.

6 Press the Enter key.

Send your results to a report file

1 On the Query Designer toolbar, click the Query Destination button.

2 In the Query Destination dialog box, click the Report button.

The Open Report screen appears.

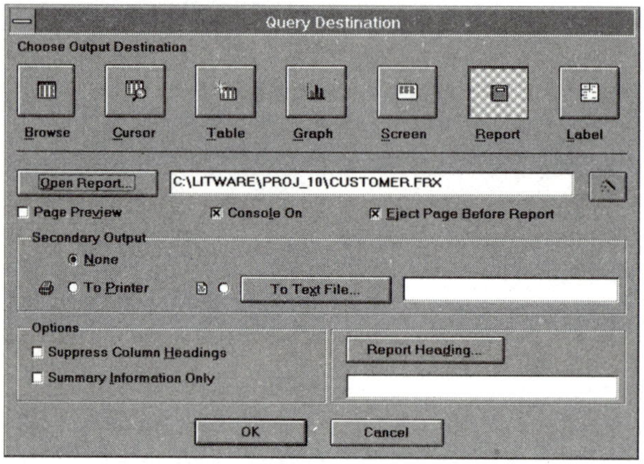

3 Click the Page Preview button.

4 Click the Open Report button.

The Open dialog box appears.

5 In the Select Report File Name text box, select customer.frx.

6 Click the OK button.

7 In the Query Destination window, click the OK button.

8 From the Query menu, select Run Query.

The Report Designer appears with the customer report displaying the queried data.

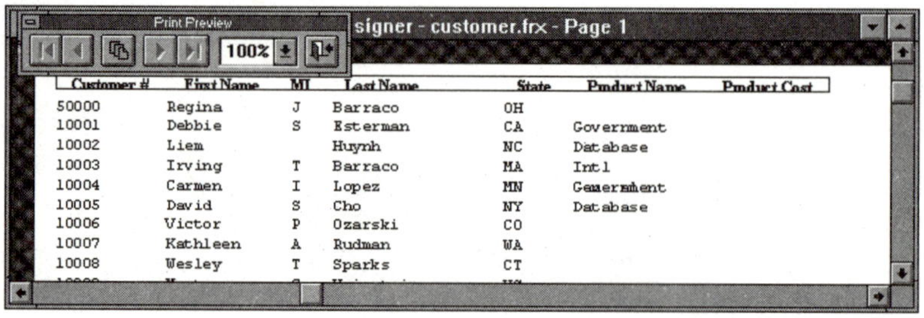

9 Click the Close Preview button on the Report Designer.

10 Save and close the Query Designer.

Run a query from Project Manager

1 Locate and click Query on the Data tab.

2 Click on the Customer query.

The query should be the report query you saved previously.

3 Click the Run button.

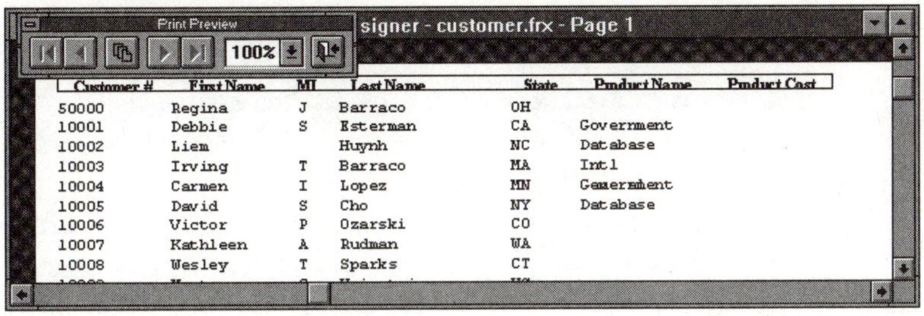

4 Close the Report Designer.

Select specific groups for a query

With Query Designer, you can be more selective in your choice of what to include in the query. In this exercise, you will modify the query to select only those customers from the state of New York.

1 Locate and click Query on the Data tab.

2 Click on the Customer query.

3 Click Modify.

Having

4 In the Group By dialog box, click the Having button.

The Having dialog box appears.

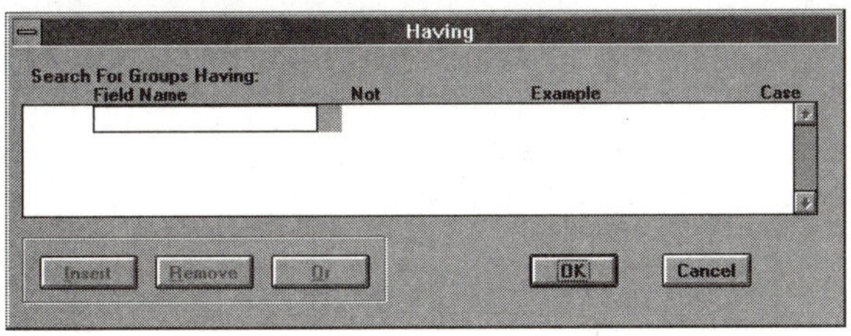

5 Click the list box next to Field Name.

6 Scroll to find the customer.cstate field. Click customer.cstate to select it.

Do not change the Equal selection. This option provides only the names of states that equal the one you type for the query.

7 Click the Example text box.

8 Type **NY**

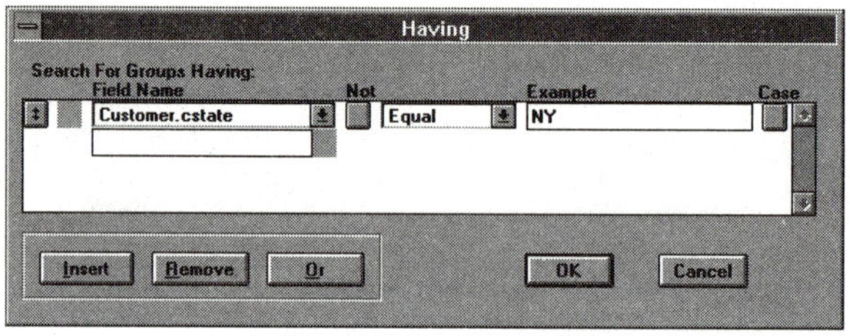

9 Click the OK button.

10 From the Query Designer toolbar, click the Query Destination button.

11 In the Query Destination dialog box, click Browse.

12 Click OK.

13 Run the Query.

14 From the View menu, select Browse custquer.

The query appears, listing only customers from New York State.

15 Save the query.

16 Close the Query Designer.

One Step Further: Comparing Views and Queries

Views and queries are not the same. Queries are read-only and are not able to be updated, while Views are dynamic sets of information from one or more tables that can be updated. Views allow you to control the changes you make to a remote data source and to update the remote data source. When you update or change a set of records retrieved by a View, Visual FoxPro updates the source tables. Building views is similar to building queries. In One Step Further, you will build a View and update data in the Customer table.

You can update data in a View by editing the data in a View Browse window. Visual FoxPro then automatically updates the source tables. Creating views is similar to creating queries, so in this exercise you will walk through a truncated process to build a view of the LitWare Customer table.

Update a table using a View

1 In the Project Manager, click the Data tab.

2 Click the custinfo database under databases.

3 Click the Local Views under custinfo database.

4 Click the New button on the Project Manager.

A New Local View dialog box appears.

5 Click the New View button.

The View Designer appears.

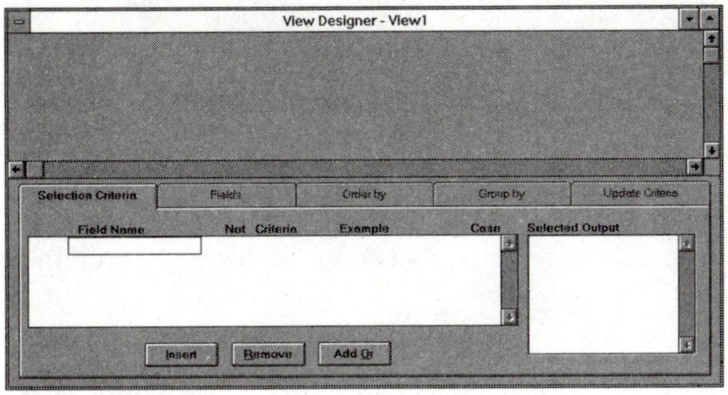

6 Select the Customer table.

7 Click the OK button.

The Customer table appears on the View Designer.

8 Click the Selection Criteria tab.

9 Under Field Name, click the Field Name text box.

10 Select Customer.clastname.

11 Repeat the procedure:

Customer.cfirstname
Customer.ccity
Customer.cstate
Customer.cpostalcode

12 Click the Fields tab and select Add All.

13 Click the Order By tab and select customer.cstate.

14 Click Add.

15 Click the Group By tab and select customer.cstate.

16 Click Add.

The changes that you make in the Local View can also be made in the database source tables. To do this, you must set the Update Criteria Options.

Set the Update Criteria options

1 Click the Update Criteria tab.

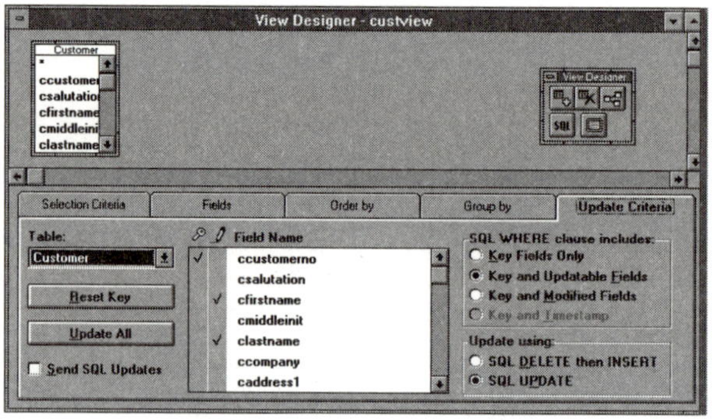

Before any of the source tables can be modified from a View, you must select a key index field to identify the unique records and fields that can be updated. Since LitWare uses a unique customer number for each customer, you will use customerno as the key index.

2 Double-click on the gray bar under the key and in front of customerno.

A check and a key appear at the top of the column to indicate that you have selected a key field. This field cannot be updated. You can now select the fields that can be updated when data is changed in the View.

3 In the gray bar under the pencil, double-click in front of the following fields:

clastname
cfirstname
ccity
ccstate
cpostalcode

4 Click the Key and Updatable Fields option.

This selects the option, and states that the Key Field cannot be updated but the other selected fields can be updated.

5 Save the Query using the file name custview.

Preview the custview View

1. From the Query Menu, click Run Query.
2. Find and highlight Hector (last name Bermudez).
3. Change the name Hector to **Heather.** Press Enter.
4. Close the View Designer.
5. Open the Customer table to view the change.
6. Close the Customer table.

If you want to continue to the next lesson

1. Click File on the Menu bar.
2. Select Close.

If you want to quit Visual FoxPro for now

1. Click File on the Menu bar.
2. Select Exit.

Lesson Summary

To	Do This
Create a query	Open the LitWare Project Manager. Click Query on the Data tab, and then click New.
Add tables to a query	Click Add Table. Add needed tables.
Add fields to a query	Select desired fields, and then click Add.
Order query results	Select desired fields, and then click Add.
Group query results	Select desired fields, and then click Add.
Save a query	Type the name of the query, and then click Save.
Output a query	Select the destination of the query, and then run the query.
Run a query	From the Query menu, select Run Query.
Select specific group	In the Group By dialog box, click the Having button, type in the example, and then run the query.
Update a table using a View	Select the database, select Local Views, select the table, and then select the fields.

For online information about	From the Visual FoxPro Help Menu, choose Contents, select "Using Visual FoxPro," and then
Queries and Views	Select the topic "Queries and Views"

For more Information on	See in the *Microsoft Visual FoxPro Developer's Guide*
Queries	Chapter 14, "Adding Queries and Reports"
Views	Chapter 8, "Creating Multi-Table Views"

Preview of the Next Lesson

In the next lesson you will learn how to use Visual FoxPro's Report Designer to create reports. You will build a Customer report for the LitWare executive staff that displays customers by number, name, and state. Your report will also display the products each customer owns, and the cost of each product.

Lesson

11

Creating Reports

Estimated time

45 min.

In this lesson you will you will learn how to:

- Design a report.
- Create a quick report.
- Customize a report using Report Designer.
- Preview a report.
- Print a report.

Reports display and summarize data in a printed or on-screen format. The two main components of reports are data and layout. The report data source can be a database table, a query, or a view. Queries search, order, and group the data. The report layout defines the format of the document. The report you will generate for the LitWare project will define the customers and the products they own, the date the products were purchased, and the price of each product.

Designing Reports

The first step in designing a report is to determine the data that will be displayed, and the second step is to determine the best display format for the report. You can create lists based on a single table, or based on complex reports such as the Customer Product report form used by LitWare. Report Designer is a flexible, easy-to-use tool for creating, designing, and modifying reports. As the developer for LitWare, you want to create a report that displays which customers own which products and when the products were purchased. You will use Quick Report to develop the customer list and sort by state, and then you will use Report Designer to customize the report to display customer products and purchase dates, grouped by state.

There are several types of report layouts available in Microsoft Visual FoxPro 3 for Windows:

Columnar One record per row with fields placed horizontally. Example: LitWare customer list, product list.

Row One column of records with fields placed vertically down one side. Example: LitWare customer list.

Form More complex reports showing many data relationships. Example: LitWare customer-owned product compared with inventory status to show slow moving products.

Multi-column More than one column of records. Example: LitWare customer phone directory.

Label Mailing and other types of labels. Example: LitWare customer mailing list.

For the Customer Product Report you will use the columnar, one-to-many report layout to display customer information, customer products, and date of purchase. You will create, customize, preview, and print the Customer report.

Start the lesson

1. Open Visual FoxPro.
2. From the File menu, select Open.
3. In the Drives and Directories list, select c:\litware\proj_11 directory.
4. Select litware.pjx.
5. Click the OK button.

   The Project Manager displays the LitWare project.

Creating a Quick Report

Quick Report is a time-saving tool for creating a simple report layout. Quick Report offers two report layouts:

Column Displays fields left to right across the page in the detail band.

Rows Displays fields at the left margin in the detail band.

When you select Quick Report you have the following additional options for designing your report:

Identifying a Data Source Table or database that contains the data used in the report.

Include Fields Data fields that will be used to create the report.

Label Fields Names that will be used in the column heads.

Create a Quick Report

1. From the Project Manager, select the Document Tab.
2. Select Reports.
3. Click the New button.

   The New Report window appears.
4. Click New Report.

   The Report Designer and Report Controls toolbar appear.

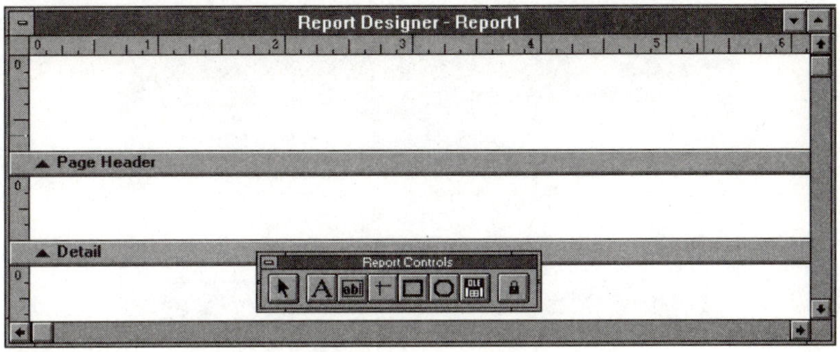

5. From the Report menu, select Quick Report.

   The open dialog box appears.
6. Select customer.dbf.
7. Click OK.

   The Quick Report appears.

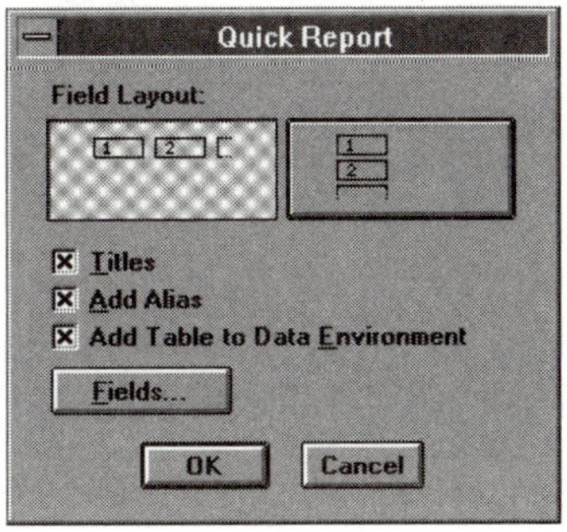

Determine report layout

1. Select the Horizontal Column Layout button, if it is not selected already.
2. Leave the Title, Add Alias, and Add Table to Data Environment option boxes checked.

Use Field Picker to select tables and fields

1. Click the Fields button.

   The Field Picker window appears.

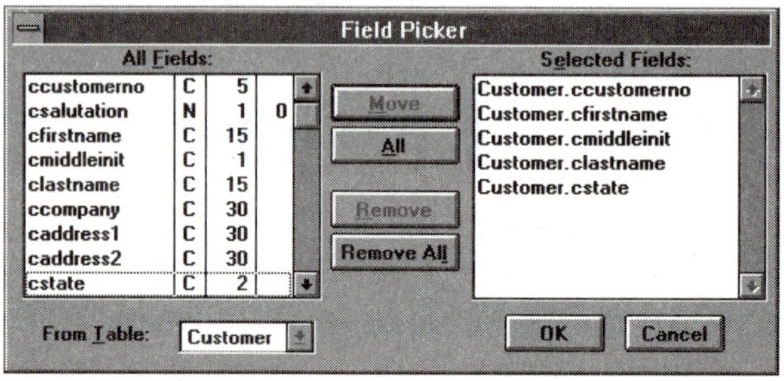

   Select fields one at a time in the order you want them to appear in the report.

   If you select a field and then wish to move it to a new location on the list, you can click the button in front of the field you wish to move and drag it to the new location in the list.

2. Select ccustomerno.
3. Click the Move button.

   Visual FoxPro moves the field to the Selected Fields column.

4. Repeat steps 2 and 3 to move the following fields to the Selected Fields column.

   cfirstname
   cmidddleinit
   clastname
   cstate

5. Click the OK button.

   The Quick Report appears.

6. Click the OK button.

   The Report Designer appears.

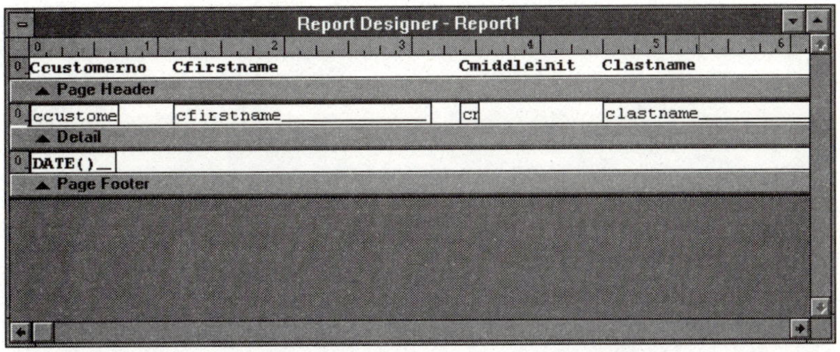

Note that Quick Report placed the fields in the order you selected.

Use Label Control to rename the page headers

Quick Report placed the field names in the Page Header bar. These names will appear as column headers on the report. In order to better describe the information in the columns, you will need to rename the column headers.

1 On the Report Control toolbar, click the Label Control button.

2 On the Page Header bar, highlight ccustomerno.

3 Type **Customer #**

4 Rename the other fields:

Current field name	**New field name**
cfirstname	First Name
cmidddleinit	MI
clastname	Last Name
cstate	State

5 Click the Select Object button.

Preview the report

1 From the View Menu, select Preview.

A preview of the report appears.

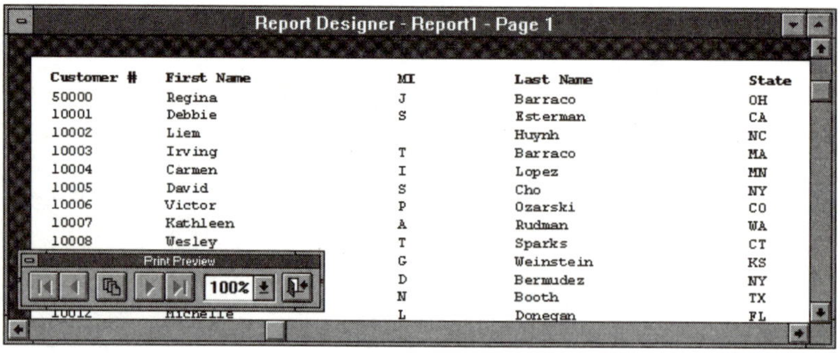

Use Print Preview Controls to zoom in or out of the report or to change pages.

Close Preview

2 Click the Close Preview button to close Print Preview.

Format the Report

Note the width of the fields. You will need to resize the fields to improve the visual presentation of the report and fit all the data columns on a single page. In the procedure below, you will resize and reposition fields.

You need to resize and move the objects on the Page Header and Detail bars to organize the columns on the report.

1 On the detail bar, click ccustomerno.

2 Use the resize handles to resize ccustomerno so that it falls between 0 and 7/8 inches on the ruler.

3 Click and drag Customer # on the Page Header and place Customer # directly above ccustomerno.

4 Resize and move the other fields as follows:

Field	**On the ruler**
First Name	from 1 inch to 2 inch.
MI	from 2 1/8 inch to 2 3/8 inch.
Last Name	from 2 1/2 to 3 7/8 inch.
State	from 4 to 4 1/2 inch.

Your layout should look like the layout in the figure below.

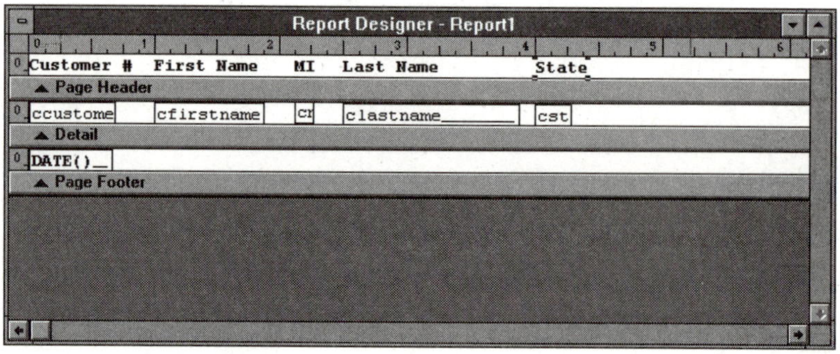

5 Preview the report.

6 Repeat step 6 as needed.

When the report looks visually balanced, you will want to save the Customer Report.

Save the report

1 Click File on the main menu.

2 Click Save.

3 Set the drive and directory to c:\litware\proj_11.

4 Type **customer** for the report name.

5 Select Save.

6 Close the Report Designer.

Using Report Designer to Modify the Report

You will use the Report Designer to customize the LitWare Customer report you just created, adding products owned and date purchased for each customer in the report. To do this you will need to access the other data tables in the LitWare project. In the following exercises you will create, add, and label new fields, and reformat the report to make room for the new fields.

Open the Report Designer

1 From Project Manager, select Document Tab.

2 Select the Reports Icon from the list of documents.

3 Select the customer report.

4 Click the Modify Report button.

The Report Designer appears, displaying the Customer report you just created.

Open the Report Designer controls toolbar

1 Click View from the main menu.

2 Click the Report Controls toolbar.

The Report Controls toolbar appears.

Adding Table Fields to the Customer Report

In order to complete the report describing the products that each customer owns, you must add fields to the report. To add fields from a table, you will first add the table containing the desired field. In this case, you will use fields from the custprod and product tables to add product names and purchase dates to the report.

Add a table

1 From the View menu, select Data Environment.

The Data Environment window appears, displaying the customer table.

2 From the Data Environment menu, select Add.

The Add Table or View window appears.

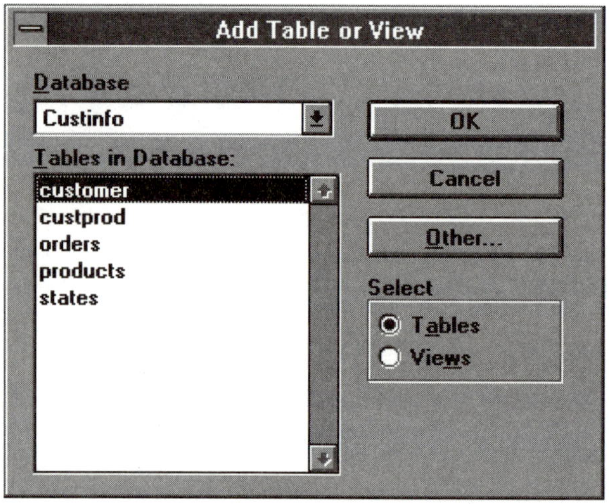

3 Select custprod.

4 Click the OK button to add the custprod table.

The custprod table appears.

5 Repeat steps 1 and 2 to add the products table.

As you add each table, the linked relationships also appear. Visual FoxPro will automatically display the links you create between tables.

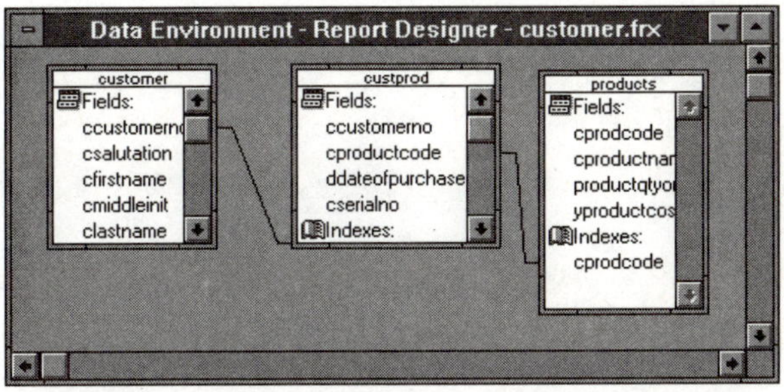

6 Close the Data Environment.

Add a field

You will add the products.cproductname (product name) and products.yproductscost (product costs) fields to display the products owned by each LitWare customer and the price each LitWare customer paid for those products.

Field

1 On the Report Controls toolbar, click the Field button.

2 Click the cursor on the detail bar where you want the product name field to be placed; in this case, place the cursor after the cstate field starting at position 4 5/8 inches on the ruler.

The Report Expression dialog box appears. This tool allows you to select and define expressions that add properties to the field.

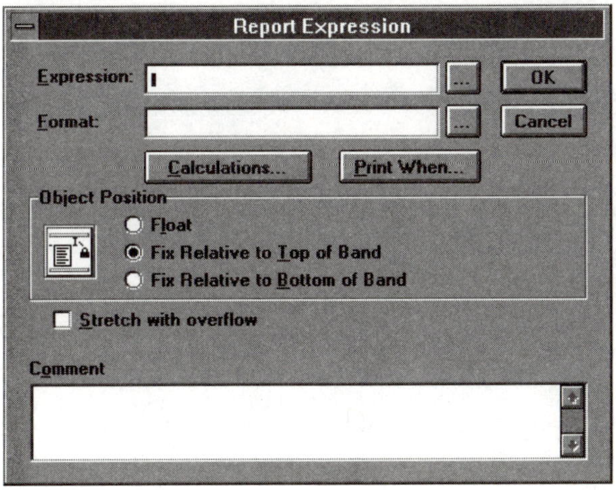

Expression

3 Click on the Expression button.

The Expression Builder appears. You will use the Expression Builder to add properties to the fields.

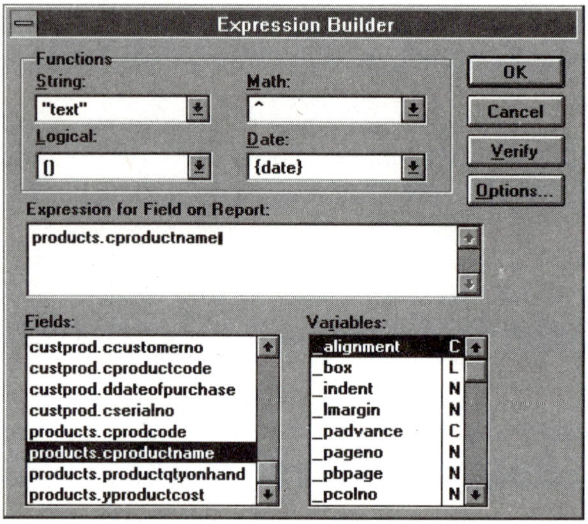

4 Scroll the list of fields and double-click products.cproductname, which appears in the Expression Field on Report text box.

5 Click the OK button.

6 Click the Format button.

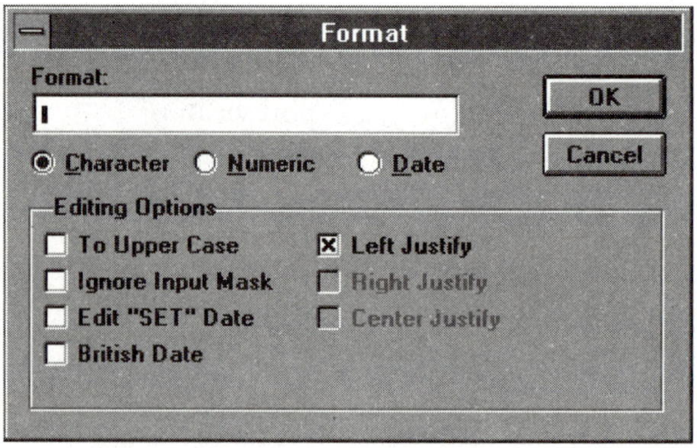

Notice that the field is a character field.

7 Click the OK button.

8 In the Report Expression dialog box, click the OK button.

cproductname appears on the detail bar.

9 Resize this field to go from 4¾ to 6½ inches.

Add a new label to appear on the report header

1 Select Label Control from the Report Controls toolbar.

2 To enter the label, click the cursor on the Page Header bar above the product name.

3 Type **Product Name**

4 Use the same process to add products.yproductscost to the detail band at position 5 6/8 inches on the ruler.

5 Add the label **Product Cost** to the Page Header.

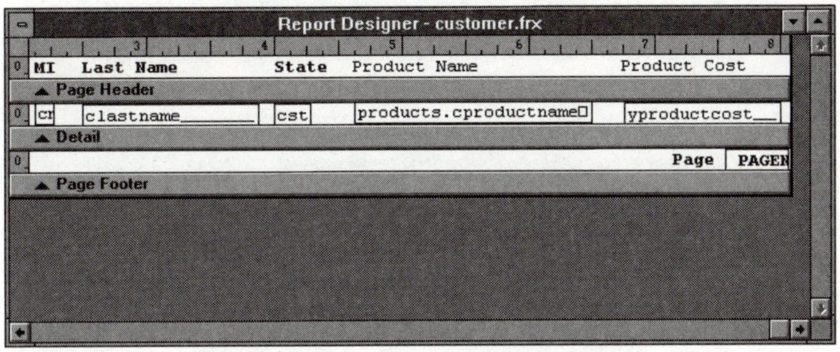

6 Select Preview from the View menu.

Use the Print Preview Controls to zoom in or out of report or to change pages.

7 Click the Close Preview button to close the Print Preview.

Formatting the Report

Formatting is the process of making the report visually appealing and functional for data calculations. When you print the report, you will need to set your printer to landscape mode for all of the columns to fit on a page.

Use page setup

1 From the File menu, select Page Setup.

The Page Setup window appears.

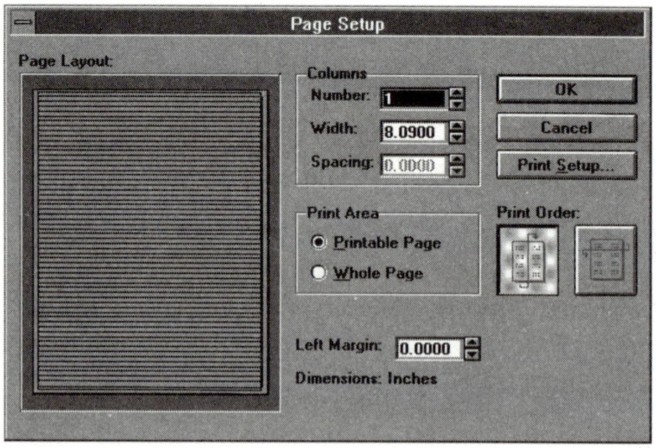

2 Click Print Setup. The Print Setup window appears.

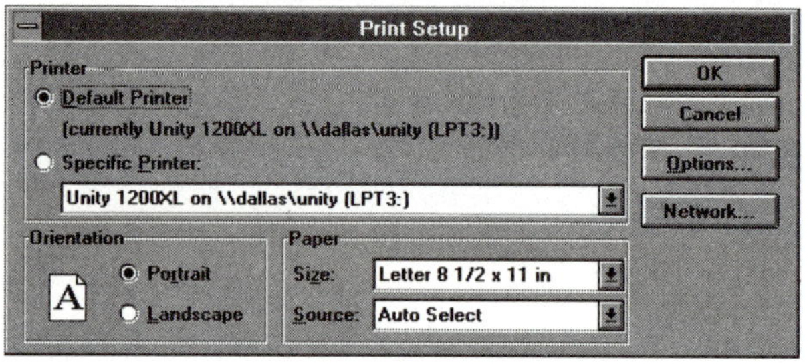

3 Select your printer from the list of printers.

4 Click Landscape under orientation.

5 Click the OK button.

The Page Setup window appears—leave all the settings intact for this LitWare report.

6 Click the OK button.

Format text

1 From the Page Header, hold down the Shift Key and click the following labels, maintaining the order.

Customer #
First Name
Middle
Last Name
State
Product Name
Product Cost

2 From the Format menu, select Font.

3 Select Times New Roman, Bold, point size 10.

4 Click the OK button.

Note the changes to the labels on the Page Header.

Place a rectangle around the header

1 On the Report Controls toolbar, click the Rectangle button.

2 Move the cursor to the lower left corner of the Page header.

3 Click and drag to draw a rectangle to enclose all of the header names.

4 Preview the report.

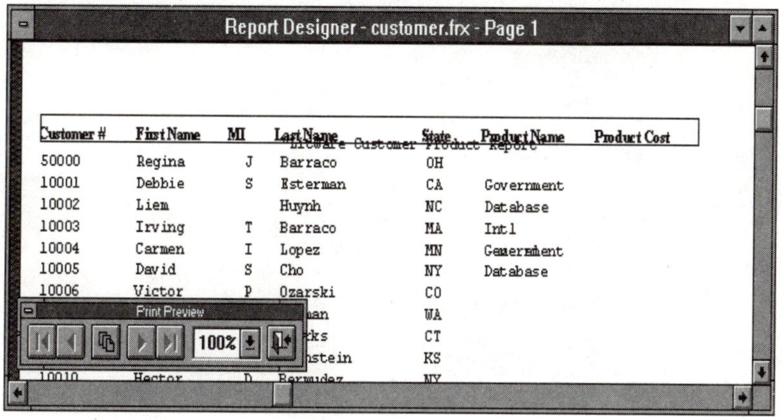

5 Resize fields as needed and preview the report.

6 Save the Report.

7 Close the Report Designer.

Using Query to Create a Report

You have just created a Customer report, and you have used Report Designer to modify the Customer report, reflecting customer products and the prices of products. In the next section of this lesson, you will learn to use Query to generate a report. The query you generated in Lesson 10 will be used to display information on your new Customer report.

Visual FoxPro provides tools to create and store queries and reports. You can generate new queries that access stored reports to display query information of any kind. Creating and storing a variety of tables saves time and makes the query-to-reporting process quick and efficient.

Create a report from a query

1 From Project Manager, select the Data Tab.
2 Click the Queries Icon.
3 Select Customer from the list of queries.
4 Click Modify.

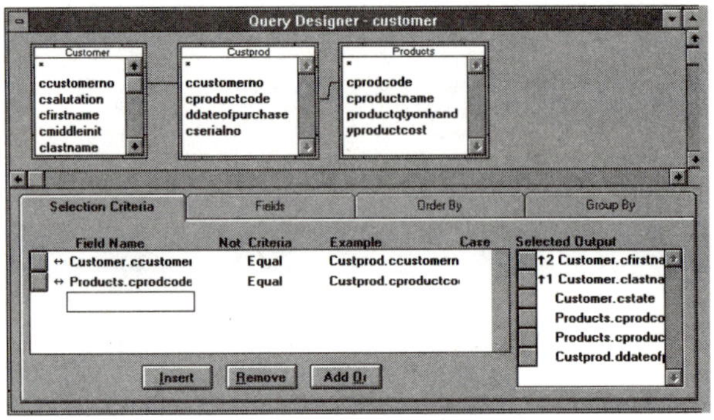

5 From the Query Menu, select Query Destination.

The Query Destination window appears.

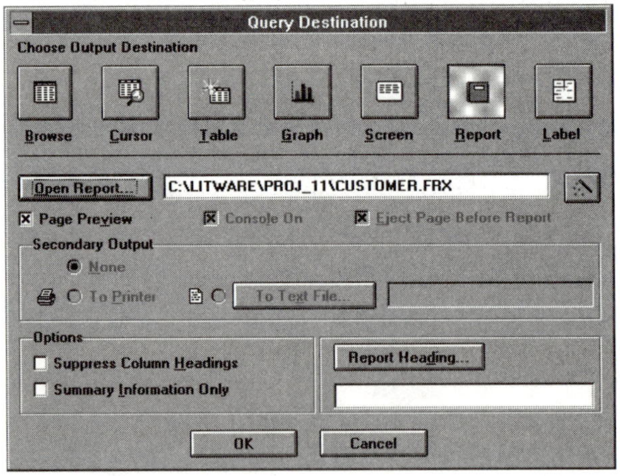

6 Click the Report button.
7 Select Open Report.
8 Set the drive and directory path to c:\litware\proj_11.
9 Select Customer from the list of reports.
10 Click OK.
11 Select Report Heading.

The Expression Builder window appears.

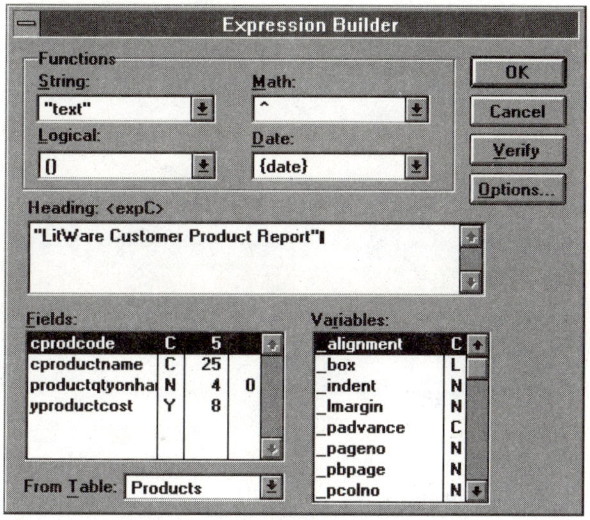

12 Type "**LitWare Customer Product Report**" (include the quotation marks) in the Report Heading text box.

13 Click the OK button.

The Query Destination window appears.

14 Click the Browse button.

15 Click the OK button.

Run the Query

1 From the Query menu, select Run Query.

The Report Designer Preview window appears with the Query Information displayed on the report.

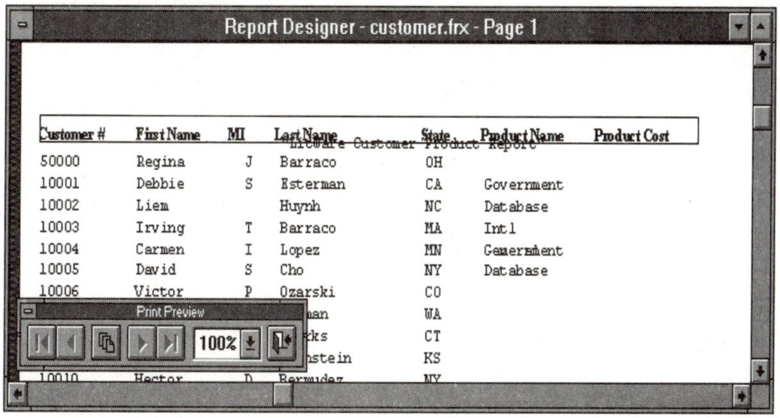

Use the Print Preview Controls to zoom in or out of the report and change pages.

2 Click the Close Preview button to close the Print Preview.

3 Close Query Designer.

4 From the Report Designer, make format changes as necessary.

5 Save the Report.

6 Close Report Designer.

One Step Further: Using a View to Create a Report

In this part of this lesson you will learn to use a View to generate a report. The View you generated in Lesson 10 will be used to display information on your new Customer report.

Create a report from a View

1 From the Window menu, select View Window.

The View window appears.

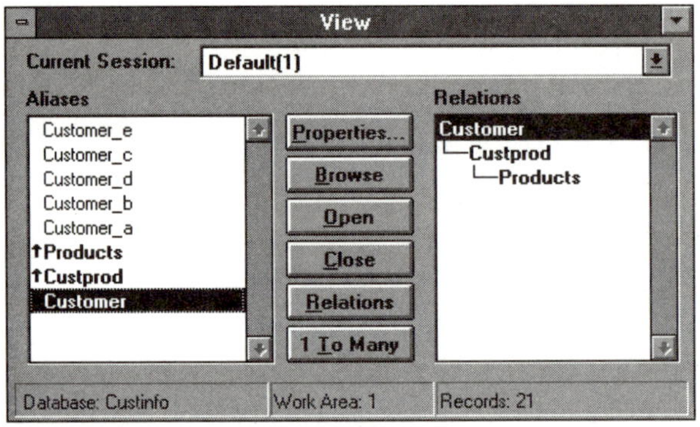

2 Click the Open button.

3 From the Select Option box, click the Views Option button.

4 Select the custview view.

5 Click the OK button.

6 Close the View window by double-clicking on the Menu Control button.

Open the report created by the view

1 Click on the Documents Tab.

2 Select the Reports button.

3 Click the New button.

The New Report dialog box appears.

4 Select New.

5 From the Report menu, select Quick Report.

The Quick Report dialog Box appears.

6 Click the OK button.

Fields from the custview view have populated the report.

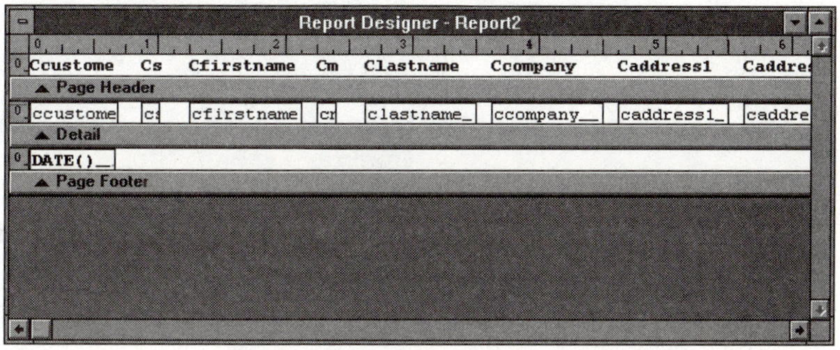

7 From the View menu, select Preview.

A preview of the new report appears.

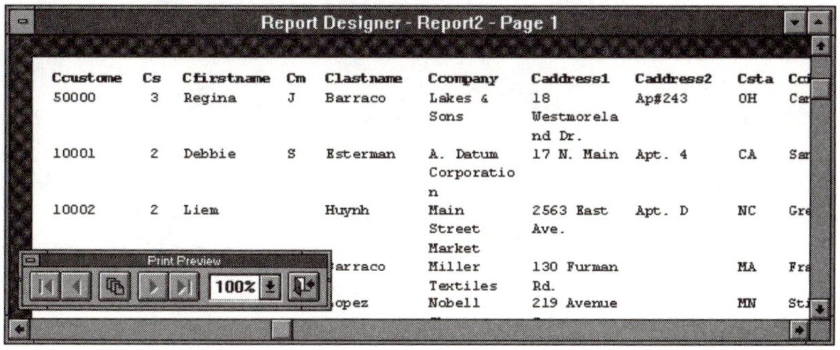

8 Close the Report Designer.

The Save Changes dialog box appears.

9 Select NO to save your changes.

If you want to continue to the next lesson

1. Click File on the Menu bar.
2. Select Close.

If you want to quit Visual FoxPro for now

1. Click File on the Menu bar.
2. Select Exit.

Lesson Summary

To	Do This
Create a Quick Report	From the Project Manager, select the Data tab. Select the Report Icon, and then click New. *or* From the Report Menu, select Quick Report. Locate and select the appropriate database.
Determine the Layout.	Select the fields. Label the header. Format the report.
Modify an existing report	Open Customer Report. Add the necessary tables and format as needed.
Use a query to create a report	Open the Customer Query, and select the destination. Open the Customer Report, and run the query.

For online information about	From the Visual FoxPro Help Menu, choose Contents, select "Using Visual FoxPro," and then
Reports	Select the topic "Reports and Labels"

For more Information on	See in the *Microsoft Visual FoxPro Developer's Guide*
Reports	Chapter 14, "Adding Queries and Reports"

Preview of the Next Lesson

In the next lesson you will learn to optimize and debug an application. With all the effort you put into developing the LitWare application, you want it to run without errors, and as efficiently as possible. Using Visual FoxPro's debugging tools, you will test and debug the LitWare application.

Lesson

12

Debugging, Optimizing, and Compiling

Estimated time

45 min.

In this lesson you will learn how to:

- Use Visual FoxPro debugging tools.
- Optimize your application.
- Compile your application.

All developers, managers, and users want their application to run properly and as efficiently and quickly as possible. It is very rare however, that this goal is achieved on the first attempt. A cycle of coding, testing, and debugging is necessary to remove as many problems as possible before users access an application. Because it is difficult for a developer to duplicate the precise environments, habits, and practices of the users, it is possible that users will find additional unexpected behaviors and problems in the application. You, as the developer, need to be able to identify the causes of these problems, and fix them as quickly as possible.

Queries and reports that are run regularly should not take too long to run, and screens should respond to user requests promptly. While application performance obviously depends a great deal on the hardware on which the application runs, there is much the developer can do to maximize an application's efficiency.

Microsoft Visual FoxPro 3 for Windows provides tools for the following operations:

- The Trace window allows you to watch programs and methods in forms execute, or step through them one line at a time.
- The Debug window allows you to examine the values of settings, memory variables, and fields in tables, and to set break points (suspend execution) when those values change.
- The View window allows you to examine the environment, open tables, views, cursors, as well as various settings of the Visual FoxPro environment.

Start the lesson

1. Open Visual FoxPro.
2. From the File menu, select Open.
3. In the Drives and Directories lists, select c:\litware\proj_12 directory.
4. Select litware.pjx.
5. Click the OK button.

   The Project Manager displays the LitWare project.

Testing and Debugging Your Application

Before you distribute your application to users, you will want to make sure that it runs the way you expect it to, with no abnormal terminations, and that the menus, forms, and reports produce the desired results.

Because Visual FoxPro allows you to run forms, menus, and programs directly from the command line or Project Manager, you can do a substantial amount of testing as you develop each piece of your application.

Using the Debugging Tools

Visual FoxPro provides excellent tools for debugging your application. The Debug window allows you to view the values of variables, fields, and built-in functions as your application runs. The Trace window allows you to view programs as they execute, step through them one line at a time, and suspend execution by setting breakpoints at specific lines in the code.

View values dynamically in the Debug Window

The Debug window has three components:

- The left half is where you type the names of the fields, variables, or functions whose values you want to see.

- The right pane where is the values are displayed.
- The middle bar is where you can set a breakpoint to tell Visual FoxPro to suspend execution when the value of that line changes.

To make sure that the Visual FoxPro environment is set up as you expect, it is often helpful to view Visual FoxPro's environment settings as the application runs. Use the Debug window to view the current path, which tells Visual FoxPro where to search for programs and databases. You can also view the setting of DELETED, which tells Visual FoxPro to include or exclude deleted records from processing.

TIP When a record is deleted in Visual FoxPro, it is not permanently removed from the table, it is merely marked for deletion. With SET DELETED OFF, those records marked as deleted are processed like all others. Deleted records are permanently removed from tables with the PACK command.

Open the Debug window before running the application (because there is no Debug window option on any of the LitWare application menus):

1. From the Tools menu, select Debug window.
2. Type **SET('PATH')** and press the Enter key.

   The current path appears on the right side of the window. If there is no path set, the null string ("") is shown.
3. Type **SET('DELETED')** and press the Enter key.

   The current setting of Deleted is shown (either "ON" or "OFF").

Set break points to suspend program execution

While you are testing the LitWare application, it would be helpful to verify that an attempt to add a record to the customer table was successful, and that the new record contains the desired information. Use the Debug window to suspend execution after the record count of the Customer table changes:

1. Open the Debug window if it is not already open.
2. Type **RECCOUNT('customer')**
3. Click on the middle bar of the line you just typed.

   A breakpoint marker appears on the bar.

If the customer table is open, the number of records in the table appears in the right pane of the Debug window. If it is not open, nothing appears.

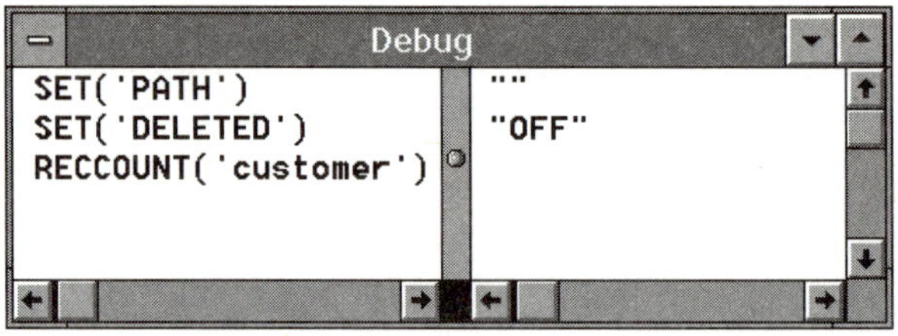

4 Press the Enter key to advance the cursor to the next line of the Debug window.

5 Run the custdata form.

6 Click the Add button.

7 Enter the following sample data:

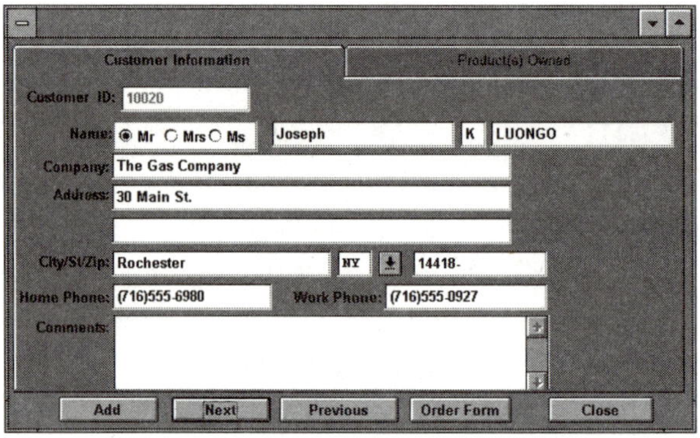

When the record is saved to the table, program execution suspends and the Command window becomes visible.

Verify that the data in the table matches your input

1 Click the Command Window to make it the active window.

If it is not completely visible, rearrange the windows on the screen.

2 Type **EDIT** to view the contents of the current record.

The following information appears:

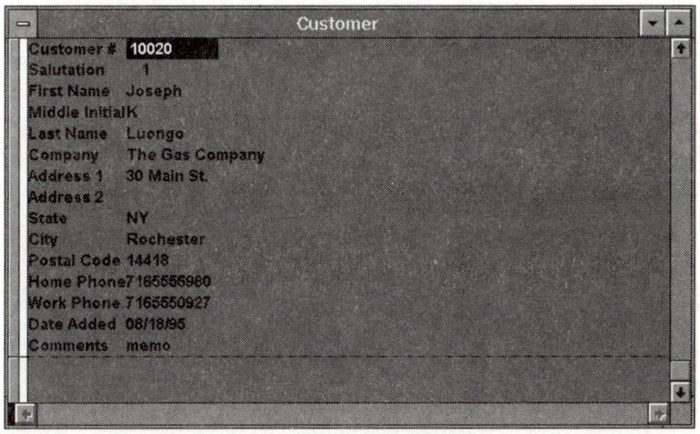

3 When you are finished verifying that the contents of the record matches your entry, press Escape to close the edit window.

4 Type **RESUME** and press Enter to resume program execution.

Close the Debug window

1 Click the Debug window to make it the active window.

If it is not visible, you can select it by selecting Debug window from the Tools menu.

2 Close the Debug window by pressing Escape or by double-clicking on the Control box in the top left corner of the window.

3 Close the custdata form.

Using the Debug and Trace Windows to Find Bugs

A sample program has been built into this lesson's files to illustrate the use of the Debug and Trace windows. The program attempts to reference a variable that has been released from memory.

NOTE When a variable is released from memory, it becomes "un-initialized." The value of that variable is lost, and that variable cannot be referenced unless it is reinitialized.

Run the program Bug1

1 Open the Project Manager.

2 Under the Code tab, select the Bug1 program.

3 Click Run.

The following error appears:

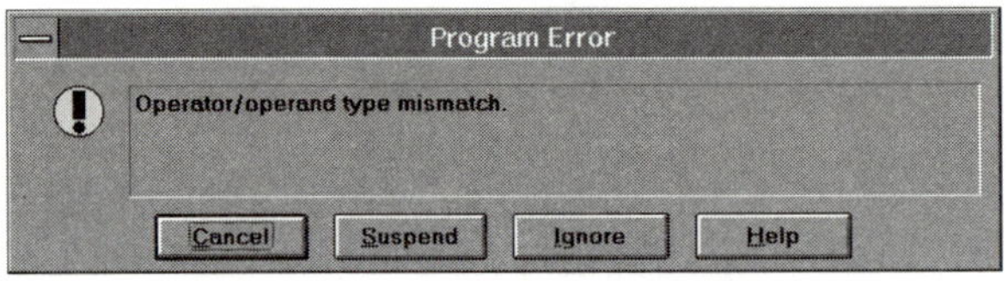

Use the Debug window to find the source of the error

To find the source of the error, use the Debug window to track the change in the type of the variable lnCounter.

1. Open the Debug window.
2. Type **TYPE("lnCounter")** in the Debug window.

   A "U" appears in the right side of the Debug window, indicating that lnCounter is not initialized (it is type U, for undefined)
3. Put a breakpoint on the line.

   This will cause a running program to suspend when the lnCounter variable is initialized.
4. Run the Bug1 program again.

   Program execution suspends when lnCounter is initialized to 0.

   Notice in the Debug window that the type of lnCounter is "N" for Numeric. At this point, you know that lnCounter has been initialized, so the cause of the error must be later in the program.

NOTE A memory variable has a type, just as a field in a table does. Variable types are the same as field types, except that memory variable types may be changed during program execution. In Visual FoxPro, the following code sequence is legal:

```
PageCount = 1
PageCount = LTRIM( STR( PageCount ) )
```

Notice the second line takes a memory variable of numeric type and assigns it a character value. This will not cause an error, but may very well lead to confusion, as later maintenance will be difficult on a variable whose type changes. For more discussion of variable types and variable naming conventions, see Appendix A.

Use the Trace window to find the cause of the error

Open the Trace window:

1. From the Tools menu, select Trace Window.

   The Trace Window appears, with the Bug1 program running.

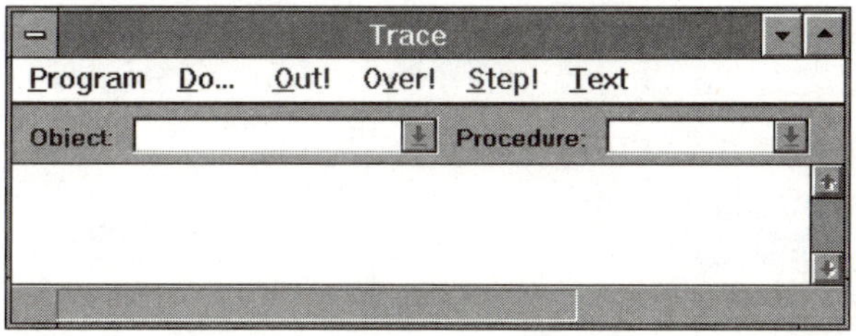

*You can open the View window from the Command window by typing **SET** and pressing Enter.*

2 Press S or click Step to execute the line.

3 Repeat step 2, watching the value in the Debug window until it changes to "U" for Undefined.

4 Notice the line that has just executed in the Trace window. The RELEASE command causes the value of the memory variable to be released from memory and the type to change back to undefined.

NOTE You can use the Trace window to view program code as it runs without stepping through it line by line. You can select Resume to run the program uninterrupted. To control the speed at which each line executes, set the speed using the Throttle option under the Program menu of the Trace window.

---

5 Click **Resume** to continue program execution.

6 Fix the error by removing the offending line.

TIP Open the program in the Program Editor, and remove the line beginning RELEASE....This will remove the cause of the error, since the variable will not be released from memory, and will be accessible to the program.

If you know that a program works until a certain point, but want to investigate execution from that point on, you can tell Visual FoxPro to suspend execution at that point.

Set a break point using the Trace window:

1 Open the Trace window.

2 Select Do.

3 Select Bug1.

The program appears. All lines of code appear, with the line about to be executed highlighted.

4 Use the cursor navigation keys (arrows, page up, page down) or the Trace window's scroll bars to position the cursor at the desired line.

5 Press the space bar or click the mouse on that line.

A breakpoint marker appears at that line.

The code will execute without interruption until it reaches the line marked by the breakpoint. When execution reaches the breakpoint, execution will suspend, allowing you to step through code one line at a time, or even execute code in the Command window.

TIP Use the Debug and Trace windows in combination to investigate problems. If you want to step through a particular program in an application, set a breakpoint on the expression **PROGRAM() = "MYPROG"** or **"MYPROG" $ SYS(16)** (program names are returned in upper case) to cause execution to suspend when that program is called, because the value will change from .f. (false) to .t. (true). You can open the Trace window by typing **ACTIVATE WINDOW Trace** in the Command window, and stepping through the program. To debug an application when the Trace and Debug Windows are not available from menus, assign them to "hot keys," as follows:

```
ON KEY LABEL F7 ACTIVATE WINDOW Debug
ON KEY LABEL F8 ACTIVATE WINDOW Trace
```

Of course, most errors are not as obvious as the one described here. Using the Debug and Trace windows can usually isolate the area where an error is occurring, as well as the specific cause of the error. From there, it is a simple matter for you to fix the error.

Use the View window to determine open tables and relations

When you are developing and debugging an application, it often useful to be able to see what tables are opened and how they are related. The View window provides a snapshot of open tables and their relations, and allows you to open and close tables and set relations. Use the View window to see what tables are open when the custdata form is running.

1 Run the custdata form.

2 From the Window menu, select View.

The View window appears:

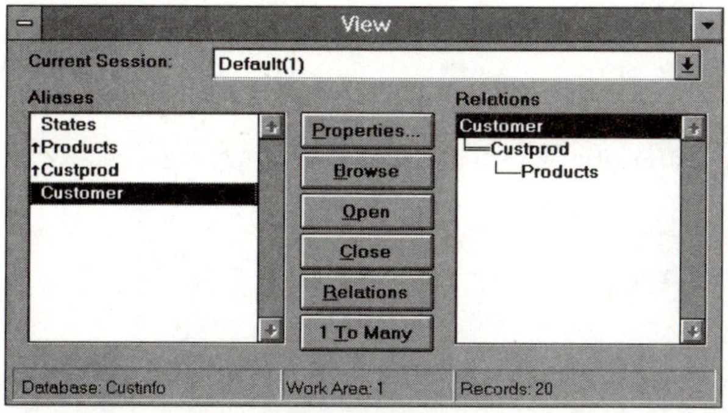

The left panel of the View window displays the open tables. The right panel shows the relationship between the tables; a single connecting line indicates a one-to-one relationship, and a double line indicates a one-to-many relationship. If you are using Data Sessions (discussed in Lesson 9), you can select the data session whose open tables you want to view by using the DataSession drop-down box in the View window.

Optimizing Your Applications

In addition to an accurate application, the user wants an application that runs as quickly as possible. There are many actions you can take within Visual FoxPro to tune the performance of the application.

Visual FoxPro uses Rushmore technology to run queries and search through tables rapidly. Rushmore works effectively if it is enabled and the indexes and commands are constructed properly.

NOTE Rushmore technology is the patented method by which Visual FoxPro optimizes searches and queries. It uses available indexes and requires no special programming.

Using Rushmore Technology

Visual FoxPro uses Rushmore technology to speed searches and queries. Rushmore uses standard indexes (IDX files and CDX tags) when available, and constructs its own internal indexes when necessary. Structural CDX files, which are opened automatically when the table is opened, allow Rushmore to use multiple index tags for the same operation, as well as to optimize queries and operations using indexes other than the currently selected index.

For example, a table may have two (or more) index tags, one on the state field and one on the last name field. The current sort sequence, or the logical order of the table, may be by last name. Any operations or queries that can be optimized by Rushmore using the state index will still be automatically optimized, without changing the master index tag of the table.

You must open IDX files with the **SET INDEX TO <indexname>** or **USE <Table> INDEX <indexname>** for Rushmore to utilize them, since they are not automatically associated with the table.

For more information about indexes and building a Visual FoxPro database, refer to Lesson 4.

Using Optimizable Expressions in Searches and Queries

Rushmore allows you to optimize access to a single table or to multiple tables. To retrieve data from a single table, use the FOR clause of an optimizable command. For example, if there is an index tag on the State field of the Customer table, the following code would be optimized:

```
SCAN FOR State = 'AL'
       *-- other code goes here
ENDSCAN
```

To retrieve data from multiple tables, use the SQL SELECT command.

Expressions may be partly optimized as well. If there is an index on the State field but none on the City field, the following code would be partly optimized:

```
SCAN FOR State = 'MI' AND City = "ROCHESTER"
       *-- other code goes here
ENDSCAN
```

To be optimizable, expressions in the command and in the indexes must match exactly. For example, if your query searches for all customers in the state of California, and you have an index on State + CustomerId, the query must match the index:

```
SELECT * FROM Customer WHERE State = "CA" is not optimizable, because the
where clause doesn't exactly match the index expression, but

SELECT * FROM Customer WHERE State + CustomerId = "CA" is optimizable,
because the where clause exactly matches the index expression.
```

The two queries will return the same results, but the second one will perform much more quickly.

TIP The UPPER() function is a potential source of confusion For example, if the index expression is **State** field, and a query's where clause is UPPER(State) = "CA", the query will not be optimizable, even if all the states are entered in upper case. The index expression and query clause/ optimizable expression must match exactly, as **WHERE State = "CA"**.

Create Index Tags on Search Fields

When you created the LitWare database, you created index tags for each of the tables. Those indexes were created to enable searching by a key field, to ensure relational data integrity, and to link tables. Another reason to create index tags is to allow queries to run faster.

LitWare management has decided to review the results of their marketing program by geographic area. The query will specify a date range and the first three digits of a zip code, and should output the number of sales made for each customer in that selection criteria. It will look like the following (ldBegDate, ldEndDate, and lcZip3 are user-input variables):

```
SELECT COUNT( custprod.cid ),  customer.cid
FROM custprod, customer ;
WHERE customer.cid = custprod.cid ;
AND custprod.date_of_purchase >= ldBegDate ;
AND custprod.date_of_purchase <= ldEndDate ;
AND LEFT( customer.cPostalCode ) = lcZip3
```

To maximize the ability of Rushmore to optimize queries and searches, there must be indexes available for each of the portions of the WHERE clause. There are already index tags in the custprod and customer tables on the cId field, but you will need to create tags for the remainder of the WHERE clause.

You can view the results of the operations in the System Status bar at the bottom of the screen.

1. Type **SET STATUS BAR ON**

   This activates the status bar at the bottom of the screen.

2. Type **SET TALK ON**

   This will cause command results to appear in the status bar.

Create the tags in the Command window

1. Type **OPEN DATABASE CustInfo**

   The database box under the System menu reflects that the custinfo database is open.

2. Type **USE Customer EXCLUSIVE**

   Remember that exclusive use is required to create an index tag.

3. Type **INDEX ON LEFT(cPostalCode, 3) TAG cPostal3**

   The status bar shows the number of records indexed.

NOTE For Rushmore purposes, the index tag name (the portion following the keyword TAG) is irrelevant; the index expression is searched. You could also name the index tag IndexTag1, and Rushmore would work just as well. However, when you want to set the active tag programmatically, you need to know the tag name, as in **SET ORDER TO TAG cPostal3.**

A tag name may be up to 10 characters long.

4 Type **USE CustProd EXCLUSIVE**

5 Type **INDEX ON date_of_Purchase TAG PurchDate**

The status bar shows the number of records indexed.

TIP If there are likely to be deleted records in your application's tables and you don't want them processed (SET DELETED is ON), create an index tag for each of your tables on the deletion marker: **INDEX ON DELETED() TAG Deleted** makes SET DELETED ON an optimizable condition.

Writing Efficient Code

In addition to using Rushmore optimization whenever possible, there are many other actions you can take to maximize system performance. The less work Visual FoxPro has to do in terms of opening and closing files, sending and retrieving information across a network, and updating the screen, the more resources it can devote to processing, and the faster overall operation becomes.

Minimize network and hard disk traffic

Visual FoxPro creates and maintains temporary files for its own use, as it swaps information to disk and otherwise manages memory. If your application runs on a network, it is much faster to have those temporary files exist on a local hard drive than on a network drive. You can only set the location of temporary files in the FoxPro configuration file, CONFIG.FPW.

The SYS(2019) function returns the name of the configuration file being used (which may be useful for a developer with CONFIG.FPW files in multiple directories on the hard disk).

1 Type **MODIFY COMMAND SYS(2019)** and press Enter.

The CONFIG.FPW file appears.

2 Make sure it contains the following line: TEMPFILES=C:

3 Close and save the file.

Opening and closing files slows execution, especially on a network. If you want optimal speed, it is good practice to open tables at the beginning of an application, and close them only at the end. Visual FoxPro provides 32,767 work areas for open tables, so it is unlikely that you'll run out of work areas in which to open tables. Also, as mentioned in Lesson 9, locking and unlocking tables and records causes network traffic, so it is a good idea to minimize and control lock attempts whenever possible.

TIP Visual FoxPro allows 32,767 work areas per data session. Actual work areas opened will be limited by your computer's memory and other considerations (such as the FILES setting of CONFIG.SYS).

Reducing Code Lines

Multiple lines of code take longer to execute than single lines. For example, you can code a table update using either of the following methods:

```
REPLACE field1 WITH value1
REPLACE field2 WITH value2
REPLACE field3 WITH value3
```

or

```
REPLACE field1 WITH value1, ;
        field2 WITH value2, ;
        field3 WITH value3
```

NOTE The second option is one code line because the first two lines end with a semi-colon, which indicates it is continued on the next line.

The second way is more efficient for two reasons: First, one code line executes faster than three lines of code. Second, the first set of instructions needs to access the disk three times, while the second method writes to the hard disk only once. Since hard disk performance is a major bottleneck, especially on a network, this can result in an appreciable performance improvement.

There are times when the tradeoff is not so obvious. LitWare has just opened an office in Iowa, and must now collect sales tax from all customers there. The Customer table needs to be updated to reflect the tax rate change. Consider the following two code examples:

Example 1:

```
IF FLOCK()
      REPLACE taxrate WITH .05 FOR State = 'IA'
ENDIF
UNLOCK
```

Example 2:

```
SCAN FOR State = 'IA'
        DO WHILE NOT RLOCK()
        *-- wait for this record to be locked
        ENDDO
        REPLACE taxrate WITH .05
        UNLOCK
ENDSCAN
```

There are several considerations here. The second method has more code and executes one record lock and unlock for each customer record processed, so it will process more slowly than the first code block. Another consideration, however, is the likelihood of success of a file lock as opposed to a record lock. At any time another user may have a customer record locked, which will prevent anyone else from locking the file. In this situation, you would be locking the whole file, but may be processing only a few of the records in it. There's no single answer for this dilemma. It is a tradeoff that needs to be considered for each situation.

Compiling Your Application

Before you distribute the LitWare application, you should build it into one file that Visual FoxPro can run. End users do not need access to source code, only to the running (compiled) version. Visual FoxPro allows you to build an .APP file that you can distribute to users, and all they need is a copy of Visual FoxPro, not the individual program files. If the users do not have Visual FoxPro, you can create an .EXE (using the Professional Edition of Visual FoxPro) to distribute so that the users can run the application just as they run any other Windows application. The .APP or .EXE is built from the project you've been working with in the Project Manager; Visual FoxPro automatically resolves references and builds the necessary files into the compiled code.

Selecting a Main program

The Main program in a project is the first one executed when the application runs. For example, you are building the LitWare application, and the file you distribute may be LITWARE.APP or LITWARE.EXE; however, the first program executed in the application is the one you designate as the main program, regardless of its name. It may be a program (.PRG) file, a menu (.MNX), or a form (.SCX) file, and it should contain code that provides the user access to the rest of the application.

Set the Main Program in the Project Manager

Use the System menu to set the Main program in the Project Manager. The Main program in the LitWare application is the system menu—Main menu:

1. In the Project Manager, open the LitWare project.
2. Select the LitWare menu under the Other tab.

3 From the Project menu, select Set Main.

A bullet appears next to the LitWare menu item, indicating that it is the main program for the application.

Building an Application or an Executable

The .APP or .EXE file is the only Visual FoxPro-executable file that users need to run the LitWare application. It contains all the object code for the application, including programs, forms, queries and reports. It may also contain tables that are not user-modifiable, such as lookup tables (state listings, error codes, and other system information).

Excluding Modifiable Files

Files that are built in to the project are read-only; the application cannot update the data in those tables. Therefore, tables containing data that can be updated by the user (customer, products, orders) should not be built in to the project. They can be excluded from the project using Project Manager. This allows those files to be listed in Project Manager, while still not being built in to the distributed application.

When a table is built in to the project, it becomes part of the executable application and does not need to be distributed separately. Tables that serve as lookup tables and that don't normally need to be updated within an application can be included in the application (such as a table of state abbreviations). Tables that are not built in to the project must be distributed separately so the application can access them. This means that the developer has to make provisions to distribute empty data tables with the application, since those files will not be built in to the distributed application.

In the LitWare application, include the States free table, since it does not to be updated by CSRs.

The Visual FoxPro default is for tables and databases to be excluded from a project.

Include the States table

1 In the Project Manager, open the LitWare project.

2 Select the States table from under the Custinfo database.

3 From the Project menu, select Include.

The symbol disappears from next to the States table, indicating that it is included in the project. Tables excluded from the project are marked with the Æ symbol.

Build the LitWare application from the Project Manager

As all applications do, the LitWare application will run faster when installed on a user's local hard drive instead of a network drive, because the application does not have to travel over the network. To create a single file to be installed on each CSR's hard disk, create an .APP file.

1 In the Project Manager, click Build.

The Build Options dialog window appears.

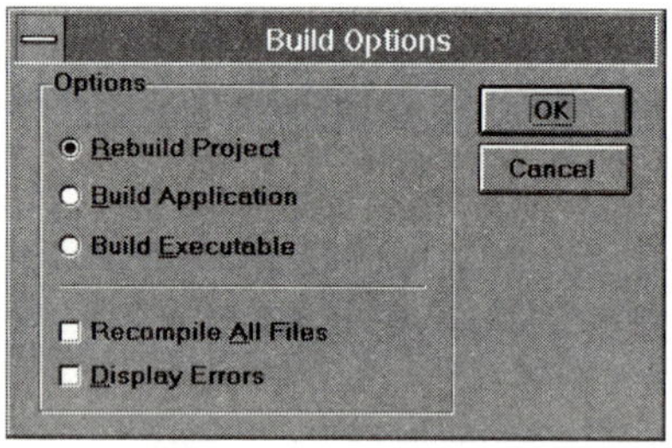

2 Click Build Application.

NOTE Selecting Rebuild Project generates any components that have been updated since the last build and resolves references to called programs and files. Selecting Build Application does that as well, and builds the FoxPro executable .APP file.

---

3 Click the OK button.

The Save As dialog window appears with the default name of LitWare.app.

4 Click Build Application to generate the .APP file.

You can now run the LitWare application file by typing **DO LitWare** in the command window.

One Step Further: Writing the Startup Routine

You will develop the routines to be called when the LitWare application starts. Such routines typically include verification that the tables necessary to run the application exist (the customer, custprod, and prodinfo tables), as well as the necessary index tags for each of the tables.

Write the startup routine

1 In the Project Manager, open the LitWare project.

2 Click the Code tab.

3 Click Programs.

4 Click New.

5 Type the following code:

```
*-- verify the existence of the Database container
IF NOT FILE('custinfo.dbc')
 *-- the database container does not exist
 =MESSAGEBOX('The database container file is missing; Cannot run
  application')
 RETURN
ENDIF

*-- verify the existence of the relevant tables
IF NOT FILE('customer.dbf') OR ;
 NOT FILE('products.dbf') OR NOT FILE('custprod.dbf')

 *-- one of the tables is missing
 =MESSAGEBOX('One or more of the data files are missing; Cannot run
  application')
 RETURN
ENDIF

*-- verify the existence of the relevant indexes
IF NOT FILE('customer.cdx') OR
 NOT FILE('products.cdx') OR NOT FILE('custprod.cdx')

*-- one of the index files is missing
 =MESSAGEBOX('One or more of the index files are missing; Cannot run
  application')
 RETURN
ENDIF

*-- verify the existence of the relevant tables
IF NOT FILE('customer.dbf') OR ;
 NOT FILE('products.dbf') OR NOT FILE('custprod.dbf')

 *-- the one of the tables is missing
 =MESSAGEBOX('One or more of the data files are missing; Cannot run
  application')
 RETURN
ENDIF

*-- open the database
OPEN DATABASE CustInfo

*-- all the necessary files are there; run the application by calling
the menu
DO Main.MPR
```

6 Close the program, and save it as LitWare.PRG.

Make LitWare.prg the main program in the application

LitWare.prg contains code that should run before the menu runs, and it runs the menu to provide access to the rest of the application. It is therefore a good candidate to be the main program of the LitWare application.

1. In the Project Manager, open the LitWare project.
2. Click the Code tab.
3. Click Programs.
4. With the right mouse button, click the LitWare program.

   A menu appears.

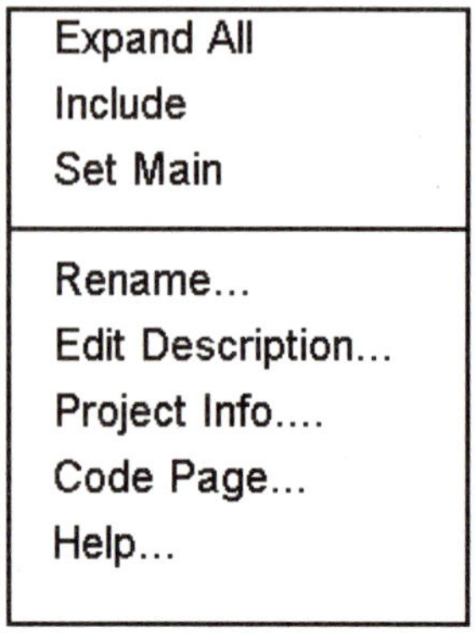

5. Select Set Main.

   A bullet appears next to the LitWare program item, indicating that it is the main program for the application.

If you want to quit Visual FoxPro for now

1. Click File on the Menu bar.
2. Select Exit.

Lesson Summary

In this lesson you learned how to debug an application using the Trace and Debug Windows. Both allow you to view the "behind-the-scenes" of an executing application, and to set breakpoints so you can interact with the application while it is running. The View window allows you to see which tables are open and how they are related to each other. You also learned how to speed up the execution of your application by taking advantage of Visual FoxPro's Rushmore technology, which uses indexes to optimize searches and queries. And to create a single file that can be distributed to end users, you learned how to use Project Manager to build an application (.APP) file.

To	Do This
Open the Debug window	Select Debug Window from the Tools Menu.
View a value in the Debug Window	Type the name of a variable, field, or Visual FoxPro function in the Debug window, and press the Enter key.
Cause program suspension when a value changes Window.	Type the name of a variable, field, or Visual FoxPro function in the Debug Press the spacebar on the center bar.
Open the Trace window	Select Trace Window from the Tools Menu.
Run a program from the Trace Window	Click Do in the Trace window, and select the program to run.
Set a breakpoint in the Trace Window	Go to the desired line in the Trace Window, and Click or press the spacebar.
Use Rushmore Optimization	Make sure the expression to be optimized matches an index expression exactly.
Exclude a file from a project	Select the file in the Project Manager. Select Exclude from the Project menu.
Build an Application	Click Build in the Project Manager. Select Build Application. Name the application to be generated, and click Build.

For online information about	From the Visual FoxPro Help Menu, choose Contents, select "Using Visual FoxPro," and then
Reports	Select the topic, "Reports and Labels"
Testing and Debugging Applications	Select the topic, "Testing and Debugging"
Compiling	Select the topic, "Compiling"

For more information on	See in the *Microsoft Visual FoxPro Developer's Guide*
Reports	Chapter 14, "Adding Queries and Reports"
Testing and Debugging	Chapter 16, "Testing and Debugging Applications"
Compiling	Chapter 15, "Compiling an Application"

Part

3

Review & Practice

You will review and practice how to:

- Control data access.
- Set buffering.
- Create a query.
- Add tables.
- Select fields.
- Run a query.
- Create a report.
- Print a report.

In this Review and Practice section, you will practice the skills you learned in Part 3: controlling access to the Survey table, querying the Survey table, and producing a survey report.

Scenario

Trace DelRio, the customer service department manager, wishes to analyze the data collected in the Survey table. She has asked you to write a query to find out which customers are dissatisfied with the service that they received. She wants a report sorted by state which will show the customer's name and phone number and any comments made. The report will be used to initiate a customer call-back form to follow up on complaints.

Step 1: Control Data Access

1. From c:\LitWare\P3Review, open the LitWare project.
2. Make the access to the Survey table exclusive.
3. Use optimistic buffering on the survey form.

For more information on	See
Access methods	Lesson 9
Buffering	Lesson 9

Step 2: Create Queries

To select data in the Survey table for analysis, you will need to create a query.

1. From the Project Manager, create a new query.
2. Select the Survey table.
3. Add the Customer table to the query.
4. Add the customer first name, last name, state, and home phone number fields to the query.
5. Add the answer to question one and the comments from the survey table to the query.
6. Order the query by customer last name and first name.
7. Group the query by state.
8. Select only customers who have answered no to question one on the survey.
9. Output your query to a table.

For more information on	See
Creating a query	Lesson 10
Adding tables to a query	Lesson 10
Adding fields to a query	Lesson 10
Selecting records for a query	Lesson 10
Displaying results of a query	Lesson 10

Step 3: Creating a Report

To analyze the data in the Survey table, you will need to create a report.

1. From the Project Manager, create a new report.
2. Select the horizontal column layout for the report.
3. From the Customer table add the customer first name, last name, state, and home phone number.
4. From the Survey table, add the answer to question one to the report.
5. Position the fields on the report to make the Report Designer look like the one below.

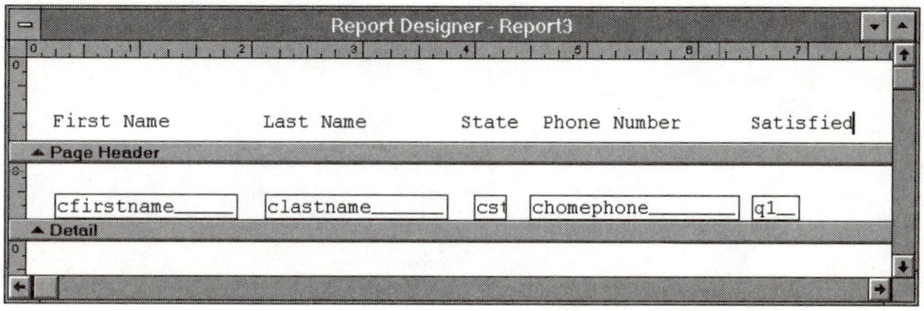

6. Preview the report.
7. Print the report.

For more information on	See
Creating a report	Lesson 11
Laying out a report	Lesson 11
Printing a report	Lesson 11

Smart Naming Strategies

Visual FoxPro 3 presents a new development approach, and with that, a chance for using a standard set of naming conventions. Proposals presented here are not earth shattering or totally new; they have been formulated and fine-tuned with the knowledge gained in developing FoxPro, Access, and Visual Basic for Windows applications.

When the interface for applications is consistent, users move from one application to another with ease and speed. Consistency facilitates the learning process and minimizes the need for training when new applications are introduced into the workplace, resulting in increased productivity. The same strategy applies to writing code. Code often survives the author and becomes the author's professional legacy.

Change is frequently the norm; developers need to understand the application code not only today, but next month or next year. Even the simplest applications will require occasional attention. A loosely defined naming strategy can be difficult to understand and it has a direct effect on productivity. Coding standards are formatting rules set up to make code more readable. While variable naming is a small part of programming, it's well worth the effort to use naming standards when writing code. This ensures that the application can be easily read, understood, and maintained.

Naming Conventions Used in this Book

Visual FoxPro 3 is moving toward the Visual Basic view of objects, which uses similar naming conventions to ease the way of a developer when moving between Microsoft products.

Program identifiers fall into the following categories:

Visual FoxPro 3 commands
Variables
Field names
Filenames and aliases
Functions and procedures
Manifest constants (#define)
Objects

There are several conventions for indicating the nature of an identifier (numeric, character string, array, etc.), and you should use these conventions to help you write clear, readable code. In development, especially with multiple developers, consistency is important; you must follow proper standards and guidelines and you should make liberal use of comments.

Visual FoxPro 3 has extended its preprocessor and now supports include files and manifest constants. Manifest constants define names for constants and can be referred to by that name throughout the program. The name is replaced by its value at compile time. The directive, #INCLUDE, tells the preprocessor to treat the contents of the specified header files as though they appeared in a Visual FoxPro 3 program.

This example is from the Visual FoxPro 3 sample, TESTRADE.h.

```
*-- Common include file
*?
#INCLUDE "\VFP\FOXPRO.H"
#INCLUDE "STRINGS.H"
#DEFINE DEBUGMODE     .F.
#DEFINE INIFILE       "TASTRADE.INI"
```

Object Naming Conventions

In keeping with Visual Basic standards, each object begins with a three-character, lower-case prefix that denotes the type of object. Each distinct word in the name should be capitalized without underscores.

Variable Naming Conventions

The capability of using and manipulating object names directly without the need to assign a variable to each object reduces variable use. Each Visual FoxPro 3 variable begins with a two-character, lowercase prefix. The first character denotes the variable scope, the second represents the variable type. Each key word in the variable name should be capitalized without underscores. Note that an object will use only one character, "o", for a designation. An object contains both its scope and type.

Scope

The scope of an identifier is where the identifier exists. In other words, where it is visible, or it specifies the range of reference for the variable. For example, the variable lnCounter is a local variable and can be accessed only by the procedure in which it was defined, while the variable gnOldRecno is a public variable and can be accessed from anywhere in the application.

When working with identifiers, your goal is to know something about the identifier context. An example is a loop counter, lnCounter. From its name, we know two properties: the prefix l states that it is a local variable (and is limited to only this program), and the second prefix n states that the variable data type is numeric.

The choices for scope are:

Scope	Description	Example
l	Local	lnCounter
p	Private (default)	pnStatus
g	Public (global)	gnOldRecno
t	Parameter	tnRecNo

The prefix scope, as described, is recommended but not required. In some cases, explicit scoping does not apply. For example, in the main program of a standalone application, there is no difference in visibility for variables scoped as public or private.

Type

Data types in Visual FoxPro 3 include all the regular FoxPro language data types plus a few new types. The original group may be saved in a data table except for the unknown (u) datatype.

Type	Description	Example
c	Character	cLastName
d	Date	dBirthDay
l	Logical	lFlag
n	Numeric	nCounter
u	Unknown	uValue unknown or undefined
a	Array	aMonths exists only as a variable

Visual FoxPro 3 has added the following new types:

Type	Description	Example
y	Currency	yCurrentValue
t	Datetime	tLastModified
b	Double	bValue
f	Float	fInterest
o	Object	oEmployee exists only as a variable

The following chart derives the variable prefix from the context with which it is used and shows an example of an identifier.

Context	**Type**	**Example**
Public/Global	g	gcUserName
Private	p	pcState
Local	l	lnCounter
Static (Class Variable)	s	snLoops
Form	f	fnInstance
Form Set	t	ttOpened
Object Instance	o	oJanitor
Class	<none>	Customer
Constant (#DEFINE)	ALLCAPS	TRUE

A data table is composed of fields, and the same type and name conventions can be used as field names.

The choices for Type are:

Type	**Description**	**Example**
c	Character	cLastName
d	Date	dBirthDay
t	Datetime	tLastMod
b	Double	bRate
f	Float	fValue
g	General	gPicture
l	Logical	lSellMail
m	Memo	mComments
y	Currency	yYearTDate
n	Numeric	nItems
i	Integer	iCustID

Example: Extract the root file name from a directory list

```
= ADIR (laTemp_,"*.txt")           && get list of all the TXT files
FOR lnCnt=1 TO ALEN(laTemp_,1)     &&  for each row
    lcName=  laTemp_[lnCnt,1]      && extract the name
    lnLoc= AT('.', lcName)         && locate the period
    lcRoot = SUBS(lcName,1,lnLoc-1) && extract the root name
                                   && more processing
       NEXT
```

This structure follows the notation and object naming standards called Hungarian notation. The notation uses several prefix conventions for indicating the nature of a named variable (numeric, character string, array, etc.). It's an elaborate system that can run from a single letter for an integer, to four or five letters for complex variables.

Guidelines

Programming conventions are subject to personal style, but the most important rule is to be consistent. Pick a convention and stick with it. We have reviewed several FoxPro/ Xbase books and have found some general standards:

- FoxPro keywords are capitalized.
- Field and variable names have the first letter capitalized.
- Procedure and user-defined functions have the first letter capitalized.
- Variables use a mix of scope and/or data type to form the name.
- Use FoxDoc to help format your code.
- Popups are named after DBF or PRG.
- Windows have the same name as an SCX file.
- Browse windows are not named after the table.
- Indentation levels on continuation lines are two columns minimum.
- Lines are 80 characters or less.
- First choice for character strings is Double quotes (""):
  then Square brackets ([]); and then Single quotes ('').
- Make liberal use of inline comments (&&) and comments at the closure of logical control structures.
- Use Initialization procedures to:
  set up standard defaults (SET commands)
  declare system wide variables
  set up hot keys (ON KEY LABEL),
  use local settings, e.g., currency, date, and phone number templates.
- Data Table file names are of the form XXYYYYnn as in ARCUST99, where :
  XX module code of the parent = AR
  YYYYY data file designator = CUST
  nn company number of the parent = 99
- Use the underscore suffix to identify array names, i.e., aArray_.

Conclusion

The discussion in this appendix stresses the importance of using a clear and consistent coding style. Using a coherent and efficient naming strategy can make your application easy to use and can save you weeks of work.

Glossary

This glossary includes some of the acronyms, abbreviations, buzzwords and programming jargon that you might encounter as you use this book.

alternate index A candidate index that was not chosen as the primary key. See also candidate index, primary key.

append To add records to the end of a table.

application A collection of Visual FoxPro programs, forms, menus, and other files that are compiled into a single program. Applications are built with the Program Manager and have an APP extension.

base class A class that is internally defined by Visual FoxPro and can be used as a basis for other user-defined classes. For example, Visual FoxPro forms and controls are base classes that you can expand with your own functionality to create new classes. See also subclass.

breakpoint A position in a program at which execution pauses and control returns to you. In Visual FoxPro, you set breakpoints in the Debug window.

browse To view a table and its contents.

buffer A temporary holding area in memory where information can be stored. Visual FoxPro provides buffering in two locking modes: pessimistic buffering and optimistic buffering. These choices determine when one or more records are locked, and how and when they are released.

builders Visual FoxPro tools that help the user set properties or create expressions.

candidate index An index that has no null or duplicate values and can become a primary key.

check box A control that indicates whether an option is on or off or a value is true or false. An X appears in the box when it is selected.

child table The related or controlled table in a one-to-one or one-to-many index relationship.

class A template or blueprint that defines the characteristics of an object and describes how the object should look and behave.

class hierarchy A structure for the logical organization of parent and child classes.

class library A collection of classes stored in a single file. In Visual FoxPro, every class is stored in a class library. Class libraries have a VCX. extension.

cleanup code Code that is executed after the menu definition code in an MRP file. Cleanup code can include user-defined functions and procedures.

click To press and release a mouse button once to make a selection.

client/server A description for applications that have a local (client) user interface but access data on a remote server. The application distributes the work between the local machine and the server, depending on the strengths of the front-end and back-end products.

clipboard An area in the computer's memory that functions as a holding place for what was last cut or copied from a file. Information contained on the clipboard can be inserted (pasted) into other documents and other applications.

combo box Contains the combined functionality of a text box and a list box.

command button A button pressed by the user that causes Visual FoxPro to perform an action. (e.g., Cancel, OK, Save).

command button group A control array of command buttons that can be treated as a unit.

connection A definition stored in a database, which you can then refer to by name when you create a remote view. You can also set properties to the named connection definition to optimize the communication between Visual FoxPro and the remote data source.

container classes Visual FoxPro base classes that group other similar classes together. For example, a form class consists of a group of several control classes, which can be treated as a unit.

container hierarchy A structure for the logical organization of an object through all of its nested containers.

Data Definition Language (DDL) The language used to declare the structure of a database to the database management system.

data dictionary A table containing information about all the tables in a database. The information stored in a data dictionary is meta-data or, data about the data, such as long table and field names, validation rules and triggers, and definitions for database objects such as views and named.

data environment All the tables, views, and relationships that are to be opened when you run or modify a form or report. The data environment is saved with the form or report and can be modified in the Data Environment Designer.

data session A current work environment/work session.

database A file consisting of a number of records (tables), each of which is constructed of fields together with a collection of operations that facilitate searching, sorting, recombination, and other activities.

database table A table contained in a database.

debug To look for and determine the cause of an error or problem in a computer program.

design time The mode of operation when an application is being created. At design time, you build the components of your application and set their properties.

dialog box A special window displayed by the system or application that asks a question requiring a response from the user.

double click To press and release a mouse button twice, generally used when opening applications or files.

drag and drop A feature that enables you to drag one object onto another to perform an action. You can drag an object and, while holding down the mouse button, move it to a new location. When you are satisfied with the location, you release the mouse button to drop the object.

edit box A button on the control toolbar that is used to create a text box that provides a place for the user to enter or view text.

encapsulation An object-oriented programming term for the ability to contain and hide information about an object, such as internal data structures and code. Encapsulation isolates the internal complexity of an object's operation from the rest of the application. For example, when you set the caption property on a command button, you don't need to know how the string is stored.

event Any action recognized by an object, such as clicking the mouse.

event code Code that is executed when an event occurs. The code can also be called programmatically.

event driven A mode of programming emphasizing event code rather than the sequential code used in procedural programming.

expression A combination of variables, operators, constraints, functions, and names of fields, controls, and properties that translates to a single value. You use expressions as settings for many properties, and to set criteria or define calculated fields in queries.

field-level rule A validation rule, associated with a field, that is activated when the field value is inserted or changed, and most often used to verify data entry and correctness. Field-level rules are activated before record-level rules and trigger, and work during buffered updates.

form A container class that behaves like a standard window or dialog box with predefined areas for entering or changing information.

form set A container class that is a collection of related forms.

free table A table that is not contained in a particular database.

function A pre-programmed calculation that can be carried out on request from any point in a Visual FoxPro program. Because a function takes in one or more arguments and returns a single value, it can be embedded in an expression. Functions contain a pair of parentheses that distinguish them from commands. For example, ROW ( ) is a function. Functions can be from Visual FoxPro or user-defined.

grid A control that creates a grid allowing you to present data in a tabular format. Grid controls contain column headers, columns, and column controls.

handle A number assigned to a window that is used by the operating system to keep track of the window, or in a C or C++ library, as a pointer to a pointer. Handles are used in library routines constructed with the Library Construction component of the Professional Edition of Visual FoxPro.

index A set of pointers that is logically ordered by the values of a key. Indexes provide quick access to data and can enforce uniqueness on the rows in a table. Indexes in Visual FoxPro are maintained in an index file.

inheritance An object-oriented programming term. The ability of a subclass to take on the characteristics of the class it's based on. If the characteristics of the parent class change, the subclass inherits those characteristics. For example, if you add a new property, IsBold, to an editing control, any subclasses based on your control will also have an IsBold property.

instances An object-oriented programming term. An object created from a class definition. Unlike a class, which is just a definition, an instance actually exists as an object that can be used to perform tasks. For example, a text box on a running form is an instance of the TextBox class.

label A control that contains text to describe areas of the form or other controls. Sometimes referred to as a prompt.

link An OLE term. A connection between a source document and a destination document. A linked object is a placeholder for information from the source document and maintains the connection between the two documents. When the information changes in the source document, the changes are reflected in the destination document.

list box A control that provides a list of items to choose from.

locked The condition of a record or table that makes it read-only to all users except the one who is currently entering data in it.

main program The program that is executed in a compiled application. Typically, the main program sets the application's operational environment, runs menu programs or forms to display the application's interface, and establishes the event loop of the application with the READ EVENTS command.

many-to-many relationship A relationship between tables where records in each table have multiple matching records in the related table. This type of relationship may require changes in your database design.

memory variable A location in the computer's memory where data is stored. You can change the contents of a variable but its name and storage are reserved for use until you end the Visual FoxPro session or release the variable. Variables and their values are lost unless you save them to disk before quitting Visual FoxPro.

menu A list of items, such as commands and file names, that drops down when you choose a menu title from the menu bar.

menu item A menu command or file name listed on a menu. You can create and define menu items for your applications using the Menu Designer.

menu system The combination of the menu bar, menu titles, menus, and menu items.

method An action that an object is capable of performing. For example, list boxes have methods called Additem, Removeitem, and Clear, for maintaining list contents.

modal A window or form is modal if it retains the focus until you deliberately close it. Dialogs and messages are usually modal. For example, in a modal dialog box, you can't access another window until you choose OK in the dialog box.

modeless A window or form is modeless if it does not require you to close it before switching to another form or window. For example, the Command window and toolbars are modeless.

naming conventions Naming scheme and typographical conventions used to standardize names throughout a program to a better understanding of the program.

null Having no explicitly assigned value. Null is not equivalent to zero or blank. A value of null is not considered to be greater than, less than, different than, or equivalent to any other value, including another value of null.

object An instance of a class, containing both data and procedures. For example, a control on a running form is an object.

object hierarchy A structure for the logical organization of objects.

Object Linking and Embedding (OLE) A protocol by which an OLE object, such as an Excel spreadsheet or a Word document, can be linked to or embedded in a Visual FoxPro table or form.

object-oriented A description of a system or language that supports the use of objects.

Object-Oriented Analysis (OOA) A method of analysis that examines requirements from the perspective of classes and objects.

Object-Oriented Design (OOD) The process of grouping a program into objects and establishing relationships between them.

Object-Oriented Programming (OOP) A programming paradigm in which a program is viewed as a collection of discrete objects that are self-contained collections of data structures and routines that interact with other objects.

one-to-many relationship A relationship between tables in which each record in the primary table can be associated with many records in the related table (each primary key value can appear many times in the related table).

one-to-one relationship A relationship between tables in which each record in the primary table can be associated with only one record in the related table.

optimistic buffering An efficient way to update records because locks are only applied at the time the record is written, thus minimizing the time any single user monopolizes the system in a multi-user environment. When you use record or table buffering on remote tables, Visual FoxPro imposes optimistic locking.

page A container class used to create tabbed dialog boxes. One screen or sheet of a form that has a collection of controls. Only one form page can be active at a time within the form.

parent table The primary or controlling table in a one-to-one or one-to-many relationship.

pixel The smallest physical element of a digitizied image.

polymorphism An object-oriented programming term. The ability to have methods with the same name, but different functions for related classes. The procedure to use is determined at run time by the class of the object. For example, related objects might both have Draw methods. A procedure, passed such an object as a parameter, can call the Draw method without needing to know what type of object the parameter is.

primary index An index that never permits duplicate values within a field or expression. Primary indexes are principally used within the primary or "referenced" table for establishing referential integrity in a persistent relationship. You can create only one primary index for a table. Visual FoxPro returns an error if you specify a primary index on any field that already contains duplicate data.

primary key The column or columns whose values uniquely identify a row in a table.

procedure A set of instructions that work as a unit, a subroutine.

project A file that keeps track of all programs, forms, menus, libraries, reports, labels, queries, and other types of files that are needed to create an application. Projects are maintained in the Project Manager and have a .PJX file extension.

property An attribute of a control, field, or database object that you set to define one of the object's characteristics or an aspect of its behavior. For example, the Visible property affects whether a control can be seen at run time. You can change an objects property settings with the Property Window.

query A request for the retrieval of information from a database, using criteria to extract specific records. Queries are created with the Query Designer.

record A unit of storage in a table. Every table can contain a large number of records, each record is comprised of fields.

record-level rule A validation rule, bound to a record, that is activated when a record is inserted or changed, and most often used to verify data entry and correctness. Validation rules do not apply when records are deleted. Record-level rules are activated after field-level rules, and before triggers, and work during buffered updates.

referential integrity Rules for governing data consistency, specifically the relationships between primary keys and foreign keys of different tables. Visual FoxPro addresses referential integrity with user-defined field and record-level rules. The Referential Integrity Builder helps you set up rules to control how records are inserted, updated, or deleted in related tables.

regular index An index that is not unique, primary, or candidate. You use a regular index for ordering and seeking records, but not to enforce the uniqueness of the data in those records. You also use regular index as the "many" side of a one-to-many persistent relationship.

related table The tables that make reference to another table's columns.

relation A link between tables that allow data to be accessed from more than the currently selected table. The link is the join condition.

remote view A view that allows you to view and update a set of records from a table(s) located on another server. The results are sent back to the source tables.

report band An area in a report that can contain text, data from table fields, calculated values, or user-defined functions, as well as pictures, lines, and boxes. Several different types of bands can appear in a report.

report detail band The area between the page header and the page footer, consisting of detail lines based on the records from the selected table or tables.

run time The time during which an application is running. During run time, you can interact with an application.

Rushmore technology A data access technique that permits sets of records to be accessed very efficiently.

scope The range of reference for an object or variable or a range of records in a view or table. For example, local variables can be referenced only within the procedure they were defined. Public variables are accessible from anywhere in the application. Objects, such as the current database, are in scope if they are in the defined search path. Record ranges can be specified with a Scope clause in many commands.

setup code The portion of a program that executes before the menu definition code in an MPR file. Setup code might include code to open files, declare memory variables, or place a previous menu system on a stack so it can be retrieved later without redefining it.

sort order The order in which records are displayed, either ascending (0-100) or descending (100-0). Alphabetic sort order depends on the locale.

subclass A new class definition of an object which uses another class definition, the parent class, as a starting point. This definition inherits any changes to the parent class.

tab A user interface element that looks like the top of a file folder. You click the tab to select the page. Create tabs in Visual FoxPro using the page control tool in the Form Designer.

table The fundamental structure of a relational database management system. In Visual FoxPro, a table stores data in records (rows) and fields (columns). The data is usually about a particular category of things, such as customers, customer orders, employees, or inventory parts. Each Visual FoxPro table can be stored in its own file with a .DBF extension or contained in a database.

text box A control that allows you to enter or view text in a form. Typically, text boxes hold a single line of text.

toolbars A set of buttons that you click to carry out common tasks. Toolbars can float in their own window, or you can dock them at the top, bottom, or sides of the main Visual FoxPro window. You can customize the toolbars provided with Visual FoxPro and you can create toolbars of your own design by using the base toolbar class provided with Visual FoxPro.

transaction processing A series of processing steps that results in a specific function or activity being completed, ensuring that a set of actions is treated as a single unit of work.

trigger Record level event code that runs after an insert, update, or delete action is requested. Different actions can be attached to the different events. Triggers run last, after rules, and do not run during buffered updates unless TABLEUPDATE() is issued. They are most often used for cross-table integrity.

user-defined class Similar to Visual FoxPro base classes, but defined by the user, and available for subclassing. This type of class has no visual representation.

user-defined function Code created by a user that returns a value. User-defined functions include stand-alone programs saved with .PRG extensions, as well as procedures and functions contained inside a program.

view A customized virtual table definition that can be local, remote, or parameterized. Views reference one or more tables, or other views. They can be updatable, and they can reference remote tables.

wizard A sequence of dialog boxes that present specific questions about what you want to create. Once you answer the questions, the wizard completes the task.

Index

Special Characters

G

H

N

T

IMPORTANT — READ CAREFULLY BEFORE OPENING SOFTWARE PACKET(S).
By opening the sealed packet(s) containing the software, you indicate your acceptance of the following Microsoft License Agreement.

Microsoft License Agreement

MICROSOFT LICENSE AGREEMENT
(Single User Products)

This is a legal agreement between you (either an individual or an entity) and Microsoft Corporation. By opening the sealed software packet(s) you are agreeing to be bound by the terms of this agreement. If you do not agree to the terms of this agreement, promptly return the book, including the unopened software packet(s), to the place you obtained it for a full refund.

MICROSOFT SOFTWARE LICENSE

1. GRANT OF LICENSE. Microsoft grants to you the right to use one copy of the Microsoft software program included with this book (the "SOFTWARE") on a single terminal connected to a single computer. The SOFTWARE is in "use" on a computer when it is loaded into temporary memory (i.e., RAM) or installed into permanent memory (e.g., hard disk, CD-ROM, or other storage device) of that computer. You may not network the SOFTWARE or otherwise use it on more than one computer or computer terminal at the same time.

2. COPYRIGHT. The SOFTWARE is owned by Microsoft or its suppliers and is protected by United States copyright laws and international treaty provisions. Therefore, you must treat the SOFTWARE like any other copyrighted material (e.g., a book or musical recording) except that you may either (a) make one copy of the SOFTWARE solely for backup or archival purposes, or (b) transfer the SOFTWARE to a single hard disk provided you keep the original solely for backup or archival purposes. You may not copy the written materials accompanying the SOFTWARE.

3. OTHER RESTRICTIONS. You may not rent or lease the SOFTWARE, but you may transfer the SOFTWARE and accompanying written materials on a permanent basis provided you retain no copies and the recipient agrees to the terms of this Agreement. You may not reverse engineer, decompile, or disassemble the SOFTWARE. If the SOFTWARE is an update or has been updated, any transfer must include the most recent update and all prior versions.

4. DUAL MEDIA SOFTWARE. If the SOFTWARE package contains both 3.5" and 5.25" disks, then you may use only the disks appropriate for your single-user computer. You may not use the other disks on another computer or loan, rent, lease, or transfer them to another user except as part of the permanent transfer (as provided above) of all SOFTWARE and written materials.

5. LANGUAGE SOFTWARE. If the SOFTWARE is a Microsoft language product, then you have a royalty-free right to reproduce and distribute executable files created using the SOFTWARE. If the language product is a Basic or COBOL product, then Microsoft grants you a royalty-free right to reproduce and distribute the run-time modules of the SOFTWARE provided that you: (a) distribute the run-time modules only in conjunction with and as a part of your software product; (b) do not use Microsoft's name, logo, or trademarks to market your software product; (c) include a valid copyright notice on your software product; and (d) agree to indemnify, hold harmless, and defend Microsoft and its suppliers from and against any claims or lawsuits, including attorneys' fees, that arise or result from the use or distribution of your software product. The "run-time modules" are those files in the SOFTWARE that are identified in the accompanying written materials as required during execution of your software program. The run-time modules are limited to run-time files, install files, and ISAM and REBUILD files. If required in the SOFTWARE documentation, you agree to display the designated patent notices on the packaging and in the README file of your software product.

LIMITED WARRANTY

LIMITED WARRANTY. Microsoft warrants that (a) the SOFTWARE will perform substantially in accordance with the accompanying written materials for a period of ninety (90) days from the date of receipt, and (b) any hardware accompanying the SOFTWARE will be free from defects in materials and workmanship under normal use and service for a period of one (1) year from the date of receipt. Any implied warranties on the SOFTWARE and hardware are limited to ninety (90) days and one (1) year, respectively. Some states/countries do not allow limitations on duration of an implied warranty, so the above limitation may not apply to you.

CUSTOMER REMEDIES. Microsoft's and its suppliers' entire liability and your exclusive remedy shall be, at Microsoft's option, either (a) return of the price paid, or (b) repair or replacement of the SOFTWARE or hardware that does not meet Microsoft's Limited Warranty and which is returned to Microsoft with a copy of your receipt. This Limited Warranty is void if failure of the SOFTWARE or hardware has resulted from accident, abuse, or misapplication. Any replacement SOFTWARE or hardware will be warranted for the remainder of the original warranty period or thirty (30) days, whichever is longer. Outside the United States, these remedies are not available without proof of purchase from an authorized non-U.S. source.

NO OTHER WARRANTIES. Microsoft and its suppliers disclaim all other warranties, either express or implied, including, but not limited to implied warranties of merchantability and fitness for a particular purpose, with regard to the SOFTWARE, the accompanying written materials, and any accompanying hardware. This limited warranty gives you specific legal rights. You may have others which vary from state/country to state/country.

NO LIABILITY FOR CONSEQUENTIAL DAMAGES. In no event shall Microsoft or its suppliers be liable for any damages whatsoever (including without limitation, damages for loss of business profits, business interruption, loss of business information, or any other pecuniary loss) arising out of the use of or inability to use this Microsoft product, even if Microsoft has been advised of the possibility of such damages. Because some states/countries do not allow the exclusion or limitation of liability for consequential or incidental damages, the above limitation may not apply to you.

U.S. GOVERNMENT RESTRICTED RIGHTS

The SOFTWARE and documentation are provided with RESTRICTED RIGHTS. Use, duplication, or disclosure by the Government is subject to restrictions as set forth in subparagraph (c)(1)(ii) of The Rights in Technical Data and Computer Software clause at DFARS 252.227-7013 or subparagraphs (c)(1) and (2) of the Commercial Computer Software — Restricted Rights 48 CFR 52.227-19, as applicable. Manufacturer is Microsoft Corporation, One Microsoft Way, Redmond, WA 98052-6399.

This Agreement is governed by the laws of the State of Washington.

Should you have any questions concerning this Agreement, or if you desire to contact Microsoft for any reason, please write: Microsoft Sales and Service, One Microsoft Way, Redmond, WA 98052-6399.

097-000-681

The *Step by Step* *Practice Files Disk*

The enclosed 3.5-inch disk contains timesaving, ready-to-use practice files that complement the lessons in this book. To use the practice files, you'll need the Windows 95 operating system.

Each *Step by Step* lesson uses practice files from the disk. Before you begin the *Step by Step* lessons, read the "Getting Ready" section of the book for easy instructions telling how to install the files on your computer's hard disk. As you work through each lesson, be sure to follow the instructions for renaming the practice files so that you can go through a lesson more than once if you need to.

Please take a few moments to read the License Agreement on the previous page before using the enclosed disk.

Register your Microsoft Press® book today, and let us know what you think.

At Microsoft Press, we listen to our customers. We update our books as new releases of software are issued, and we'd like you to tell us the kinds of additional information you'd find most useful in these updates. Your feedback will be considered when we prepare a future edition; plus, when you become a registered owner, you'll get Microsoft Press catalogs and exclusive offers on specially priced books.

Thanks!

I used this book as

- ◯ A way to learn the software
- ◯ A reference when I needed it
- ◯ A way to find out about advanced features
- ◯ Other____________________

I consider myself

- ◯ A beginner or an occasional computer user
- ◯ An intermediate-level user with a pretty good grasp of the basics
- ◯ An advanced user who helps and provides solutions for others
- ◯ Other____________________

I purchased this book from

- ◯ A bookstore
- ◯ A software store
- ◯ A direct mail offer
- ◯ Other____________________

I will buy the next edition of the book when it's updated

- ◯ Definitely
- ◯ Probably
- ◯ I will not buy the next edition

The next edition of this book should include the following additional information:

1● ____________________

2● ____________________

3● ____________________

The most useful things about this book are ____________________

This book would be more helpful if ____________________

My general impressions of this book are ____________________

May we contact you regarding your comments? ◯ Yes ◯ No

Would you like to receive a Microsoft Press catalog regularly? ◯ Yes ◯ No

Name____________________

Company (if applicable) ____________________

Address ____________________

City__________ State __________ Zip __________

Daytime phone number (optional) (_____) ____________________

Please mail back your feedback form—postage free! Fold this form as described on the other side of this card, or fax this sheet to:
Microsoft Press, Attn: Marketing Department, fax 206-936-7329

FOLD THIS FLAP TOWARD CENTER AND TAPE TO OPPOSING FLAP

TAPE SIDES (NO STAPLES PLEASE)

TAPE SIDES (NO STAPLES PLEASE)

FOLD HERE

NO POSTAGE
NECESSARY
IF MAILED
IN THE
UNITED STATES

BUSINESS REPLY MAIL

FIRST-CLASS MAIL PERMIT NO. 108 REDMOND, WA

POSTAGE WILL BE PAID BY ADDRESSEE

ATTN: MARKETING DEPT
MICROSOFT PRESS
ONE MICROSOFT WAY
REDMOND WA 98052-9953

FOLD HERE

TAPE SIDES (NO STAPLES PLEASE)

TAPE SIDES (NO STAPLES PLEASE)

FOLD THIS FLAP TOWARD CENTER AND TAPE TO OPPOSING FLAP

Register Today!

Return this
Microsoft® Visual FoxPro® 3 for Windows®
Step by Step
registration card for:

- ✔ a Microsoft Press® catalog
- ✔ exclusive offers on specially priced books

U.S. and Canada addresses only. Fill in information below and mail postage-free. Please mail only the bottom half of this page.

1-5615-846-7A ***Microsoft Visual FoxPro 3 for Windows Step by Step*** ***Owner Registration Card***

NAME

INSTITUTION OR COMPANY NAME

ADDRESS

CITY STATE ZIP

NO POSTAGE
NECESSARY
IF MAILED
IN THE
UNITED STATES

BUSINESS REPLY MAIL

FIRST-CLASS MAIL PERMIT NO. 53 BOTHELL, WA

POSTAGE WILL BE PAID BY ADDRESSEE

MICROSOFT PRESS REGISTRATION
MICROSOFT VISUAL FOXPRO 3
FOR WINDOWS STEP BY STEP
PO BOX 3019
BOTHELL WA 98041-9946